RESEARCH IN GOVERNMENTAL AND NONPROFIT ACCOUNTING

Volume 7 • 1992

Research in
Governmental and Nonprofit Accounting

James L. Chan and James M. Patton, *Editors*

EDITORIAL BOARD

RESEARCH IN GOVERNMENTAL AND NONPROFIT ACCOUNTING

A Research Annual

Editors: JAMES L. CHAN
*The University of Illinois
at Chicago*

JAMES M. PATTON
University of Pittsburgh

VOLUME 7 • 1992

 JAI PRESS INC.

Greenwich, Connecticut *London, England*

CONTENTS

LIST OF CONTRIBUTORS

Nissim Aranya	University of Tel Aviv
Dennis M. Bline	Bryant College
James M. Buchanan	George Mason University
Sharon L. Green	University of Wisconsin–Madison
Yuhchang Hwang	University of Pittsburgh
Robert W. Ingram	University of Alabama
Rowan H. Jones	University of Birmingham, England
James M. Kurtenbach	Iowa State University
Klaus G. Luder	Postgraduate School of Administrative Sciences, Speyer, Germany
Wilda F. Meixner	Southwest Texas State University
James M. Patton	University of Pittsburgh
Walter A. Robbins	University of Alabama
Robin W. Roberts	University of Missouri–Columbia
Marc A. Rubin	Miami University

INTRODUCTION

This seventh volume of *Research in Governmental and Nonprofit Accounting* presents several sets of papers:

Financial Reporting: The idea of "interperiod equity," which has assumed a key role in discussions of alternative governmental financial reporting models, is analyzed from an economic perspective by Yuhchang Hwang and James Patton. Robin Roberts and James Kurtenbach's paper examines lobbying activities before the Governmental Accounting Standards Board. The Board's User Needs Survey is reanalyzed, in part, by Robert Ingram and Walter Robbins.

Public Choice: Marc Rubin's paper surveys recent studies in public choice to encourage their application by governmental accounting researchers. With a greater historical perspective, Rowan Jones links issues in national governmental accounting to James Buchanan's concern about government's tendency to engage in debt financing of deficits in a democracy. Buchanan's contributions to public choice and economics, which led to his Nobel Prize in Economics in 1986, are evident from writings over the last fifty years. We are grateful to Professor Buchanan for sharing a bibliography of his writings with us. Klaus Luder's paper, with its emphasis on the political and administrative environment, is in some ways also inspired by public choice. In a more specific way, Dennis Bline, Wilda Meixner and Nissim Aranya investigate the impact of the public sector work environment on accountants' organizational and professional commitment.

Literature Analyses: Sharon Green provides an assessment of the behavioral literature in governmental and nonprofit accounting, along with suggestions for the future. We have also included the abstracts of 52 accounting doctoral dissertations on governmental and nonprofit topics to update a similar section in Volume 4 of RIGNA. Information about these dissertations comes from *Dissertation Abstracts International*, Volume 47, No. 10 (April 1987) to Volume 52, No. 12 (June 1991). The dissertation titles and abstracts are published with the permission of University Microfilm International, publishers of Dissertation Abstracts International, and may not be reproduced without their prior permission. Further information about purchase of dissertations is available from University Microfilm International, 300

North Zeeb Road, Ann Arbor, Michigan, 48106, or by telephoning 800-521-3042. The order number has been included with each abstract to encourage the greater use of dissertations. We also hope that the Author/Title Cumulative Index for Volume 1 to 7 of *Research in Governmental and Nonprofit Accounting* will be useful to the reader.

Beginning with Volume 8, *Research in Governmental and Nonprofit Accounting* will publish collections of papers on specific topics, such as public choice, international comparisons, Federal Government accounting, nonprofit accounting. Readers are urged to refer to the newsletter of the American Accounting Association's Government and Nonprofit Section for periodic calls for papers and status reports. James Chan would like to thank James Patton, coeditor for the last three volumes, and the members of the Editorial Board and reviewers for their service. We also appreciate the assistance of Zhilong Fang, Mrs. Betty H. Tillmon and Ms. Jo Ann S. Burgess in preparing Professor James Buchanan's bibliography, Zhilong Fang in compiling the doctoral dissertation abstracts, and Raju Ayal in preparing the cumulative index.

Suggestions for future volumes and other editorial communications should be addressed to:

Professor James L. Chan, Editor
Research in Governmental and Nonprofit Accounting
College of Business Administration (M/C 006)
University of Illinois at Chicago
P.O. Box 4348, Chicago, IL 60680
Tel: (312) 996-2650; Fax: (312) 996-4520.

James L. Chan
James M. Patton

PART I

GOVERNMENTAL AND
NONPROFIT RESEARCH

_____

AN ECONOMIC ANALYSIS OF INTERPERIOD EQUITY IN GOVERNMENTAL FINANCIAL REPORTING

Yuhchang Hwang and James M. Patton

ABSTRACT

The Governmental Accounting Standards Board (GASB) has selected the measurement of "interperiod equity" (IPE) as a primary objective of financial reporting by governments. However, the concept of IPE is not yet well understood. This paper develops a precise operational definition of IPE and applies it to examine the desirability of alternative bases of accounting for governmental activities in various circumstances. In addition, the risk-sharing efficiency implications of accounting policy choices are also discussed. The results show that the appropriate basis of accounting generally depends on the funding concept chosen and on the distribution (mean, variance) of the measures of the underlying economic events. However, in some cases an allocation basis of accounting dominates the cash or accrual bases regardless of the funding concept used.

Research in Governmental and Nonprofit Accounting, Vol. 7, pages 3–23.
ISBN: 1-55938-418-2

I. INTRODUCTION

Since it was established in 1984, the Governmental Accounting Standards Board (GASB) has spent considerable resources developing a conceptual framework for governmental accounting standards. The GASB [1987] concluded in Concept Statement No. 1 that accountability is a basic foundation for governmental reporting and that measuring interperiod equity is an essential part of accountability.

In its Statement No. 11 "Measurement Focus and Basis of Accounting— Governmental Fund Operating Statements," GASB [1990] cites interperiod equity as one of the reasons for proposing the "flow of financial resources" measurement focus for governmental funds' operating statements. The GASB [1990, par. 23] concluded, "An accrual basis of accounting generally is necessary to measure interperiod equity because it recognizes the effects of transactions or events when they take place...regardless of when cash is received or paid." However, the specific assumptions and logic underlying this conclusion have not been adequately analyzed to date.

We believe that the GASB's implicit equity concept and the related concept of measuring interperiod equity suffer from several potential drawbacks as a criterion for choosing among alternative accounting principles. Specifically, the concepts are ambiguous, inconsistent, and ex post in nature. In addition, GASB has not directly addressed the possible equity-efficiency tradeoffs that may be necessary in setting Governmental Generally Accepted Accounting Principles (GGAAP). The purposes of this paper are: (1) to examine the definitions and implications of equity and measuring interperiod equity in the context of Governmental Generally Accepted Accounting Principles (GGAAP) and, (2) to examine the possible equity-efficiency trade-offs that an accounting standard setter may confront in choosing GGAAP. In doing so, this paper seeks to provide a conceptually sound framework for studying the equity and the efficiency implications of the choice of governmental GAAP based on citizens' welfare. It also identifies those situations in which efficiency-equity trade-offs have to be confronted in the choice of governmental accounting standards. The paper thus hopes to provide valuable information to the GASB for evaluating economic consequences of alternative GGAAP.

II. INTERPERIOD EQUITY AND MEASURING INTERPERIOD EQUITY

A. GASB's Definitions

GASB's notion of interperiod equity is based on governments' legal tradition of balanced budgets. GASB Statement No. 11 states that ". . . the general objective of these laws is that the current-year citizens should not be able to shift the burden of paying for current-year services to future-year taxpayers.... The Board [GASB] refers to this concept as interperiod equity" [GASB 1990, par. 14]. As to the issue of measuring interperiod equity, GASB [1990, par. 20] proposed that "Measuring interperiod equity requires comparing the revenue obtained by the government entity with a financial measure of the services it provides."

B. Observations Concerning GASB's Definition of Equity and Measuring Interperiod Equity

GASB's notion of interperiod equity is ambiguous because some of its under-lying assumptions and implications are not explicit enough. For example, the equity concept adopted by the GASB is essentially a *funding* concept based on an assumption of who *should pay* for services provided. In particular, GASB focuses on matching the services provided by the government with the burden of paying for them. As a result, a normative funding concept underlines GASB's equity concept and, therefore, its choice of a basis of accounting. Although GASB [1990, par. 13] cites the spirit of governmental balanced budget laws and acknowledges that some budgetary practices are designed to achieve interperiod equity, GASB does not emphasize the fact that a funding concept is essential for defining its equity concept. However, in order to operationalize the GASB's approach to measuring interperiod equity, one must first develop a set of acceptable funding concepts for various governmental activities.[1] As the choice of a particular funding concept must be a matter of value judgment, in a given situation there may be various defensible funding concepts available. Thus, the choice of a funding concept and related basis of accounting will continue to be difficult and controversial.

GASB's definition of interperiod equity also appears to be inconsistent. GASB Statement No. 11 [1990, par. 23] states that "An operating statement measurement focus that measures the relationship between aggregate revenues and aggregate services within a particular time period...is appropriate for measuring interperiod equity." Later [par. 25] it proposes the concept of "financial resources obtained during a period...sufficient to cover claims incurred during that period against financial resources" in defining the measurement focus. These two approaches to interperiod equity are not necessarily consistent: one focuses on matching revenues and services, while the other focuses on revenues and all claims against the government. This inconsistency is further revealed in later sections of GASB Statement No. 11 where the GASB hesitated to strictly apply its earlier conclusion concerning accruals in other governmental operating situations, for example, compensated absences [par. 214]. While noting this apparent inconsistency, later in this paper we provide conceptual support for using a variety of approaches.

The equity concept adopted by GASB is also ex post rather than ex ante. An ex post equity concept is based on *outcome-equity* (or end-state fairness), while ex ante equity is based on *opportunity-equity* (or the procedural notions of fairness). GASB adopted an ex post equity concept by requiring a matching of the actual services that have been provided with the actual financial burden incurred in each generation. The issue of whether an equity concept should be defined in terms of an ex post (end-state) fairness, or in terms of ex ante (opportunity) fairness has been debated by philosophers, politicians and economists for decades [Baumol, 1987]. GASB has implicitly adopted the ex post approach to interperiod equity. However, we believe that an ex ante equity concept may be appropriate for selecting governmental accounting standards for several reasons. First, the ex ante approach is widely accepted as a goal of public policy [Lev, 1988]. Also, as accounting measurements are normally imperfect at the time when events or transactions occur (e.g., measurement errors in estimating the service provided by an asset), even ex post funding and equity concepts will retain some level of uncertainty. Thus the apparent advantage of the ex post approach in eliminating uncertainty is, in part, an illusion. Finally, as accounting policies in general must be adopted before events occur, the interperiod equity aspects of an accounting method choice should be ex ante as well.

Due to the budgetary constraints in governmental environment (i.e., balanced budgets), real resource allocations will generally be affected by the accounting basis adopted. Therefore, the choice of governmental accounting standards will have public policy implications. To evaluate whether a public policy would improve social welfare, economists often examine *both* the equity and the efficiency impacts of the policy. Different approaches are available to evaluate the efficiency implications of a policy. For example, in the choice of governmental accounting standards, efficiency could be measured in terms of the administrative costs for the system, the incentive implications for the city manager's spending policies, and so forth. In this paper we consider the effects of the choice of governmental accounting standards on the economic efficiency of risk sharing across generations. The choice of an accounting standard and a particular funding concept will affect resource allocations across generations, if they are applied on a consistent basis across generations. Consequently, they implicitly provide a vehicle for reallocating resources among generations, which in turn affects the risk sharing efficiency across generations. Hence, we believe that in choosing a basis of accounting policy, one should consider the potential risk sharing efficiency implications as well as its equity effects. This point is amplified and analyzed in Section IV.

C. An Overview: Definitions and Relationships Among Basic Concepts

Our goal is to propose and analyze an unambiguous, consistent, ex ante concept of interperiod equity for governmental financial reporting, while considering efficiency implications as well. In order to analyze such a model it is first necessary to define a variety of related concepts and procedures. These definitions will serve as a foundation for later development of a formal model.

As was discussed in Section II.B, underlying GASB's notion of interperiod equity is a funding concept. A funding concept, defining who *should pay* for the services provided by the government, is normative in nature. There exist at least three basic funding concepts in practice that define how obligations might be shared by citizens:

F1. when the legal obligation or claim is created,
F2. as the services or goods are provided, and
F3. when actual cash payment is made by the government to service providers.

An accounting basis is descriptive by its nature. GASB [1990, par. 36] defines an accounting basis as "*when* a transaction or an event is recorded." In practice there are three accounting bases commonly available:

i. Accrual Basis: The accrual basis records events at the time when the legal obligation associated with the event is created; for example, when a firetruck is acquired by a city. Note that often the actual obligation realized in the future may differ from the estimated amount recorded at the time when the event originally occurred. An adjustment for the difference is made at the time when the final obligation is realized.

ii. Allocation Basis: The allocation basis records the effects of an event systematically over a number of periods of time; for example, depreciation of a firetruck as it is used. A final adjustment for the difference between the actual and estimated obligations may also be required at the time the final obligation is realized if the initial estimate proves incorrect (measurement error).

iii. Cash Basis: The cash basis records an event when the actual cash outflows associated with the event occur; for example, a firetruck is paid for.

GASB refers the measurement focus as to *what* is to be measured or presented in financial statements. GASB [1990, par. 2] also notes that "basis of accounting is an essential part of measurement focus."

Governments' budgetary mechanisms tie accounting numbers to the appropriation of real resources. Although governments have different budgetary laws and practices, governmental budgets are often required by law to be in balance. To simplify the analysis, we define "balanced-budget" to mean that sufficient revenue has to be raised (ex post) to meet whatever obligations are recorded in an accounting period.

We next briefly note some linkages among the various concepts defined above. Although the definitions of an accounting basis and a funding concept may appear to be similar, it is important to note one fundamental difference. The choice of a funding concept must be based on a *value judgment*; in contrast, an accounting basis is descriptive in nature. Also, assessing interperiod equity requires the choice of an accounting basis and a measurement focus such that the accounting measurement reflects whether the equity/funding objective chosen by the government has been fulfilled. Thus, the measurement of interperiod equity ultimately depends on the specific equity/funding concept that is adopted.

In Section III, assumptions and operational definitions used in our model are briefly described. Our analysis explicitly assumes a balanced budget and adopts the ex ante approach to defining equity. In addition, we examine equity concepts (funding concepts) other than the one implicitly adopted by GASB. We then provide an operational approach to measuring interperiod equity. In Section IV we develop a formal model for analyzing measurement of interperiod equity in governments. We analyze the equity implications of various accounting bases based on the proposed equity concepts. We also investigate the potential efficiency implications of choosing an accounting basis under the assumption of balanced-budget. We note the possible trade-offs that may be necessary between the equity and efficiency criteria in choosing accounting bases in governments.

III. ASSUMPTIONS AND OPERATIONAL DEFINITIONS

A. Basic Assumptions

Assume there is an infinite but countable number of generations of citizens. Generation t is identified with the time period t; $t \, \varepsilon \, T = \{$set of all integers$\}$. Citizens are assumed to be identical in all relevant aspects (for example, socioeconomic status), both within a generation and across generations. They are also assumed to have preferences over net wealth or consumption, (c_t). If π_t is the amount of per capita tax levied by the government on generation t, then the *ex ante* expected utility of a citizen in the t generation is: $V_t = EU[c_t]$; where $c_t = w - \pi_t \geq 0$, and w is the *exogenous equilibrium endowment (income)* distribution and π_t is the per capita tax paid by each citizen. We further assume that citizens are risk averse, having the following form of preferences over the net wealth: $U[c_t] = - \exp\{-[c_t]\}$.

Given the assumption of a balanced-budgeting mechanism, obligations recorded in period t are assumed to be financed in full through a tax collection π_t (e.g., property tax) from citizens by the government during period t. Note that since the amount of obligations recorded in each generation is determined in part by the accounting basis adopted, the basis of accounting chosen will affect the per capita tax levied and the amounts available for consumption by each generation.[2]

Denote the basis of accounting as Ri, $i = 1,2,3$ such that:

R1 = Accrual Basis, R2 = Allocation Basis, and R3 = Cash Basis.

Restating the above: Consumption c_t and taxes π_t of generation t are functions of the basis of accounting adopted; that is, $c_t = c_t(Ri)$ and $\pi_t = \pi_t(Ri)$ where Ri is the accounting basis.

Denote an economic event or transaction which occurs in period t as e_t. Also, denote y_t as the estimated obligation caused by a event or transaction in period t. The actual cash outflows Y_t, associated with event e_t, are paid at time $t + m$. For simplicity, m is assumed to be constant in our model. The cash outflows associated with an event are assumed to follow a linear statistical model: $Y_t = b\,e_t + \varepsilon_t$; where the ε_t are independently and identically distributed random variables with mean 0 and variance Ω.

At the occurence of e_t, we assume that the government can make an unbiased and linear estimate of the future cash outflows as $E(Y_t | e_t) = b\,e_t$ with $Var(Y_t | e_t) = \Omega$. Note that the assumption of unbiased estimates (a zero mean and a constant variance) for the measurement error term implies that there is no political manipulation or systematic misestimating by the government in our model. A vector of events $E_t \equiv (e_{t-k}, e_{t-k+1}, \ldots, e_t)$ is asumed to have a multivariate normal distribution with a variance/covariance matrix that is time independent. The mean of e_t is denoted as μ_t.

In summary, our model assumes that a funding/equity concept, a budgeting mechanism, a distribution of events/transactions across generations, and measurement errors inherent with each type of accounting basis are given. Our analysis focuses on the effects of choosing different accounting bases on a citizen's ex ante expected utility and, consequently, the equity and efficiency implications.

B. Operational Definitions

We now translate the concepts discussed in Section II.C into operational terms. The ultimate purpose of this subsection is to provide an operational definition of "measuring interperiod equity." As was discussed in II.C, the basic notion of measuring interperiod equity requires an ex ante equity/funding concept. Our operational definition of measuring interperiod equity is based on the following concepts: (1) citizen's ex ante preference order, (2) a Bench Mark Measure, and (3) a neutral accounting method.

An ex ante preference order of a citizen is defined as follows: Assume that a citizen of generation t is allowed to choose (ex ante) a generation in which to live. Given a balanced-budget mechanism, a distribution of events/transactions, and a basis of accounting Ri, $P_t(Ri) = \{\ldots, j, k, t, \ldots\}$ defines the citizen's ex ante preference order over generations. In this example, citizens of t generation reveals $... \geq V_j \geq V_k \geq V_t \geq ...$, where $V_j = E \ U[c_j(Ri)]$. This means a citizen feels either better-off or indifferent if she or he were in generation j versus k, and so forth. Thus, the preference order in our model involves preferences concerning which generation or period in which to live.

For each of the three funding/equity concepts (Fi) we proposed a corresponding $M(Fi)$ or "Bench Mark Measure" in which no measurement errors are created during the measurement process, that is, perfect foresight about the realization of final outcomes.

We define a basis of accounting Ri as "neutral" under the assumption of funding concept Fi if, and only if, the induced preference order $P_t(Ri)$ has the property $P_t(Ri) = P_t[M(Fi)]$. In other words, an accounting basis Ri is "neutral" if it induces the same preference order with respect to generations as the Bench Mark Measure. A neutral accounting basis associated with a given equity/funding concept Fi is denoted as $Ri^*(Fi)$.

Measuring interperiod equity can now be defined in our model as follows: For a given funding concept Fi, there exists a corresponding neutral accounting basis, Ri*(Fi). A financial report that discloses the difference between the amount of outflows during a period recorded using the actual basis of accounting Rj and the neutral accounting basis Ri*(Fi) is said to measure interperiod equity. This definition of measuring interperiod equity is based on the fact that for a given economic event, budgeting process, and equity/funding concept, a neutral accounting basis will preserve a citizen's preference order over different generations. In other words, if an accounting basis is neutral, a citizen would choose the same most preferred generation to live in as if the basis used had been the bench mark basis. A neutral basis of accounting introduces no additional equity distortions during the measurement process. With a given equity/funding concept and a neutral basis as a yardstick, one can then measure the potential equity distortion that may be created by using the given accounting basis. The next section provides a formal analysis based on this model. It also compares our operational definition of equity to that used by economists.

IV. ECONOMIC ANALYSIS

A. Equity Implications

Our basic result concerning the equity effects of accounting bases using the model described above is summarized in Proposition 1.

Proposition 1. *Given that the assumptions of III.A hold, and events' distributions are not identical over time, the neutral accounting basis for funding* concepts F1, F2, and F3 are the Accrual Basis, Allocation Basis and Cash Basis, respectively.

Proof: See Appendix 1.

Proposition 1 implies that the choice of a neutral accounting basis depends on the underlying equity/funding concept adopted for an event. The intuition supporting Proposition 1 is that different funding concepts imply different patterns of wealth allocation across generations and, consequently, different preference orders for citizens. As it is not likely that a citizen's preference orders would be the same across different wealth allocations, one accounting basis is not likely to be neutral for multiple funding concepts. Thus, in most cases, a specific accounting basis can serve as a neutral basis for only one particular funding concept. Because only a neutral basis of accounting can fairly reflect the equity implications of events across generations, an important implication from Proposition 1 is that: There is no single accounting basis that can serve the purpose of measuring interperiod equity for various equity/funding concepts assumed. Thus, if different equity/funding concepts are applied to different types of events/transactions in government, then different accounting bases will be required for the purpose of measuring interperiod equity.

The equity concept adopted in the earlier analysis differs in form from the conventional definition of equity concept in economic literature. Therefore, we next compare the equity/funding concepts discussed in our model with a definition of equity often used by economists.

B. Neutrality and Envy-Free Equity

One of the most widely cited equity concepts in the economics literature is the concept of "envy-free" equity. Economists define the concept of *envy* as follows: In a given allocation, an agent i envies an agent j if i prefers the bundle of j to his own [Varian, 1974]. If there are no *envious agents*, the allocation is said to be envy-free (or fair or equitable). In the situation discussed in this paper, the choice variable for each citizen would be the generation in which she or he prefers to live. Therefore, a cross-generation wealth allocation induced by a particular accounting basis would be said to produce envy-free equity if, and only if, no generation of citizens would prefer to live in any generation other than to her or his own. We now link the concept of "neutrality" adopted in our model to this "envy-free" equity concept as follows:

Observation 1. *Given that the assumptions of III.A hold, and the equity/funding concept adopted is Fi; if a specific basis of accounting Ri induces an envy-free wealth allocation among citizens of different generations, the* *accounting basis chosen must be neutral with respect to the assumed funding concept Fi.*

Proof: See Appendix 2.

As noted in the proof of Observation 1, an envy-free allocation can exist if, and only if, the distribution (ex ante) of economic events is identical over generations. This is because the existence of different expected utility values in different generations automatically creates "envious agents."

In the special situation of identical event distributions, the envy-free and neutrality notions of equity are practically and conceptually equivalent; a neutral accounting basis creates no envious citizens. However, as it is unrealistic to assume that economic events will always have an identical distribution pattern over time, the application of the envy-free equity criterion is extremely limited in assessing interperiod equity characteristics of alternative bases of accounting. In contrast, the criterion of neutrality (which is consistent with the spirit of envy-free criterion) does not impose restrictions on the distribution of economic events. Broadening the class of cases in which the equity concept applies is the motivation for using the neutrality criterion for defining the concept of measuring IPE in our model. In summary, neutrality is consistent with the envy-free notion of equity when both concepts work. In addition, neutrality can also be used to evaluate equity in a broader class of cases. Thus we adopt and apply neutrality as a criterion for assessing equity in our model. This point is made clear later in Proposition 3, where the distribution of events/transactions is not identical over generations.

Although the choice of a funding concept can have an important effect on the choice of an appropriate neutral basis of accounting, *governmental accounting standard setters do not have available an obvious set of unambiguous funding concepts to guide policy.* As the choice of a funding concept is itself a matter of value judgment, it would be controversial for accountants to decide which funding concept should be used. One analytical approach to this dilemma is to separate situations in which significant equity effects due to different accounting bases are likely to exist from those situations where various accounting bases are not expected to cause significant equity effects, regardless of the funding concept used. In the first case (i.e., significant equity effects exist), both equity and efficiency must be considered in choosing GGAAP, whereas in the second case (i.e., significant equity effects do not exist) a standard-setter can simply focus on the efficiency issue alone.

C.   Risk-Sharing Efficiency Implications

Based on the above discussion, a natural question to ask about our model is: Are there situations in which the criterion of efficiency rather than equity should be emphasized? Such a situation would exist when different accounting bases have the same equity implications. In those cases, social welfare and risk sharing efficiency across generations can be improved if the accounting standard and the corresponding funding concept adopted by the government can spread the economic risk among generations. For example, an allocation basis might be used to record the costs of infrequent natural disasters (for example, hurricane, earthquake). Thus, we are looking for situations where either a particular accounting basis can provide a neutral measurement no matter which funding concept is used; or, one where multiple accounting bases can serve as a neutral basis. The following Corollary summarizes our findings on this topic:

Corollary 1. *Given that the assumptions of III.A hold, if the events' distributions are identical over generations, regardless of the funding concept assumed, any one of the accounting bases Ri, i=1,2,3 is a "neutral" basis, if it is used consistently over different generations.*

Proof: See Appendix 3.

Corollary 1 indicates a case where efficiency rather than equity should be emphasized in choosing GGAAP. This is because in this special situation, any accounting basis will be a neutral basis, if it is used *consistently* over time. Thus, different accounting bases can serve the same purpose of measuring interperiod equity. As a result, a standard setter should focus on the efficiency rather than the equity implications of using various bases of accounting.

Corollary 1 is driven by the assumption of identical events distributions and by consistency in applying the accounting basis. The two assumptions together imply that a citizen would be ex-ante indifferent to living in any generation for any funding concept Fi assumed. This is because under the assumption of identical distributions, any accounting basis will give a citizen (ex ante) the same expected utility level no matter which generation he selects. This implies that a citizen's set of preference order is independent of the accounting basis used, regardless of the funding concept assumed. Therefore, any accounting basis, if it is used consistently, can serve as a neutral basis and serve the purpose of measuring interperiod equity under these circumstances. We can therefore focus on efficiency implications in such a setting. The following proposition summarizes our finding concerning efficiency:

Proposition 2. *Given the assumption of Corollary 1, if we further assume that the occurrence of events are not perfectly correlated over different generations, citizens in any generation t will prefer the Allocation Basis to either the Cash or the Accrual Bases.*

Proof: See Appendix 4.

Proposition 2 states that under the assumption of identical distributions for economic events, citizens in different generations would unanimously prefer the Allocation Basis to either the Cash or the Accrual Basis of accounting. The intuition behind this proposition is straightforward: Because of the identical distributions of economic events, any one of the accounting bases is neutral and, consequently, equitable. However, the Allocation Basis provides more efficient risk sharing because it spreads the claims associated with the occurrence of an economic event to multiple generations. Because the citizens are assumed to be risk averse, the Allocation Basis (ex ante) can thus provide an indirect mechanism for sharing the risk among different generations. As all of the accounting bases are neutral under this scenario, an Allocation Basis will dominate other accounting bases because of its favorable risk-sharing characteristics.

The policy implications of Proposition 2 are potentially significant. If a particular type of economic event fits the above assumptions, then the Allocation Basis dominates all the other accounting bases. This is because the Allocation Basis can improve the risk sharing for citizens in different generations without sacrificing the goal of measuring interperiod equity.

In contrast, if the distributions of the events do not satisfy the above assumptions (e.g., if event distributions are not identical), a standard-setter has to confront the issue of equity-efficiency trade-offs in choosing accounting bases. An example is given in the next section to illustrate this case.

D. Equity Efficiency Trade-offs

Corollary 1 covered the situation where multiple accounting bases can serve as a neutral basis (and thus have the same equity effects) for a given funding concept. As was discussed in Proposition 2, in this setting, the issue of efficiency effects should be emphasized by the accounting standard-setter in the choice of an accounting basis. In contrast, if event distributions are not identical, a standard-setter may have to face the dilemma of potentially conflicting equity-efficiency trade-offs. We provide an example (in Proposition 3) that demonstrates the existence of conflicts between the equity and efficiency effects of choosing an accounting basis. To simplify our analysis, we assume that the mean of the distributions of economic events increases (but not necessarily in a strict monotone sequence) over generations. We also assume (for illustration purposes) that a particular funding concept, $F3$, is adopted (i.e., obligations are shared by citizens when actual cash payments are made by the government). In summary, we have a scenario in which expected governmental cash outflows increase over time. Following the result in Proposition 1, the only "neutral basis" under these circumstances is the Cash Basis (because of the assumption of the funding concept $F3$). Thus if we invoke the concept of interperiod equity, the use of the Cash Basis of accounting is indicated. However, if the occurrence of the events are extremely volatile, there may exist an Allocation Basis of accounting such that citizens across generations would prefer it unanimously over any other accounting basis available. This result is summarized in Proposition 3.

> **Proposition 3.** *Assuming that (a) the distributions of economic events have a sequence of means which increases over time, (b) funding concept F3 is used and, (c) assumptions in III.A hold, there exists an allocation mechanism such that citizens across generations prefer an Allocation Basis to the other accounting bases if the variance of the event distribution is large.*

Proof: See Appendix 5.

The above proposition shows that pursuit of the goal of interperiod equity may not always be in the best interest of citizens. In Proposition 3, although the Cash Basis can serve as a "neutral" basis and, consequently, by definition can serve the purpose of measuring interperiod equity, citizens (ex ante) may still unanimously prefer an Allocation Basis of accounting if the benefits of increased risk-sharing outweigh the concern of inequity. In other words, citizens are willing to forgo an "equitable" allocation in exchange for an alternative allocation that is not equitable but gives all citizens a higher expected utility level (due to improved risk sharing). If the occurrence of economic events is relatively certain (i.e., low volatility) the contribution of an Allocation Basis to improving risk-sharing efficiency is limited. As its use may cause equity distortions for citizens in different generations, it may not be the preferred basis. If the benefit from improving risk-sharing is marginal, one can have a situation where none of the competing accounting bases will dominate the others in terms of citizens' expected utility level. Under these circumstances, a standard-setter will have to directly confront the equity-efficiency value judgment in choosing an accounting basis.

One important point that should be mentioned is that the analysis presented earlier was based upon the assumption of consistent application of whatever accounting basis is chosen. Any inconsistency in the application of any accounting basis can cause inequity among generations, if appropriate adjustments are not provided at the time of the change. A simple example is provided next to demonstrate this point.

Let us return to the assumptions given in Corollary 1 and also assume that the funding concept is *F3*. Corollary 1 tells us that either the Cash or the Accrual Basis will be a neutral basis. Assume now that in period t a city manager makes switch from the Cash to the Accrual Basis. The effect of the change will be to increase the burden of the citizens of t generation while reducing the obligation of the $t+m$ generation. Inconsistency thus generates a set of preference orders which differs from the one that is generated by the bench mark measure. This simple example shows that changing the basis of accounting will inevitably lead to interperiod inequity unless an appropriate adjustment is made at the time of change. Thus, for a standard-setter, it is important to know that any accounting change will create equity distortions unless it is accompanied with an appropriate adjustment at the time of change.

In summary, the efficiency analyses provided in this section show that an Allocation Basis can serve as an indirect mechanism for improving risk-sharing among citizens in different generations. Thus, if different accounting bases have the same equity implications, accounting standard setters should consider adopting an Allocation Basis. Also, if different accounting bases have different equity implications, accounting standard setters should again consider the Allocation Basis if the events are extremely volatile. However, in the cases where equity and efficiency are mixed, standard setters will have to use their own judgment in choosing an accounting basis.

V. DISCUSSION

A. Summary and Implications

In this section we present a brief summary of our principal findings and discuss their policy implications. We began by pointing out that the issue of interperiod equity in governmental accounting must be based on a normative funding concept; for example, who should pay for government services. For a given equity/funding concept, we then defined a corresponding neutral accounting basis as one that will faithfully measure equity implications. Within our model we find: (A) In most cases, different "neutral" accounting bases are associated with different funding concepts for the purpose of measuring interperiod equity (see Proposition 1). This is because, except in the unusual case of identical events' distributions (i.e., Corollary 1), a single basis of accounting can not be neutral with respect to multiple funding concepts. (B) Although the Allocation Basis of accounting may not be "neutral" with respect to some funding concepts, it can improve risk-sharing efficiency among citizens across generations, if the occurrence of the economic events is relatively uncertain (see Propositions 2 and 3).

The accounting policy implications of the above findings are potentially significant. The first finding suggests that to address the issue of measuring interperiod equity, it is important to recognize the role that funding concepts play in the choice of a neutral basis of accounting. Although we believe that it would be controversial for GASB to take on the role of determining the appropriate set of funding concepts for various types of events (who should pay), accounting policy must consider the effects of funding concepts if interperiod equity is the basic objective of governmental accounting. For example, citizens in a city may feel that different types of events/transactions require different funding concepts. In this case, strict application of a uniform accounting basis for all events would be inappropriate. This suggests that the GASB may need to use its due process procedure to address the basic role of funding concepts in financial reporting. It also serves as a conceptual justification for GASB's reluctance to impose one basis of accounting for various types of events. A similar point can be made about citizens in different jurisdictions. If different governments adopt different funding concepts for the same event, our analysis would suggest that the governments should adopt different bases of accounting for the event. If GASB were to require uniform treatment across governments, the goal of measuring interperiod equity in some cities would not be achieved.

Our results also illustrate a well-known theme in welfare economics; viz., in many situations equity-efficiency trade-offs must be confronted in setting public policy. To the extent that efficiency is an important criterion, it may be appropriate for the GASB to expand the objectives of financial reporting to include efficiency rather than just focusing on interperiod equity. For example, if an event's probability of occurrence is expected to have identical distribution across generations, an allocation basis of accounting would provide a strong risk-sharing mechanism without sacrificing the goal of measuring interperiod equity.

Finally, our model can provide some guidance concerning the appropriate choice of accounting basis or bases by GASB for certain types of economic events. Table 1 summarizes our results:

1. Regardless of the type of funding concept assumed, if the occurrence of an event is highly uncertain, but the event has a relatively regular distribution over time (for example, law suits in a non-inflationary economy; cell 1 in Table 1), an Allocation Basis can provide a mechanism for improving risk sharing among different generations without sacrificing the goal of measuring interperiod equity.
2. In the case where the mean of the events' distributions has a monotone increasing (or irregular) sequence over time, the Allocation Basis *may* still dominate the other accounting bases, if the occurrence of events is extremely volatile (cells 2 and 3 in Table 1).
3. If the events' distributions have relatively low volatility (cells 4,5,6 in Figure 1), standards-setters should focus primarily on the issue of measuring interperiod equity rather than on the issue of efficiency. This is because under these circumstances the Allocation Basis can provide only marginal benefit for improving risk-sharing among citizens in different generations. In such cases, the neutral basis of accounting corresponding to the normative funding concept is the basis that shall be adopted.

B. Limitations and Extensions

There are several important limitations inherent in the conclusions of this research.

Variance σ^2 Mean μ	e_t Has High Volatility	e_t Has Low Volatility
Identical Means Over Generations	(1): $R2$ why: efficiency concern e.g.: natural disasters, law suits against city	(4): $R1,R2$, or $R3$ why: same equity, efficiency implications e.g.: recurring events

Monotone Increase Means	(2): $R2$ or depends on Fi
	why: efficiency concern might
	    outweight equity
	
	e.g.: pension with inflation
		(5): Ri depends on Fi
		why: equity concern might
		    outweight efficiency
		
		e.g.:recurring events with inflation

Irregular Means	(3): $R2$ or depends on Fi why: IPE - efficiency trade off e.g.: extraordinary events	(6): Ri depends on Fi why: equity concern might outweight efficiency e.g.: irregular events

Notes: e_t, event at t. Within a cell: The first line indicates the preferred basis of accounting; $R1$: Accrual, $R2$: Allocation, $R3$: Cash, Depends on Fi: depends on funding concept adopted. For example, if the funding concept is F1, an Accrual Basis is appropriate. The second line indicates why that basis is preferred. The third line indicates a potential example event that fits the cell.

Figure 1.   Choice of an Accounting Basis As a Function of
Event Characteristics

1.   No political manipulation concerning the timing and measurement of events was considered in the model. An interesting extension of our model would be to allow politicians to choose different reporting methods with different degrees of precision from a set of GGAP.

2.   The results obviously depend on the equity concept definition used in the analysis. Although the equity concept defined in the paper is derived from the funding concepts, other alternative definitions of equity could be explored.

3.   Intergenerational transfers (for example, bequests or gifts across genera-tions) are not allowed in this model. Although the results of this paper may still hold if a one time intergenerational transfer (for example, fixed percentage bequest to the next generation) is introduced into the model, the formal analysis of the impact of such complications is left to further research.

4.   The focus of this paper is on the choice of a basis of accounting from the view point of an accounting policymaker (i.e., the GASB) rather than the disclosure behavior of the city managers or mayors. One possible extension of the research would be to analyze the strategic interactions among generations based on municipal disclosures in an overlapping-generations model as in, for example, Dye [1988], Barro [1974], Alesina and Cukierman [1987].

5.   Finally, no debt financing is considered in our model. The effects of debt versus tax financing can be expected to be extremely complicated. For example,

macroeconomic theory suggests that issuing debt could affect the household's consumption, saving, interest rate, and so on. Whether issuing a bond is equivalent to a tax financing depends on the perfectness of private capital markets, the uncertainty about future tax liability, and so forth [for example, Barro, 1974]. Modeling the effects of these complications on the choice of GGAP is also left for subsequent research.

APPENDIX 1: PROOF OF PROPOSITION 1

Note that a t-generation citizen's ex ante expected utility is a function of the basis of accounting, Ri, adopted:

$$V_t(R_i) = E\left[-\exp\left(-(w - \pi_t(R_i))\right)\right]$$

An Allocation Basis ($R2$) first estimates an amount of future cash flow $E(Y_t \mid e_t)$ at time t when the event/transaction occurs. It then systematically allocates the estimated obligation to the next k periods of time, such that each one of the $t+j$ subsequent generations share a portion of obligation $\alpha_j E(Y_t \mid e_t)$ where $\sum_{j=0}^{k-1} \alpha_j = 1$.

A final adjustment for the difference between Y_t (the actual payment) and $E(Y_t \mid e_t)$ (the estimated obligation) is also required at time $t + m$ when the actual cash outflows of e_t is realized. Thus, the ex post aggregate obligations that a t-generation citizen should pay is:

$$\pi_t = \sum_{j=0}^{k-1} \alpha_j E(Y_{t-j} \mid e_{t-j}) - (E(Y_{t-m} \mid e_{t-m})) + Y_{t-m}$$

By letting $\alpha_0 = 1$ and $\alpha_j = 0$, $\forall\, j = 1,\ldots, k-1$, an Allocation Basis of accounting becomes an Accrual Basis. Similarly, a Cash Basis can also be defined by letting $\alpha_m = 1$ and $\alpha_j = 0$, $\forall\, j \neq m, j = 0,\ldots, k-1$. Denote the net consumption of a t-generation citizen as $c_t = W - \pi_t$. The assumption of joint normal distribution implies that the ex ante expected utility of a t-generation citizen V_t is monotonically increasing in $[\text{Mean}(c_t) - \text{Var}(c_t)/2]$. Hence, a citizen's preference order can simply be ranked by the order of $[\text{Mean}(c_t) - \text{Var}(c_t)/2]$.

Denote the mean and the variance of the event e_t as μ_t and σ^2 respectively, and denote the correlation coefficient of any two events e_t, e_{t+j}, as ρ. Assume that $Y_t = be_t + \varepsilon_t$, where $\varepsilon_t \sim N(0,\Omega)$. Under the assumption of an Allocation Basis (R2), one has

$$\text{Var}(c_t) = b^2 \sigma^2 \left[\sum_{j=1}^{k-1} \alpha_i^2 + \sum_{j=0}^{k-1} \sum_{i=0}^{k-1} \alpha_i \alpha_j \rho \right] + \Omega, j \neq i; \qquad (1)$$

$$\text{Mean}(c_t) = W - \sum_{i=0}^{k-1} \alpha_i \mu_i \tag{2}$$

The proof of Proposition 1 can now proceed as follows: First, start with funding concept $F3$. A funding concept of $F3$ implies that $\alpha_m = 1$ and

$$\pi_t = \alpha_m \, E(Y_{t-m} \mid e_{t-m}) + [Y_{t-m} - E(Y_{t-m} \mid e_{t-m})].$$

Denote $M(F3)$ be the corresponding bench mark measure for funding concept $F3$. Thus, we have

$$\text{Mean}[c_t(M(F3))] - \text{Var}[c_t(M(F3))]/2 = \mu_{t-m} - b^2\sigma^2/2 \tag{3}$$

However, a Cash Basis would imply:

$$\text{Mean}[c_t(R3)] - \text{Var}[C_t(R3)]/2 = \mu_{t-m} - (b^2\sigma^2 + \Omega)/2 \tag{4}$$

Since a Cash Basis has no measurement error; i.e., $\Omega=0$. Therefore, (3) and (4) induce the same set of preference order. Thus, a Cash Basis is a neutral accounting basis under the assumption of $F3$. In addition, one can show that no other bases can provide the same set of preference order under funding assumption $F3$. For example, a preference order set induced by (1) and (2); that is, the allocation basis obviously differs from the one induced by (3).

Next, assume that the funding concept is $F1$, then the corresponding bench mark measure gives us:

$$\text{Mean}[c_t(M(F1))] - \text{Var}[c_t(M(F1))]/2 = \mu_t - b^2\sigma^2/2 \tag{5}$$

Under the assumption the Accrual Basis, we also have

$$\text{Mean}[c_t(R1)] - \text{Var}[C_t(R1)]/2 = \mu_t - (b^2\sigma^2 + \Omega)/2 \tag{6}$$

For any given t and $t - j$

$$\text{Mean}[c_t(M(F1))] - \text{Var}[c_t(M(F1))]/2 > \text{Mean}[c_{t-j}(M(F1))] - \text{Var}[c_{t-j}(M(F1))]/2$$

implies that

$$\text{Mean}[c_t(R1)] - \text{Var}[c_t(R1)]/2 > \text{Mean}[c_{t-j}(R1)] - \text{Var}[c_{t-j}(R1)]/2$$

Hence, the preference order $P_t(R1)$ induced by the basis of $R1$ is the same as the one induced by $M(F1)$; that is, $P_t(M(F1))$; and vice versa. Thus, an Accrual Basis is neutral with respect to funding concept $F1$. By following a similar procedure, one can also prove that the Allocation Basis is a neutral basis under funding assumption $F2$. Thus, we have proved that different "neutral" accounting bases are associated with different funding concepts.   Q.E.D.

APPENDIX 2: PROOF OF OBSERVATION 1

Let Ri be the accounting basis which indues an envy-free cross generation allocation. This implies that

$$V_t(Ri) \geq V_{t+j}(Ri), \quad \forall\, j,\, t. \tag{7}$$

Since citizens are assumed to have identical preference, (7) implies that

$$V_t(Ri) = V_{t+j}(Ri), \quad \forall\, j,\, t. \tag{8}$$

From the computation of citizen's expected utility (see Appendix 1), (7) and (8) imply that for any given t, events' distributions have constant means across generations. Also, the ex ante expected utilities under different accounting bases satisfy: $V_t(Ri) = V_t(R) +$ "a constant," for any $R \in \{Rj, j \neq i\} \cup \{M(Fi), i,j = 1,2,3\}$. Therefore, $V_t(M(Fi)) = V_{t+i}(M(Fi))\ \forall\, t,\, i$. Hence we conclude that $P_t(Ri) = P_t(M(Fi))$. By the definition of a neutral basis, Ri must be neutral under the funding concept Fi. Q.E.D.

APPENDIX 3: PROOF OF COROLLARY 1

The assumption of identical distributions for the economic events implies that $\mathrm{Mean}(c_t(Ri))$ and $\mathrm{Var}(c_t(Ri))/2$ are constants across t. Thus, a citizen is ex ante indifferent among alternative generations in which he might live; that is, $V_t(Ri) = V_j(Ri),\ \forall\, t,\, j,\ and\ Ri$. Also, under the assumption of identical distribution the bench mark measure has $V_t(M(Fi)) = V_j(M(Fi));\ \forall\, t,\, j,$ and Fi. Therefore, we have $P_t(Ri) = P_t(M(Fi));\ \forall\, Ri$ and Fi. Thus, by definition, any one of the accounting bases is a neutral basis regardless of the funding concept assumed.   Q.E.D.

APPENDIX 4: PROOF OF PROPOSITION 2

The assumption that events are not perfectly correlated implies that the correlation coefficient $\rho \neq 1$. From equation (1) of Appendix 1 an Allocation Basis implies that:

$$\mathrm{Var}(c_t) = b^2\sigma^2 \left[\sum_{j=1}^{k-1} \alpha_i^2 + \sum_{j=0}^{k-1}\sum_{i=0}^{k-1} \alpha_i\alpha_j\rho \right] + \Omega, \quad j \neq i;$$

By assuming that $\alpha_m = 1\ (\alpha_0 = 1)$ and $\alpha_j = 0,\ \forall\, j \neq m(j \neq 0)$, we have the variance term for the Cash (Accrual) Basis as: $\mathrm{Var}(c_t(R1)) = b^2\sigma^2 + \Omega = \mathrm{Var}(c_t(R3))$. Under the assumption of identical distributions, we also have

$$\mathrm{Mean}(c_t(R2)) = W - [\Sigma\, \alpha_j\mu_{t-j}] = W - \mu,\ \text{since } \mu_t = \mu,\ \forall\, t.$$

Thus, we conclude:

$$\text{Mean}(c_t(R2)) = \text{Mean}(c_t(R1)) = \text{Mean}(c_t(R3)).$$

Note that $\alpha_i, \alpha_j, \rho < 1$; therefore, $\text{Var}(c_t(R2)) < \text{Var}(c_t(R1)) = \text{Var}(c_t(R3))$, we therefore have $V_t(R2) > V_t(R1) = V_t(R3)$, $\forall\ t$. Thus, citizens prefer the Allocation Basis to either the Cash or the Accrual Basis.   Q.E.D.

APPENDIX 5: PROOF OF PROPOSITION 3

By the assumption of monotonicity, $t > s$ implies that $\mu_t \geq \mu_s$. Comparing the Cash Basis versus the Allocation Basis, we have

$$\text{Mean}(c_t(R2)) = W - [\Sigma\ \alpha_j\ \mu_{t-j}] < \text{Mean}(c_t(R3)) = W - \mu_{t-m}, \text{ if } m < k.$$

From Appendix 4, if the events are not perfectly correlated, we also have

$$\text{Var}(c_t(R2)) = b^2\sigma^2[\Sigma\ \alpha_i^2 + \Sigma\ \Sigma\ \alpha_i\alpha_j\ \rho] + \Omega < \text{Var}(c_t(R3)) = b^2\sigma^2 + \Omega.$$

Therefore, for given ρ, Ω and b, there must exist a $\sigma^{2*} > 0$ such that for any $\sigma^2 > \sigma^{2*}$

$$\text{Mean}(c_t(R3)) - \text{Var}(c_t(R3))/2 < \text{Mean}(c_t(R2)) - \text{Var}(c_t(R2))/2.$$

Q.E.D.

ACKNOWLEDGMENT

The authors gratefully acknowledge the helpful comments of participants in accounting workshops at the University of Pittsburgh and the University of California-Berkeley.

NOTES

1. GASB's Statement No. 11 indicates that there are situations that may require different funding concepts. For example, paragraph 30 says " . . . the Board intends to explore whether budgetary funding methods designed to achieve interperiod equity for certain types of expenditures meet the test of being "systematic and rational" and, therefore, warrant uses for expenditure recognition and measurement purposes."

2. The above assumptions imply that (ex ante) citizens are uncertain about their future tax burdens and that the objective of citizens is to minimize their expected tax burdens. A similar model could be developed to analyze the setting where there is uncertainty concerning the benefit that a citizen can expect to receive from the government. Without loss of generality, our model assumes that a citizen's utility from the specific services provided by the government is known and constant across generations. It is the per capita tax burden which a citizen has to share in each generation that is not known with certainty (ex ante).

REFERENCES

Alesina, A. and A. Cukierman, "The Politics of Ambiguity," Working Paper, [Carnegie-Mellon University, 1987].

Barro, R.J., "Are Government Bonds Net Wealth?," *Journal of Political Economy* [1974], pp. 1095–1117.

Baumol, W. J., "Applied Fairness Theory and Rationing Policy," *American Economic Review* [September 1982], pp. 639–651.

———, *Superfairness* [MIT Press, 1986].

Dye, R.A., "Earnings Management in an Overlapping Generations Model," *Journal of Accounting Research* [Autumn 1988], pp. 195–235.

Governmental Accounting Standards Board, *Statement No. 11*, "Measurement Focus and Basis of Accounting—Governmental Fund Operating Statements," (MFBA) *Governmental Accounting Standards Series* [May 1990].

———, "Concept Statement No. 1 of Governmental Accounting Standards Board," *Governmental Accounting Standards Series* [May 1987].

Ives, M.,"Pension Accounting the Controversy Continues," *Government Financial Review* [December 1988], pp. 13–17.

Lev, B., "Toward a Theory of Equitable and Efficient Accounting Policy," *The Accounting Review* [January 1988], pp. 1–22.

Pazner, E.A., "Pitfalls in the Theory of Fairness," *Journal of Economic Theory* [1977], pp. 458–466.

Varian, H.R., "Equity, Envy and Efficiency," *Journal of Economic Theory* [1974].

AN ANALYSIS OF LOBBYING ACTIVITIES BEFORE THE GOVERNMENTAL ACCOUNTING STANDARDS BOARD

Robin W. Roberts and James M. Kurtenbach

ABSTRACT

Prior research investigating the lobbying behavior of parties affected by proposed accounting and auditing standards has focused on the corporate sector standard-setting process. Our research examines the incentives of financial statement preparers and attestors to lobby before the Governmental Accounting Standards Board (GASB). Incentives to lobby before the GASB are expected to vary somewhat from those in the corporate sector because (1) there is no regulatory body to enforce compliance with standards, (2) different agency relationships are present in the public sector, and (3) the underlying motivation for public sector financial reporting is not identical to that in the corporate sector. We use agency theory and the economic theory of regulation as a conceptual framework to develop expectations concerning why and

Research in Governmental and Nonprofit Accounting, Vol. 7, pages 25–40.
ISBN: 1-55938-418-2

when financial statement preparers and attestors might submit comment letters to the GASB. These expectations concerning lobbying behavior are empirically tested using data from comment letters received by the GASB in response to their *Statement No. 5* exposure draft on pension disclosures. Our empirical tests show that the GASB received a significantly larger proportion of comment letters opposing the exposure draft. This result suggests that preparers and attestors considered information production costs, flexibility in financial reporting, and audit fees in their lobbying positions.

I. INTRODUCTION

Numerous studies have investigated the lobbying behavior of parties affected by the implementation of new professional standards. Prior research has focused on lobbying activities before the Financial Accounting Standards Board [Deakin, 1989; Puro, 1984; Watts and Zimmerman, 1978], the Auditing Standards Board [Geiger, 1989; Kinney, 1986], and the Accounting Standards Committee in the United Kingdom [MacArthur, 1988]. With the exception of Kinney [1986], these studies examined comment letters received by these standard-setting bodies. In this study we extend prior research by examining comment letters submitted to the Governmental Accounting Standards Board (GASB).

Although the GASB comment letter process is similar to that used by other standard-setting bodies, differences in the composition of their constituents and in the standard setters' willingness to consider constituents' arguments may result in different levels of constituent participation and influence. Also, the governmental accounting standard-setting process may be expected to differ from the corporate process because: (1) there is no regulatory body in the public sector, such as the Securities and Exchange Commission, to enforce compliance with standards, (2) different agency relationships are present in the public sector, and (3) the underlying motivation for public sector financial reporting is not identical to that in the private sector (i.e., there is less emphasis on income effects in the public sector).

This study should be of interest to governmental accounting standard setters, regulatory authorities, accountants, auditors, and financial statement users. An evaluation of the incentives of these parties to influence the regulation of governmental accounting standards will increase our knowledge of the dynamics of the GASB standard-setting process. In our study, the economic theory of regulation and agency theory are employed to provide some insights into why and when governmental financial statement preparers and attestors may participate in the GASB standard-setting process (by submitting comment letters). The insights gained through applying these theories are used to analyze the content of comment letters received by the GASB regarding GASB *Statement No. 5*, "Disclosure of Pension Information by Public Employee Retirement Systems And State and Local Government Employers." GASB *Statement No. 5* was selected because a relatively large number of comment letters regarding this exposure draft (ED) were received.

Although analyzing a single ED with an above-average number of responses reduces our ability to generalize our findings, the selection insured that we analyzed an ED that generated significant interest among GASB constituents.

The rest of the paper is organized as follows. Section II presents the conceptual foundations of our study, reviews prior research on lobbying in the accounting standard-setting process, and states our expectations regarding the incentives of financial statement preparers and attestors to lobby for or against the GASB *Statement No. 5* ED. Section III explains our research design, and Section IV presents our results. The conclusions, limitations, and suggestions for future research are presented in Section V.

II. CONCEPTUAL FOUNDATIONS AND PRIOR RESEARCH

We develop our expectations concerning the lobbying positions of financial statement preparers and attestors regarding the GASB *Statement No. 5* ED through: (1) analyzing evidence from prior research on accounting standard lobbying, and (2) revising the conceptual bases used in prior research to address some of the incentives that may influence lobbying in the governmental sector.

A. Prior Research

Prior research has provided evidence that accounting standards are created through a political process [Deakin, 1989; Puro, 1984; Watts and Zimmerman, 1978]. Given a political process, parties affected by changes in the standards may be expected to try to influence the proposed standards. Puro [1984] analyzed auditor lobbying behavior before the Financial Accounting Standards Board using two models, an economic regulation model and an agency theory model. Salient features of each of these models and prior research related to accounting standard lobbying are discussed below.

1. The Economic Theory of Regulation

The economic theory of regulation, first introduced by Stigler [1971], maintains that economic regulation exists to forward the private interests of politically effective groups. The theory holds to the general economic premise that people act in their own self-interest and do so in a rational manner. Outcomes of the regulatory process can be explained by understanding the determinants of demand and supply for economic regulation. Puro believed that the economic theory of regulation provides a particularly proper foundation for developing expectations of auditor lobbying positions on accounting standards dealing with *new disclosure* requirements. Results of her empirical tests were consistent with her analysis. Although the economic theory of regulation has not been used extensively in public sector accounting research, it has the same basic appeal for investigating the GASB standard-setting process that it held for Puro [1984] in her study of the FASB process.

2. Agency Theory

Agency theory is an economic theory that is rooted in the same basic assumptions as those of the economic theory of regulation (i.e., people act in their own self-interest and are rational in their decisions). Principals (e.g., owners or voters) assume that agents will act in their own best interests and enter into contracts with the agents to align the agent's interests with those of the principals. Thus, an agent's opportunities to act in a purely self-interested manner are limited by his or her contract with the principal.

Agency theory has been used in the corporate sector to propose hypotheses concerning management lobbying decisions [Watts and Zimmerman, 1978]. Factors explored in prior agency-based studies include debt, taxes, regulation, management compensation, firm contracts, information production costs, and political costs [Deakin, 1989; Watts and Zimmerman, 1978]. Puro [1984] posited that the agency theory perspective was particularly appropriate for analyzing auditor lobbying positions on standards that proposed *standardization* of accounting methods. Her results were consistent with agency theory expectations regarding auditor lobbying on standardization proposals.

Agency theory has been applied extensively in public sector research. Zimmerman [1977] used the Jensen-Meckling agency model to define principal-agent relationships in the municipal sector. Elected officials were viewed as agents of the voting public and bureaucrats as agents of the elected officials.[1] Baber [1983] analyzed the role of auditing in the public sector. His work, based on the monitoring demand for auditing, viewed auditors as agents employed by elected and appointed officials to add credibility to the financial statements they make available to their principals (the voters).

Our ability to use an agency theory perspective to develop specific expectations about the lobbying positions of financial statement preparers and attestors concerning the GASB proposals for standardizing accounting practices depends on the principal-agent relationships operating within the public sector. For example, if voters (principals) are actually interested in the GASB standard-setting process (because it affects the amount and the types of financial information they receive from elected and appointed officials, i.e., agents), then the officials may have sufficient incentives to lobby (as agents of the voters) for accounting standards that provide the financial information desired by the voters. On the other hand, if voters do not appear concerned about the standardized accounting standards, then the officials may be motivated to lobby in a more self-interested manner, consistent with the economic theory of regulation.

B. Public Sector Lobbying in Accounting Standard Setting

From our review of prior research we conclude that the economic theory of regulation and agency theory provide similar (but not identical) perspectives from which to develop some expectations about why financial statement preparers and attestors may decide to participate in the GASB standard-setting process. Like Puro [1984], we will develop our expectations of lobbying behavior separately for GASB proposals (1) for new disclosure standards and (2) for standardizing accounting methods.

In order to gain some initial understanding of the nature of the lobbying activities before the GASB, we decided to first identify which GASB constituencies could be considered politically active groups. Once the active lobbying groups were identified, we then developed expectations (based on the economic theory of regulation and/or agency theory) of why and when a group would lobby before the GASB.

In order to determine which constituencies are actively involved in the standard setting process, we obtained from the GASB lists of individuals and organizations that wrote comment letters regarding six different GASB projects. Using the respondent category scheme adopted by the GASB, we developed four broad categories for respondents—financial statement preparers, attestors, users, and others. The number of comment letters written by each group for each GASB project is presented in Table 1.

The frequencies of comment letter submissions by financial statement users and by others (i.e., educators) are very low. For the six GASB projects analyzed in Table 1, financial statement users represent only 6.2 percent of the respondents and "others" represent only 4.0 percent. Thus, preparers and attestors make up almost 90 percent of the GASB comment letter respondents for these six GASB projects. The low frequencies for users seem even more dramatic because there are many more potential financial statement users than preparers or attestors. One reason for this low rate of participation by users and others may be found in the economic theory of regulation. The economic theory of regulation holds that regulation exists to benefit those who are regulated—in this case, financial statement preparers and attestors. Financial statement users and others are not expected to be involved in the standard-setting process because they do not have as much to gain as preparers and attestors have to gain from trying to influence the regulatory process. In any case, based on the data presented in Table 1, we decided to limit our analysis to financial statement preparer and attestor lobbying activities before the GASB.

1. *Lobbying Positions of Financial Statement Preparers*

For state and local governments, financial statement preparers are the elected and appointed officials responsible for the management of public sector entities. As rational actors, elected officials are expected to make decisions that maximize

Table 1. Frequencies of Responses by GASB Constituents to Selected GASB Exposure Drafts

	Preparers		Users		Attestors		Others		
GASB Project	No.	(%)	No.	(%)	No.	(%)	No.	(%)	Total
1. GASB Project No. 4 (Measurement Focus)	111	(58.1)	7	(3.6)	62	(32.5)	11	(5.8)	191
2. GASB Project No. 20 (FASB statement # 93)	73	(71.6)	3	(2.9)	23	(22.6)	3	(2.9)	102
3. GASB Project No. 5-1 (Pension Disclosures)	57	(57.6)	9	(9.0)	29	(29.3)	4	(4.1)	99
4. GASB Project No. 12 (Financial Institutions)	44	(47.8)	8	(8.7)	34	(37.0)	6	(6.5)	92
5. GASB Project No. 10-1 (Business-Type Activities)	47	(64.4)	3	(4.1)	22	(30.1)	1	(1.4)	73
6. GASB Project No. 3-3 (Reporting Entity)	40	(52.6)	9	(11.8)	26	(34.1)	1	(1.3)	76
Total	372	(58.8)	39	(6.2)	143	(31.0)	26	(4.0)	633

Source: Governmental Accounting Standards Board

their chances for reelection. Appointed officials are expected to make decisions that maximize the probability that they will be reappointed to their current position and/or improve their status in the public sector managerial labor market [Evans and Patton, 1987].

In deciding whether or not to lobby before the GASB, it seems logical that officials will assess (1) the time and effort it takes to develop their arguments into a comment letter, (2) their ability to influence the outcome, and (3) the severity of the costs associated with having to implement a new accounting standard. The costs associated with new standards may include (1) explicit costs imposed on the public sector entity in order to generate financial statements that comply with the new standard, and (2) the implicit costs associated with restricting officials' choices regarding what, and how much, financial information should be revealed.

Under the economic regulation view, preparers might be expected to oppose new governmental accounting standards that increase financial disclosures. Their objections would stem from the additional production costs associated with generating the new types of financial information. Given the budget constraints that most governments operate under, officials may lobby against a disclosure-related ED because the higher financial reporting costs may divert resources from programs that are more likely to increase their chances of reelection. On the other hand, officials who already voluntarily disclose information similar to the proposed requirements may welcome the guidance and authoritative support provided by a GASB pronouncement.

Government officials might be expected to view GASB standardization proposals as restrictions on the alternatives available to them when deciding what, and how much, financial information should be revealed. The economic theory of regulation perspective leads us to believe that officials who have used an accounting method that would be eliminated by the adoption of a standardization exposure draft will probably oppose the ED. On the other hand, officials currently using the proposed method would not be expected to oppose that particular ED and might even support the standard for comparability reasons.

From an agency theory perspective, we believe that government officials would tend to support the positions of their voters. If certain existing disclosures or reporting methods that are preferred by the voters would be changed by a new GASB standard, then we would expect most officials to oppose the related ED. Conversely, if voters found new disclosure or reporting requirements to be beneficial, officials would be inclined to support the GASB proposal. This would be especially true if both the voters and the officials held the same beliefs. However, given that voters are likely to have divergent views regarding the desirability of a new standard, the mixed voter preferences in a political market complicate the prediction of officials' lobbying behavior. In addition, the appropriateness of using the agency theory perspective to develop expectations concerning officials' lobbying positions may be suspect because of the low level of user participation in the GASB standard setting process; see Table 1. If this lack of interest stems from a lack of use of financial statements as a monitoring device by voters, the descriptive power of agency theory in this setting could be relatively low.

Our analysis of financial statement preparer (i.e., government officials) lobbying incentives leads us to conclude that neither the economic theory of regulation nor agency theory provide unambiguous predictions of financial statement preparers' lobbying positions regarding disclosure-related or standardization-related sections of the GASB *Statement No. 5* ED. Because we have no way to predict ex ante whether officials who oppose or support sections of the ED are more likely to write a comment letter, we decided to test whether or not there was an equal distribution of financial statement preparer comments "supporting" versus "opposing" these sections. The statistical null hypotheses used to test our expectations are:

E1: *There is no significant difference between the proportion of financial statement preparers' comments supporting versus opposing the disclosure-related sections of the GASB Statement No. 5 exposure draft.*

E2: *There is no significant difference between the proportion of financial statement preparers' comments supporting versus opposing the standardization-related sections of the GASB Statement No. 5 exposure draft.*

2. Lobbying Positions of Attestors

Although Puro's model of audit firm lobbying was developed for the private sector standard-setting process, we think the incentives of public accounting firms and governmental audit agencies are similar enough to use her model as a basis for discussing some of the reasons why public accounting firms and state audit agencies may participate in the GASB standard-setting process. Just as Puro expects public accounting firms to seek increased revenues, we expect governmental auditors to prefer increased auditing budgets. Audit fee research supports this contention through the findings stating that audit firms price public sector and private sector audit engagements in a similar manner [Rubin, 1988] and that state audit agencies use a similar approach when charging local governments for their audits [Copley, 1989].

The preceding discussion leads us to believe that, from an economic theory of regulation perspective, attestors of the financial statements of public sector entities, as a group, would be inclined to favor the adoption of governmental accounting standards that result in an increased demand for attestation services. According to Puro [1984], this is more likely to be the case when new disclosure-related standards are being proposed than when an ED is related to the standardization of accounting methods. However, it appears to us that the degree to which this would hold true for a particular disclosure-related standard would be complicated by other firm-specific and client-related concerns. For example, an auditor may have only a few clients that would be affected by a new, complicated disclosure standard. These auditors may believe that the additional training required for them to continue to serve these few clients would cost more than they could collect in additional audit fees. In addition, lobbying positions on standardization-related issues are probably more complicated. When an audit firm is deciding its position on a standardization issue, the ultimate decision may depend upon whether or not the firm has already developed expertise in the accounting method chosen to be the standard and/or their assessment of the balance between the short-run costs associated with implementing the change and the long-run costs savings that may result from standardization.

Puro [1984, p. 625] explained that when analyzing auditor lobbying behavior, the agency theory perspective differs from the regulation model by "emphasizing ways in which the interests of clients and the interests of auditors can overlap." Instead of auditors focusing only on the impact of a prospective accounting standard on the demand for attestation (i.e., private interests), they recognize their role as agents of financial statement preparers when determining their lobbying position on a new accounting standard.

Using the agency theory paradigm, attestors view their wealth as being strongly linked to the wealth of their clients. Puro [1984], in describing the Watts and Zimmerman [1981] arguments, states that auditors are inclined to lobby for accounting standards that are in the best interests of their clients because clients produce audit revenues. Any standard that reduces client wealth may negatively impact the wealth of the audit firm. Given that clients will lobby in their own best interests, auditors may be inclined to adopt lobbying positions that are similar to those of their clients. Under this agency-based scenario, preparers and attestors could achieve mutually desirable outcomes from the standard-setting process.[2] It was Puro's opinion that an agency theory analysis of auditor lobbying would be a better predictor of auditor lobbying on standardization issues rather than disclosure issues.

We have no way to predict ex ante whether auditors who oppose or support sections of the ED are more likely to participate in the ED process. Thus, the null hypotheses used to test our expectations concerning attestor lobbying positions are nondirectional:

E3: *There is no significant difference between the proportion of attestors' comments supporting versus opposing the disclosure-related sections of the GASB Statement No. 5 exposure draft.*

E4: *There is no significant difference between the proportion of attestors' comments supporting versus opposing the standardization-related sections of the GASB Statement No. 5 exposure draft.*

III. RESEARCH DESIGN

To test our expectations regarding preparer and attestor lobbying positions, we analyzed the comment letters received by the GASB concerning key parts of the *Statement No. 5* ED. This section of our paper provides (1) a description of the key parts of the ED that were used as the basis for our empirical tests and a description of the comment letters received by the GASB, (2) an explanation of our comment letter analysis, and (3) a description of our empirical tests.

A. GASB *Statement No. 5* Exposure Draft

The parts of the GASB *Statement No. 5* ED relevant to our study were taken from Appendix E, Basis For Conclusions. The Basis for Conclusions section of the ED summarizes the key components of the draft, the alternatives considered by GASB, and the rationale for GASB's decisions. For the GASB *Statement No. 5* exposure draft, the Board discussed seven key issues. Six of the issues relate to increasing pension disclosure requirements or to standardizing the measure for the accumulated benefit obligation that is presented in the disclosures. A seventh issue related to the GASB's timing in addressing pension disclosure and is not considered in our analysis.

Three key issues discussed by the GASB in the ED would substantially increase the quantity of pension *disclosures* in governmental financial statements. The three issues are:

1. *Sensitivity Analysis*—GASB proposed the disclosure of a sensitivity analysis of a one percent increase and decrease in the interest rate used to calculate the discounted benefits obligation.
2. *Supplementary Information*—GASB proposed the disclosure of a ten-year historical trend in both dollar amounts and ratio analysis.
3. *Cost-Sharing Multiple-Employer*—GASB proposed that PERS disclosure is required in full detail if the employer is the dominant employer (25%) in a PERS and in summary if the employer is not the dominant employer.

We categorize the following three ED issues as attempts by the GASB to *standardize* the methods used to generate pension disclosure amounts:

1. *Frequency of Actuarial Updates*—GASB proposed to preclude the use of actuarial valuations undertaken more than 24 months prior to the balance sheet date. Also, a new actuarial valuation is required when there are changes in the benefit provisions.
2. *Measure*—GASB proposed a single, standardized measure of the accrued pension benefit obligation for disclosure.
3. *Attribution Approach*—GASB proposed the use of the credited projected benefits attribution approach prorated on service as the standardized measure for disclosure.

We combined respondents' comments to the disclosure-related ED issues to form the data used to test expectations E1 and E3. Respondents' comments to standardization-related ED issues provided the data to test expectations E2 and E4.

The GASB *Statement No. 5* ED was formally issued on August 20, 1985. Ninety-nine responses to the ED were received. The original respondent categories, as utilized by the GASB, consisted of 11 main categories. The 11 categories were collapsed into four for the purposes of our analysis: (1) financial statement preparers, (2) attestors, (3) users, and (4) others (e.g., educators). The 99 responses came from 57 financial statement preparers, 29 attestors, 9 users, and 4 other respondents. Our analysis was performed on the 86 comment letters received by the GASB from preparers and attestors.

Approximately 80 percent of the comment letters were written by individuals or committees representing a constituent organization (e.g., a state society of CPAs, a state auditor's office, or a government finance officers association). Because our expectations regarding lobbying positions of constituents are concerned with the aggregate position of a constituency, we believe that organization sponsorship of comment letters increases the reliability of the data used in our tests. Comment letters resulting from a committee analysis and/or letters that are endorsed by organizations may better represent the aggregate position of a particular type of constituency.

B. Comment Letter Analysis

Each author independently read the comment letters and made an assessment of the comment letter author's stance on each of the key parts of the exposure draft. The analysis was planned in such a way to provide consistent, reliable measures of the respondents' views on each of the seven key issues in the GASB *Statement No. 5* exposure draft. The steps used in our analysis were as follows:

1. We studied the exposure draft to make sure we understood the pertinent features of each of the key issues. We discussed our understanding of the key issues to increase validity of our analysis.
2. We developed a coding scheme and coding sheets to use in recording our interpretations of the respondents' views on each of the key issues. For each issue, the respondent's view was coded as "for," "against," "neutral," or "no mention."
3. We independently read each of the comment letters and recorded our personal interpretation of each respondent's view on each of the seven key issues.
4. We compared our independent evaluations to assess the degree of consensus reached on each issue for each respondent. We agreed on 79 percent of the ratings.
5. We held a meeting to reconcile observations where our codings were not the same. Where there was disagreement on a respondent's position, we jointly read the comment letter and reassessed the respondent's view. The consensus view is presented in the paper.

C. Description of Empirical Tests

We aggregated the "for" and "against" responses concerning the three disclosure-related sections and (separately) the three standardization-related sections of the ED for the purpose of testing our expectations. This approach was necessary in order to obtain a sufficient number of observations for use in the empirical tests and seems reasonable because our expectations regarding a constituent's lobbying position within each section of the ED (disclosure-related and standardization-related) does not vary across the issues.

Our expectations concerning financial statement preparers' lobbying positions on the disclosure-related and standardization-related sections of the ED (E1, E2,

E3, and E4) were tested using a binomial test. The binomial test allows us to test whether or not the proportion of preparer comments opposing versus supporting the sections of the ED are significantly different from that of an even representation of lobbying positions. This approach seems appropriate because (1) we are concerned with the comments that result in one of only two possible outcomes, "for" or "against" and (2) a priori the probability of a respondent being for or against a specific topic is equal to .5. One problem in using the binomial test is that by combining responses across the issues for each respondent in order to satisfy sample size requirements, we were unable to satisfy one of the assumptions of the test. Specifically, because each comment letter respondent could have stated a position on as many as six key ED issues, the binomial test assumption that each response is independent was not met. Although we believe that increasing the sample sizes was necessary for us to conduct empirical tests, this violation could bias our results because respondent comments across ED issues may be correlated (i.e., a respondent that opposes/favors one aspect of the ED is also likely to oppose/favor other aspects of the ED). This bias increases the likelihood that we would find significant results.[3]

IV. RESULTS

The frequencies of responses by category (i.e., financial statement preparers or attestors) for each of the six disclosure-related or standardization-related issues are presented in Tables 2 and 3.

The summary of financial statement preparer comment letters in Table 2 reveals several interesting features. First, very few comment letters written by financial statement preparers supported any of these six key issues for the *Statement No. 5* ED. The standardized pension obligation measure received the most support with four of the 57 comment letters signifying approval with that portion of the ED. Second, many comment letters from preparers focused on only one or two key issues. As noted in the "no mention" column on Table 2, 45 comment letters did not mention the proposed change in the frequency of actuarial updates, while all but 12 discussed the ten-year supplementary information proposals. An additional finding of the comment letter analysis deals with the fact that "neutral" comments were made for some of the key issues. The neutral responses usually discussed the pros and cons of a key issue without taking a clear stance for or against that particular proposal. Our theoretical discussion did not analyze the motives underlying a neutral lobbying position and these responses are not included in our empirical tests. We speculate that a neutral comment resulted from disagreements among committee members writing the comment letter or from a lack of clear support from a sponsoring organization's membership regarding the committee stance on a key issue.

Comment letters from attestors followed a pattern similar to that of the financial

Table 2. Analysis of Comment Letters Written to the GASB by Financial Statement Preparers Regarding GASB Statement No. 5 Exposure Draft

	For	Against	Neutral	No Mention	Total
Disclosure-Related Sections					
1. Sensitivity Analysis	2	25	1	29	57
2. Ten-Year Supplementary Information	1	43	1	12	57
3. Cost-Sharing Multiple Employer	2	11	7	37	57
Standardization-Related Sections					
1. Frequency of Actuarial Up-dates	0	11	1	45	57
2. Standardized Measure of Accrued Pension Benefit Obligation	4	36	0	17	57
3. Use of Credited Projected Benefits Approach	2	31	1	23	57

statement preparers. As shown in Table 3, attestors' letters did not provide much support for the key issues. The only substantive difference between preparer and attestor responses has to do with the proposed standardization of the accrued pension benefit obligation measure. Six of the 14 attestors that mentioned the standardization issue supported its adoption. Only four of the 40 preparers commenting on this issue supported its adoption.

The binomial tests performed to test our expectations regarding the lobbying positions of financial statement preparers and attestors produced statistically significant results. The results are presented in Table 4. At a .01 level of significance, all four of the two-tailed tests allow us to reject the null hypothesis of no differences in proportions for and against the proposal. Our findings suggest that the proportion of financial statement preparer comment letters opposing the adoption of disclosure-related (E1) and standardization-related (E2) sections of the ED is sig-

Table 3. Analysis of Comment Letters Written to the GASB by Financial Statement Attestors Regarding GASB Statement No. 5 Exposure Draft

	For	Against	Neutral	No Mention	Total
Disclosure-Related Sections					
1. Sensitivity Analysis	1	11	1	16	29
2. Ten-Year Supplementary Information	2	25	1	1	29
3. Cost-Sharing Multiple Employer	0	9	6	14	29
Standardization-Related Sections					
1. Frequency of Actuarial Up-dates	0	9	1	19	29
2. Standardized Measure of Accrued Pension Benefit Organization	6	8	0	15	29
3. Use of Credited Projected Benefits Approach	1	9	2	17	29

Table 4.   Results of Binomial Tests

ED Sections	For	Against	Total	Test Result
Panel A **Financial Statement Preparers**				
1. Disclosure-Related (Expectation 1)	5	79	84	Normal Approximation to Binomial $z = +/- 8.07$ $p < 0.0001$ The probability of only 5 or more than 78 preparers being for the disclosure items, by chance, is less than .0001
2. Standardization-Related (Expectation 2)	6	78	84	Normal Approximation to Binomial $z = +/- 7.86$ $p < 0.0001$ The probability of only 6 or more than 77 preparers being for the disclosure items, by chance, is less than .0001
Panel B **Attestors**				
1. Disclosure-Related (Expectation 3)	3	45	48	Normal Approximation to Binomial $z = +/- 6.06$ $p < 0.0001$ The probability of only 3 or more than 44 attestors being for the disclosure items, by chance, is less than .0001
2. Standardization-Related (Expectation 4)	7	26	33	Normal Approximation to Binomial $z = +/- 3.31$ $p < 0.0016$ The probability of only 7 or more than 25 attestors being for the disclosures items, by chance, is less than .0016

nificantly greater than 0.5. Likewise, the proportion of attestor comment letters opposing the disclosure-related (E3) and standardization-related (E4) aspects of the GASB *Statement No. 5* ED appear to be significantly greater than 0.5 (a random chance method of predicting lobbying positions).

V. CONCLUSIONS, LIMITATIONS, AND SUGGESTIONS FOR FUTURE RESEARCH

A. Conclusions

This study was designed to develop and test expectations regarding the lobbying activities by governmental financial statement preparers and attestors before the

GASB. Although our conceptual discussion did not lead to unambiguous predictions of preparer or attestor lobbying positions on the disclosure-related and standardization-related sections of the GASB *Statement No. 5* exposure draft, our empirical tests indicate that most preparers and attestors opposed these sections of the ED. Our application of agency theory and the economic theory of regulation suggests that preparer opposition may stem from potential increases in information production costs and/or reduced flexibility in financial reporting. Attestor opposition could be due to potential unrecoverable increases in audit costs or a concern for their clients' welfare.

B. Limitations and Suggestions for Future Research

The results of our analysis are subject to limitations. Our study investigated only one part of the lobbying process (comment letter submission) and limited the analysis to only one GASB exposure draft. Our analysis and our results may not represent the process associated with other aspects of the lobbying process and/or the comment letter process for other exposure drafts. Future studies could expand our sample to perform a more comprehensive analysis of the nature of governmental accounting standard setting. Another limitation is that we performed our empirical test of pension disclosure lobbying at an aggregate level. For example, we did not match financial statement preparers with their attestors to test specific agency theory expectations. Further research could be undertaken to test our expectations at a more micro level. Another avenue for future research in this area could address the impact of the comment letter process on the final version of the approved standard.

Finally, our results could be driven by some factors not controlled for in our tests. Specifically, one competing explanation for our results could be that a negative bias exists in the GASB comment letter process. Simply stated, it may be that some financial statement preparers and attestors write comment letters only when they oppose the exposure draft being considered. Evidence to suggest that this negative response bias is not a major factor in this case is the fact that 80 percent of the comment letters on the GASB *Statement No. 5* ED came from constituent organizations (e.g., a state society of CPAs, a state audit agency, or a government finance officers association). These organizations appear to respond to most GASB exposure drafts rather than just the ones they oppose. Future research could specifically address the extent to which such organizations routinely respond to all GASB exposure drafts.

ACKNOWLEDGMENTS

We gratefully acknowledge the helpful comments of the editor, an anonymous reviewer, and participants in the 1990 UIC Governmental Accounting Symposium.

NOTES

1. More recently, analytical studies in political science (e.g., Banks and Weingast [1989] and Banks [1990]) have modeled these relationships more carefully.

2. The Watts and Zimmerman [1978] analysis recognizes that audit firms may have clients that disagree on a given standard. They suggest that audit firms will support the lobbying position of clients that have displayed a strong interest in the standard (i.e., the firm is actively lobbying for their position). If these clients are not in agreement, audit firms are expected to support the majority position.

3. Another potential problem with our data relates to the possibility of a negative response bias (i.e., constituents only write comment letters when they disagree with key aspects of the GASB exposure draft). See the limitations section that follows.

REFERENCES

Baber, W.R., "Toward Understanding the Role of Auditing in the Public Sector," *Journal of Accounting and Economics* [December 1983], pp. 213–227.

Banks, J.S., and B.R. Weingest, "The Political Control of Bureaucracies Under Asymmetric Information," Working paper [University of Arizona, 1989].

Banks, J.S., "Agency Budget, Cost Information, and Auditing," *American Journal of Political Science* [November 1989], pp. 670–699.

Copley, P.A., "The Deteminants of Local Government Audit Fees: Some Additional Evidence," *Research in Governmental and Nonprofit Accounting* [1989] pp. 3–26.

Deakin, E., "Rational Economic Behavior and Lobbying on Accounting Issues: Evidence from the Oil and Gas Industry," *The Accounting Review* [January 1989], pp. 137–151.

Evans, J.H., III, and J.M. Patton, "Signaling and Monitoring in Public Sector Accounting," Supplement to *Journal of Accounting Research* [1987], pp. 130–158.

Geiger, M., "The New Audit Report: An Analysis of Exposure Draft Comments," *Auditing: A Journal of Practice and Theory* [Spring 1989], pp. 40–63.

Governmental Accounting Standards Board, *Statement No. 5*, "Disclosure of Pension Information by Public Employee Retirement Systems and State and Local Government Employers" [GASB, 1986].

Governmental Accounting Standards Board, *Proposed Standard*, "Disclosure of Pension Information by Public Employee Retirement Systems and State and Local Government Employers," [GASB, 1985].

Kinney, W., "Audit Technology and Preferences for Auditing Standards," *Journal of Accounting and Economics* [1986], pp. 73–89.

MacArthur, J., "An Analysis of the Content of Corporate Submissions on Proposed Accounting Standards in the UK," *Accounting and Business Research* [Summer 1988], pp. 213–226.

Puro, M., "Audit Firm Lobbying Before the Financial Accounting Standards Board," *Journal of Accounting Research* [Autumn 1984], pp. 624–646.

Rubin, M.A., "Municipal Audit Fee Determinants." *The Accounting Review* [April 1988], pp. 219–236.

Stigler, G.J., "The Theory of Economic Regulation," *Bell Journal of Economics* [Spring 1971], pp. 3–21.

Watts, R.L., and J.L. Zimmerman, "Auditors and the Determination of Accounting Standards," Working paper [University of Rochester, 1981].

Watts, R., and J. Zimmerman, "Towards a Positive Theory of the Determination of Accounting Standards," *The Accounting Review* [January 1978], pp. 112–134.

Zimmerman, J. "The Municipal Accounting Maze: An Analysis of Political Incentives," Supplement to *Journal of Accounting Research* [1977], pp. 107–144.

A PARTIAL VALIDATION OF THE GASB USER NEEDS SURVEY:
A METHODOLOGICAL NOTE

Robert W. Ingram and Walter A. Robbins

ABSTRACT

This study examines responses by municipal financial analysts to a set of financial information items included as part of the GASB survey of user needs. Our purpose is to validate the GASB findings by using a method of eliciting responses different from that used in the prior study. The approach we used is known as magnitude scaling and is designed to elicit information about the relative usefulness of survey items. Our approach overcomes several weaknesses inherent in the GASB instrument and research design. Our findings are consistent in most respects with those of the GASB. Thus, we demonstrate that the GASB results are robust to differences in survey instrument and sample.

I. INTRODUCTION

In 1985 the Governmental Accounting Standards Board [Jones et al., 1985] published its first research study titled *The Needs of Users of Governmental Financial Reports*. That study surveyed various external user groups regarding the

Research in Governmental and Nonprofit Accounting, Vol. 7, pages 41–52.

perceived importance of selected information items in annual reports of state and local governments. The purpose of this paper is to report on a partial replication of the GASB survey. The replication examined the potential for incorrect inference in the survey as a result of the instrument used to elicit responses.

In this study, we identified a sample of potential users of governmental annual reports similar to that sampled in a portion of the GASB survey. We used an instrument that included items from the GASB survey but that was designed to elicit information about the relative usefulness of survey items as opposed to the categorical scale used by the GASB. In addition to being more suitable for its purpose, our instrument provided a means of examining the internal validity of the survey that was not possible with the GASB study.

This study has implications for standard setting organizations that are interested in the opinions of users and preparers of financial reports. These organizations have often used questionnaires to obtain opinions of users and preparers. These opinions have then been used in formulating the agendas and setting the policies of these organizations. Validation of the results of these efforts is important to reduce the risk that improper conclusions may lead to erroneous policy decisions.

II. THE GASB SURVEY

The GASB surveyed various user groups to obtain information about aspects of the annual reports of state and local governments that were considered to be most important to the decisions of the users. The results of the survey were intended to provide guidance to the GASB in developing financial reporting objectives [GASB, 1986] and in developing reporting standards for governmental entities [Jones et al., 1985, p. 3].

The survey consisted of 115 items for which responses were sought on a 5-point scale. A small sample of users in each of three user categories (citizen groups, legislative and oversight officials, and investors and creditors) responded to the survey.[1]

Several problems exist with the survey. Some of these problems are inherent in survey research—self-selection bias, and the inability to assess the true beliefs of the respondents or the behavior associated with these beliefs [see Fowler 1984].[2] Other problems are associated with the survey instrument employed that is the primary concern of this study. One particular problem is the use of a subject-centered categorical scale to provide information about the relative perceived usefulness of survey items and failure of the survey to provide a means for examining measurement error.

Torgerson [1958] argued that if the research objective is to place the stimulus, not the subjects, on a continuum of interest, then a stimulus-centered scale should be used. This type of scale permits comparison across stimulus items. It is designed to measure subjects' attitudes rather than to compare responses of different subjects (subject-centered scale). Grove and Savic [1979] and Howard [1981] also asserted that since subject-centered scales require subjects to express the intensity of their attitudes about different items rather than to express their perceptions of the relative values of the items, it is improper to make statements about the relative relationship of the stimuli. Even though the GASB used a subject-centered scale to measure subjects' attitudes, an attempt was made to assess the relative usefulness of various items in the survey [Jones et al., 1985].

The 5-point categorical scale used by the GASB permits conclusions to be drawn about which groups had the strongest opinions about the usefulness of items in the survey. It was not an appropriate technique for drawing conclusions about the relative usefulness of the items as perceived by respondents.

As the GASB study attempted to draw inferences about the stimuli, the conclusions concerning the relative usefulness of the report items need to be validated. We replicated a portion of the GASB survey using stimulus-centered procedures designed to overcome these problems.

III. METHOD

A. Magnitude Scaling

Categorical scaling techniques such as the Likert and semantic differential scales are subject-centered scales, while stimulus-centered scales include the magnitude and Thurstone paired comparison scales [Torgerson, 1958]. A magnitude scale was used in our study to elicit subject responses. This technique was developed in the area of psychophysics and is advocated as a means of quantifying strengths of attitudes on a ratio scale.[3]

A salient feature of magnitude scaling is that all judgments are made explicitly relative to a reference (anchor) item. Thus, the individual respondent can gauge a response to a particular item relative to an established criterion. For example, if the researcher were interested in perceptions of the severity of crimes, robbery might provide an anchor and be given an arbitrary value of 100. Respondents would then be asked to score other crimes relative to the anchor. A crime perceived to be twice as severe as robbery would be assigned a score of 200, while one perceived to be half as severe would be assigned a score of 50.

The magnitude procedure allows the researcher to capture information about the *relative* magnitude of a stimulus. (As noted earlier, subject-centered measurement techniques are based on category scales.) These scales rely on arbitrary responses such as "very useful," "useful," or "not useful." Accordingly, respondents are inhibited from distinguishing among items that may be coded as similar but that can be differentiated in the minds of the respondents. The extent to which respondents can differentiate their responses is limited by the scale provided (a 5-point scale was used in the GASB survey). Such a scale has several limitations:

(1) We do not know whether all respondents had the same concept of usefulness in mind when they responded with a particular numerical value, "3" for example. (2) We do not know what range of usefulness is encompassed by all items for which a response of "3" was elicited. (3) We do not have a reference against which to compare the usefulness responses. For example, how useful are those items that received a response of 3 relative to those that received a response of 4?

An advantage of magnitude scaling (as noted by Howard [1978]) is that it does not require subjects to measure the stimuli using structured categories, but rather an open-ended measurement scale is provided that allows subjects to make a direct comparison of all stimulus items. Consequently, the items of interest are scaled on a "relative" basis.

Magnitude scales generate responses that are continuous, producing ratio measures. In contrast, categorical scaling results in nominal or ordinal measures. Attempts to compare responses across items are thus complicated by the measurement scale. Categorical scales often are treated as ratio scales, and distributional statistics such as means and standard deviations are used to make comparisons. However, the data often are not normally distributed and assumptions must be made about the relative differences in scale values. For example, is the difference between "useful" and "very useful" equivalent to the difference between "no opinion" and "useful"? It is also a common practice for researchers to use measures such as frequency counts to analyze categorical data. However, such distributional measures are not readily convertible to comparative measures across items.

Categorical scales do not control for different interpretations by the respondents of the meanings associated with the scale values. The researcher does not know how much more useful those items are that are rated "extremely useful" from those that are assessed as being "useful". Also, the researcher cannot determine whether one respondent's interpretation of "extremely useful" is equivalent to another's interpretation. Accordingly, any conclusions drawn from such a study about the relative usefulness of items in the survey must be very tentative.

Since the responses to categorical scales are not anchored to any specific item of known value, the researcher does not know what biases may exist in the responses. In a situation in which information costs are not considered, as in the case of the GASB survey, respondents may exhibit an upward bias in their expressed perceptions of the usefulness of information items since the extent of usefulness is measured without reference to any benchmark and since respondents are likely to prefer more information to less.

Magnitude scales provide for the direct comparison of survey items using continuous measures for which distributional properties are readily determinable. Because items are anchored to a known benchmark, problems associated with the arbitrary scale and unknown meaning of scale values do not exist. However, the selection of the anchor item and the value ascribed to this item are subjective decisions. If the researcher selects an anchor that is known (from other sources) or is theorized to be important to most respondents, those items which are identified as being relatively more important than the anchor can be assessed as being important as well. The lower limit of values that respondents can assign to survey items is zero. Therefore, the value assigned to the anchor must be sufficiently large to permit the respondents to assign values of lesser amounts to items in the survey without computational difficulty or without having to truncate the assigned values.

B. Sample

Our study utilized one of the groups identified by the GASB as a potential user of government annual reports and therefore was included in its survey. All municipal financial analysts listed in the 1987 *Membership Directory* of the National Federation of Municipal Analysts (613 individuals) were included in our survey. After an initial and follow-up mailing, responses were received from 195 analysts (response rate of 32%) during the summer of 1989. A comparison of results for those who responded to the first mailing to those who responded to the second mailing revealed no statistically significant differences on the basis of t-tests of means at a significance level of .05. Population demographics were not available as a basis to determine the representativeness of the sample. However, the demographics that were collected as part of the survey (Table 1) reveal a broad spectrum of respondents with respect to job description, experience, and education.

C. Instrument

Items included in our survey were selected from those included in the GASB

Table 1. Sample Description

	Percent
Job Title	
Vice President	34.5
Securities Analyst	23.6
Assistant Vice President	10.3
Portfolio Manager	6.9
Credit Analyst	6.9
Other	17.8
Years of Experience	
Less than 1	3.4
1 to 4	21.2
5 to 9	37.3
Over 10	38.1
Education	
Undergraduate Degree	26.9
Graduate Degree	73.1

Table 2.   Accounting and Report Items Included in Survey

Item Number	Description
1.[a]	Explanation of purposes of transfers between funds
2.	Expenditures by object of expenditure
3.	Depreciation as expense of the general fund
4.	Tax burden as a percentage of income
5.	Identification of annual surplus or deficit
6.	Details concerning costs of services provided
7.	Statement of changes in general fixed assets
8.	Fund balance available for future appropriation
9.	Statement of monthly cash flows
10.	Consolidated financial statements without fund type statements
11.	Comparison of actual with modified budget
12.	Efficiency and effectiveness data
13.	Tax abatements and cancellations
14.	Explanation of timing of revenues and expenditures
15.	Trends of employee fringe benefit costs
16.	Legal tax limits
17.	Tax burden as percentage of income
18.	Percentage of taxes by income bracket
19.	Tax abatements and cancellations
20.	Disclosure of largest employers
21.	Description of budgetary procedures and policies
22.	Explanation of differences between budget and actual
23.	Comparison of actual to budget for several years
24.	Reconciliation of GAAP to budget basis
25.	Identification of annual surplus or deficit
26.	Nonrecurring revenues or expenditures
27.	Explanation of purpose of transfers between funds
28.	Compliance with revenue bond debt service coverage
29.	Auditor attests to compliance with bond agreement
30.	Demonstration of debt service coverage on accrual basis
31.	Rates charged to related government departments and agencies
32.	Details concerning cost of services
33.	Efficiency and effectiveness data
34.	Expenditures by object of expenditure

Note: [a]Item 1 was the anchor item.

study. The items were worded in the same way as in the GASB study. Our survey contained 34 items, including seven items that were repeated twice (for tests of validity as discussed below) and the anchor item. A list of these items is provided in Table 2. The items were selected judgmentally to encompass the range of reporting areas included in the GASB survey and the range of responses (i. e., from "extremely useful" to "not useful") reported by the GASB. The survey was limited to 34 to keep the task manageable since subjects were asked to evaluate the usefulness of each item relative to one other item in the list. We believed that a longer survey would have reduced the response rate as a result of subject concerns about excessive complexity and length. A limited response rate was a problem with the GASB survey.

Item 1, "explanation of purpose of transfers between funds" was selected as the anchor item. The assessed usefulness reported in the GASB survey for this item was near the midpoint of the usefulness scale (considered to be important by about half the respondents). It was assigned a value of 100. Subjects were instructed to score the remaining items in terms of their relative importance in comparison to the anchor item. The subjects' task was to evaluate the financial condition of a government issuing general obligation bonds for purposes of assessing the default risk of the bonds.

D. Instrument Pretest

The survey procedures were pretested using 56 students enrolled in a senior-level governmental accounting course to ensure the clarity of the instructions. Two response modalities were considered in obtaining student responses. One involved the use of numerical values relative to the anchor item with an arbitrary value of 100. The other required the subjects to draw lines of lengths proportional to the value they assigned to items in the survey. The anchor item was represented by a line 50 millimeters long. All subjects used both modalities to respond to all of the items on the survey. The questionnaires were administered separately.

Using two modalities provided a means of validating responses by comparing results across modalities [see Lodge, 1981]. Results for the students were consistent across modalities, indicating that the subjects understood the task and that the results were independent of the response modality. The use of two modalities required about twice the time of a single modality. Accordingly, we decided that the use of numerical estimates would be the easiest response modality for financial analysts and would likely produce a better response rate than the use of two modalities or requiring subjects to draw lines to estimate relative values.

E. Measurement Error

We used a repeated measures design to examine the extent of measurement error in the survey responses. Respondents are likely to vary with respect to the care they take in completing surveys. Surveys that can be completed in a short time are likely to produce more accurate responses; however, the incentives and interests of respondents will vary. The responses of those who did not examine the survey instrument carefully may distort the results relative to the responses of those who were thoughtful about their true perceptions.

In our study, several questions were included twice in the survey and were inserted in random positions. The anchor item was included as one of the items requiring a response, as well. This procedure permitted us to assess which respondents read the questionnaire carefully and, therefore, were likely to have attempted to respond consistently about their perceptions. The procedure did not permit us to validate whether the responses were the true perceptions of the respondents since those who read the survey carefully could have easily compared their responses for the items that were repeated. However, the procedure did permit us to compare responses of those who appeared to have read the survey instrument carefully with those who responded more perfunctorily and to assess any resulting biases.

IV. RESULTS

Table 3 provides a summary of results of the survey of financial analysts. The scale values reported in the table are the geometric means of the responses. Geometric means are used to correct for the skewed distribution that results because the upper limit of the magnitude scale is infinity whereas the lower limit is zero. Accordingly, the range of possible scale values greater than the anchor value of 100 is much larger than the range of possible values smaller than the anchor (see Lodge [1981] for further discussion).

The items are ranked from most to least useful. Responses from the GASB survey are included for comparison. In addition to the total sample results, results for a reduced sample are provided. The reduced sample consisted of only those responses for which the difference between any of the pairs of identical items was no greater than 25 percent. Only 67 (34%) of the respondents met the criterion for the reduced sample. The small percentage of respondents who met the criterion for the reduced sample suggests that care should be used in interpreting results from this type of study and that an assessment of the care used in the responses to such a survey is important.

Results for the total and reduced samples were similar. The rank-order correlations for the two samples across all items was .967. Responses for items that were identical were similar, although these similarities were greater for the reduced sample than for the total sample as a result of the procedures used to define the reduced sample. Responses for the total sample were biased upwards in comparison to the reduced sample across all items in the survey. This bias also is apparent from observing item 27 which was identical to the anchor item. The mean response for the total sample was 115 for this item, 15 points higher than the anchor value of 100. The mean response for the reduced sample was 100.

The rank correlation between the reduced sample and the GASB survey results was .820.[4] Accordingly, the results for our survey were similar to those of the GASB and, in general, reinforce the GASB findings. The relationships are observable in Table 4. Responses are compared for each item for the reduced sample and GASB survey. Differences in some of the items are apparent (e.g., item 2, 9, 12, and 30), and attempts to draw inferences about the relative importance of the items from the GASB results are problematic. The magnitude data provide evidence about the relative importance of each of the items.

Table 3. Summary of Responses

	Total Sample		Reduced Sample[c]		GASB Survey	
Rank	Item No.[a]	Scale Value[b]	Item No.	Scale Value	Item No.	Percent Favor
1	5	269.77	25	239.88	5	98.5
2	25	255.27	5	238.23	25	98.5
3	28	255.27	28	228.03	26	93.8
4	16	231.21	8	213.80	16	90.8
5	8	230.67	16	201.37	8	87.5
6	20	223.36	20	194.54	28	86.2
7	29	206.54	29	173.38	22	83.3
8	30	172.58	30	156.31	14	83.1
9	26	162.55	26	144.88	20	80.0
10	22	159.96	22	134.59	21	78.8
11	23	148.59	23	132.13	17	76.9
12	24	133.35	24	122.18	29	76.9
13	11	132.74	11	115.88	4	76.9
14	17	130.92	4	112.98	24	74.2
15	4	126.18	17	111.69	11	72.7
16	21	117.22	2	108.89	9	71.2
17	14	116.68	34	108.64	23	69.7
18	27	115.08	14	106.66	27	68.8
19	2	110.41	21	103.04	13	66.7
20	34	106.17	27	99.77	19	66.7
21	9	85.31	13	70.96	7	61.5
22	13	78.89	19	70.47	15	56.3
23	6	77.80	9	68.71	30	56.3
24	19	76.74	15	65.01	3	53.0
25	15	76.74	7	63.53	31	46.8
26	7	72.78	32	62.09	2	46.0
27	32	71.61	6	62.09	34	46.0
28	33	67.30	33	57.41	18	33.8
29	12	66.07	12	56.49	10	23.4
30	31	64.57	18	52.48	32	21.5
31	10	57.54	10	51.29	6	21.5
32	18	56.23	31	48.75	12	13.8
33	3	49.77	3	38.73	33	13.8

Notes: [a]The following pairs of items were identical: 2,34; 4,17; 5,25; 6,32; 12,33; 13,19. Item 27 was the same
            as the anchor item (number 1).
        [b]Scale values are the geometric means of the magnitude scale responses.
        [c]The reduced sample consists of only those respondents for which none of the responses for the pairs of
            identical items differed between items by more than 25 percent.

The usefulness of the information collected from our survey relative to the
GASB survey can be observed in Table 4. The most useful item on both surveys
was "identification of annual surplus or deficit." The least useful item from our
survey was "depreciation as expense of the general fund." The annual surplus or
deficit was perceived, on average, to be more than six times as useful as general
fund depreciation expense and to be more than twice as useful as the anchor item,

Table 4. Comparison of Magnitude and GASB Responses

Item No.[a]	Magnitude Scale[b]	GASB Response[c]
5/25	239.06	98.5
28	228.03	86.2
8	213.80	87.5
16	201.37	90.8
20	194.54	80.0
29	173.38	76.9
30	156.31	56.3
26	144.88	93.8
22	134.59	83.3
23	132.13	69.7
24	122.18	74.2
11	115.88	72.7
4/17	112.34	76.9
2/34	108.77	46.0
14	106.66	83.1
21	103.04	78.8
27	99.77	68.8
13/19	70.72	66.7
9	68.71	71.2
15	65.01	56.3
7	63.53	61.5
6/32	62.09	21.5
12/33	56.95	13.8
18	52.48	33.8
10	51.29	23.4
31	48.75	46.8
3	38.73	53.0

Notes: [a]Item numbers are listed together for those items that were the same.
[b]The magnitude scale is the geometric mean of the survey responses. For those items that were the same, the arithmetic mean of the pair of magnitude scale values are presented.
[c]Percent who favored the item from the GASB survey.

explanation of purposes of transfers between funds. Such conclusions cannot be drawn from the GASB survey.

Other items that were perceived to be very useful by the respondents relative to the anchor item were "compliance with revenue bond debt service coverage," "fund balance available for future appropriation," and "legal tax limits." Other items that were perceived not to be very useful relative to the anchor included "rates charged to related government departments and agencies," "consolidated financial statements," and "percentage of taxes by income bracket." From a user needs perspective, we can say that the items rated highest on the magnitude scale were perceived as being more than four times as useful as the items rated lowest.

Comparisons were made across respondents grouped by the number of years of experience they had as analysts (less than five years, five years or more) and grouped by whether or not they had a graduate degree. Results were similar for both comparisons. A rank-order correlation coefficient of .95 was computed for both comparisons. A slight (approximately 5%) upward bias in the magnitude values was observed for respondents who possessed undergraduate degrees only, relative to those who also had graduate degrees. The bias was not observed for the experience partition.

V. SUMMARY AND CONCLUSIONS

This study replicated a portion of the GASB user needs survey using a method that was designed to elicit responses about the relative usefulness of items in the survey. The GASB study measured attitudes about the usefulness of certain governmental accounting report items in a way that permits inferences to be drawn about the differences in attitudes across groups of subjects. Extending this analysis to draw conclusions about the relative usefulness of the items is problematic. Our results provide evidence of the relative usefulness of these reporting items that could not be assessed reliably from the GASB study.

In addition, this study examined measurement error in the responses that indicated that many (over 60%) respondents did not provide consistent responses to the survey. Those respondents who were not consistent in their responses provided upwardly biased estimates of the usefulness of the report items relative to those who were more careful.

The rank-order correlation between the GASB findings and those of this study along with the consistency of the results of this study across different partitions of the subjects supports, for the most part, the conclusions of the GASB about which items were most important. This result is important since it is based on an independent analysis of user perceptions at a different point in time from the GASB survey and uses a method different from that employed by the GASB. Therefore, the results of the GASB survey appear to be robust to the choice of instrument and subjects.

NOTES

1. The response rates for the groups included in the GASB survey were not reported in Jones et al. [1985]. Our discussion with the GASB revealed that the response rates were low, about 10 percent for most groups.

2. Both the GASB and this study employed mail surveys. The inherent limitations of this method apply to both studies.

3. The technique known as magnitude scaling was originally developed by Stevens [1966 and 1975] in the area of psychophysics. Stevens believed that a subjective scale of physical stimulus (i.e., loudness) could be constructed by having subjects match numbers with the perceived intensity of the stimuli. Stevens [1975, p. 229] asserted that "magnitude measures become possible because people have a remarkable ability to match one thing to another. They can match numbers to apparent loudness or apparent loudness to numbers. They can match loudness to the strength of a vibration on the fingertip, and vice versa."

Although magnitude scaling was originally developed to scale sensory attributes, Stevens and others began to use these procedures to gauge the intensity of opinions and attitudes. Such research was founded on the belief that people could match numbers or items from any continuum to a nonsensory variable such as prestige of occupation [Stevens, 1975, p. 229]. As opinions and attitudes are hypothetical constructs rather than the sensory attributes of physical stimuli, the validity of using magnitude scaling in opinion research was examined critically (see Howard [1981] for a detailed discussion of the criticism). By using cross-modality and multimoditily matching, later research supported the use of magnitude scaling as a viable technique for obtaining data from subjects in a way that measures the intensity of attitude [Dawson and Brakes, 1971; Howard, 1981].

4. The arithmetic mean for each pair of identical items was substituted for the individual values for the reduced sample.

REFERENCES

Dawson, W., and R. Brinker, "Validation of Ratio Scales of Opinion by Multimodality Matching," *Perception and Psychophysics* [May 1971], pp. 413–417.

Fowler, F., *Survey Research Methods* [Beverly Hills, CA: Sage Publications, 1984].

Governmental Accounting Standards Board, *Concepts Statement 1*, "Objectives of Financial Reporting" [GASB, 1987].

Grove, H., and R. Savich, "Attitude Research in Accounting: A Model for Reliability and Validity Considerations," *The Accounting Review* [July 1979], pp. 522–537.

Jones, D., R. Scott, L. Kimbro, and R. Ingram, *The Needs of Users of Governmental Financial Reports* [GASB, 1985].

Howard, T., "Attitude Measurement: Some Further Considerations," *The Accounting Review* [July 1981], pp. 613–621.

Howard, T., "On the Usefulness of Alternative Reporting Formats for Municipalities," Ph.D. dissertation [Arizona State University, 1978].

Lodge, M., *Magnitude Scaling: Quantitative Measurement of Opinion* [Beverly Hills, CA: Sage Publications, 1982].

Stevens, S., "A Metric for the Social Consensus," *Science* [February 1966], pp. 530–541.

Stevens, S., *Psychophysics: Introduction to its Perceptual, Neutral, and Social Prospects* [New York: John Wiley and Sons, 1975].

Torgerson, W., *Theory and Methods of Scaling* [New York: John Wiley and Sons, 1958].

BEHAVIORAL RESEARCH IN GOVERNMENTAL AND NONPROFIT ACCOUNTING:
AN ASSESSMENT OF THE PAST AND SUGGESTIONS FOR THE FUTURE

Sharon L. Green

ABSTRACT

The purpose of this paper is to update Herhold, Parry, and Patton's 1987 review of behavioral research in governmental and nonprofit accounting. Behavioral research published in academic accounting journals between 1986 and 1990 is assessed to determine the extent that the issues raised in the earlier review have been addressed. The assessment reveals that, although considerable progress has been made, additional progress will be necessary if this type of research is to be accepted as a legitimate subfield of behavioral research in the future. A more unified research strategy, which includes replications, triangulation, and theory development, is recommended. It is also suggested that theories from other academic disciplines and additional methodological approaches may be necessary.

Research in Governmental and Nonprofit Accounting, Vol. 7, pages 53–78.
Copyright © 1992 by JAI Press Inc.
All rights of reproduction in any form reserved.
ISBN: 1-55938-418-2

In 1987, Herhold, Parry, and Patton published an overview of behavioral research conducted prior to 1986 in governmental accounting settings. Their overview outlined the strengths and weaknesses of three methodological approaches to behavioral research, provided illustrations of studies utilizing these different methodologies, and suggested additional research topics that could be explored with each methodology. Herhold, Parry, and Patton concluded that there remained "a significant need for well formulated [behavioral accounting research] in the government sector" (1987, p. 105).

The purpose of this paper is to update the work of Herhold, Parry, and Patton by assessing how well behavioral studies published in academic accounting journals between 1986 and the present have addressed the issues raised by them, and by suggesting additional ways in which behavioral research in the area can continue to be improved in the future. The remainder of the paper is organized as follows: Section I develops the operational definition of behavioral research in governmental and nonprofit accounting that was used in this paper. Section II assesses the progress that has been made since the Herhold, Parry, and Patton paper and Section III recommends ways in which such research can be improved in the future. Section IV offers some concluding comments.

I. BEHAVIORAL RESEARCH IN GOVERNMENTAL AND NONPROFIT ACCOUNTING DEFINED

In general, behavioral research seeks to "understand, explain and predict aspects of human behavior" [American Accounting Association (AAA), 1971]. More specifically, the objective of behavioral research in accounting (BRIA) is to understand, explain and predict those aspects of human behavior that are *relevant in accounting contexts*. That is, BRIA is designed primarily to explore those aspects of behavior that may affect or be affected by accounting data. Thus, BRIA can be viewed as a specialized subset of behavioral research.

As nearly all contemporary accounting research explores some aspect of human behavior, the above definition of BRIA could encompass virtually *all* types of accounting research. For example, in its broadest sense, the above definition could include studies of aggregate market-level behavior and analytical models of principal-agent behavior [Burgstahler and Sundem, 1989]. Traditionally, however, accounting research has been categorized as behavioral on the basis of three distinguishing characteristics: (1) an individual, small group or organizational unit of analysis; (2) a psychological or sociological theory base; and (3) a survey, experimental or case study methodology [Birnberg and Shields, 1989; Dyckman, Gibbons, and Swieringa, 1978; Hofstedt, 1976; Libby and Lewis, 1977].

Just as BRIA can be viewed as a specialized subset of behavioral research, behavioral research in governmental and nonprofit accounting (BRIGNA) can be viewed as an even more specialized subset of BRIA. That is, BRIGNA is associated with *both* a specific topic area within accounting research (governmental and nonprofit accounting problems) and a specific methodological approach (behavioral) for exploring these topics.[1] For purposes of this paper, BRIGNA is defined as research that seeks to understand, explain, and predict those aspects of human behavior that are *relevant in governmental and nonprofit accounting contexts.* In keeping with the traditional categorization of behavioral research, BRIGNA would have an individual, group or organizational unit of analysis, a psychological or sociological theory base and utilize an experimental, survey or case study methodology.

II. ASSESSMENT OF RESEARCH PUBLISHED 1986 TO 1990

As noted earlier, the Herhold, Parry, and Patton paper reviewed BRIGNA conducted prior to 1986. To assess how well BRIGNA researchers have addressed the issues raised by Herhold, Parry, and Patton, academic accounting journals were searched to identify all papers published between 1986 and 1990 that conformed to the preceding definition of BRIGNA.[2] A list of the journals searched is provided in Table 1. As Table 1 discloses, the journals searched were almost evenly divided between general purpose accounting journals (e.g. *The Accounting Review*) and special interest accounting journals (e.g. *Research in Governmental and Nonprofit Accounting*).

Restricting the search to academic accounting journals excludes a number of potential alternative outlets for BRIGNA, including journals in other academic disciplines (e.g. *Public Administration Review*) and practitioner journals (e.g. *Journal of Accountancy*). However, it is the intent of this paper to assess the development of that body of literature previously defined as BRIGNA. That definition restricted the search to empirical, theory-based research specifically designed to address governmental and nonprofit accounting questions. Although papers published in other outlets have contributed to BRIGNA, their assessment is beyond the scope of this paper. A survey of such publications could prove to be a valuable resource to BRIGNA researchers, however, and would be a fruitful direction for future research.

A total of 18 BRIGNA studies were published between 1986 and 1990 in the 19 journals listed in Table 1. As BRIGNA is traditionally characterized by both the nature of topic investigated and the type of methodology employed, Table 2 categorizes the studies on both of these dimensions. Table 2 suggests the existence of both breadth and depth in the BRIGNA studies published during the period. Breadth is evidenced by the five different topic areas that were explored; some

Table 1.   List of Accounting Journals Surveyed

Journal Title

General Purpose Journals:

Accounting and Business Research
Accounting Horizons
Accounting, Organizations and Society
Accounting Review
Advances in Accounting
Contemporary Accounting Research
Georgia Journal of Accounting
Journal of Accounting Literature
Journal of Accounting Research

Special Interest Journals:

Accounting, Auditing and Accountability
Advances in International Accounting
Advances in Public Interest Accounting
Auditing: A Journal of Practice and Theory
Journal of Accounting, Auditing and Finance
Journal of Accounting and Economics
Journal of Accounting and Public Policy
Journal of Business, Finance and Accounting
Research in Accounting Regulation

evidence of depth is also demonstrated by the existence of multiple studies within some of the topic areas.

While this initial evidence may appear encouraging to BRIGNA researchers, closer inspection of Table 2 indicates that development has been somewhat limited. Although five different general topic areas were investigated, only two of the topics were investigated in more than a single study. Further, although all three methodological approaches were utilized at least twice, the overwhelming majority of studies (11 of 18) were experimental. Only five studies (28%) used a survey methodology and the remaining two (11%) were case studies. The implications of these observations on the development of BRIGNA are discussed in the sections that follow.

A. Research Topics Investigated

Clearly, financial reporting issues received the most attention by BRIGNA researchers during the 1986 to 1990 period. As Table 2 discloses, 11 of the 18 studies (61%) explored financial reporting topics. Thus, financial reporting issues constituted nearly two-thirds of all BRIGNA papers published during the period. The predominant role of financial reporting topics in published BRIGNA may indicate a relative lack of maturity in the field, compared to mainstream BRIA.

Table 2. Survey of Behavioral Research in Accounting Journals, 1986 to 1990

Topic Investigated		Methodology Employed			Percent of all Published BRIGNA
General Topic Area	Specific Research Issue	Experimental	Survey	Case Study	
I. Financial Reporting	Service Efforts and Accomplishments	Reed [JAPP, 1986]			
	Pensions	Reed and Koch [RIGNA, 1989] Willets, et al. [RIGNA, 1988]	Robbins [RIGNA, 1988] Wardlow & Godfrey [RIGNA, 1989]		61%
	Depreciation*	F. Carpenter [RIGNA, 1988]			
	Alternative Types of Reports*	Gaffney [JAPP, 1986]			
	Entity Inclusion Criteria	Green [RIGNA, 1990]			
	Basis of Accounting*	Shoulders [RIGNA, 1987]			
	GAAP Adoption Decisions		Bokemeier [RIGNA, 1988]	V. Carpenter & Feroz (AH, 1990]	
II. Auditing	Audit Reports*	Herhold-Baskin [RIGNA, 1986]			
	False Sign-offs	Lynn & Gaffney [RIGNA, 1990]			22%
	Judgment Consensus		Berry et al. [AR, 1987] Meixner & Welker [AR, 1988]		
III. MIS Adoption Decisions				V. Carpenter [RIGNA, 1987]	6%
IV. Human Information Processing		Lewis et al. [AR, 1988]			6%
V. Attitudes		Meixner & Bline [AA&A, 1989]			6%
Percent of all Published BRIGNA		61%	28%	11%	100%

Notes: *Topic also investigated in Robbins, 1988
    AA&A – Accounting, Auditing and Accountability
    AH – Accounting Horizons
    AR – Accounting Review
    JAPP – Journal of Accounting and Public Policy
    RIGNA – Research in Governmental and Nonprofit Accounting

Previous reviews of BRIA point out that early BRIA was characterized by its policy orientation and its focus on financial reporting issues [American Accounting Association (AAA), 1974].

The policy orientation of early BRIA was also often criticized for a lack of theoretical underpinnings [AAA, 1974, 1979]. Partially as a response to this criticism, the focus of BRIA changed to more basic, rather than applied, research during the early to mid 1970s [Lord, 1989]. In fact, the structure of recent reviews of behavioral research on other accounting topics reveals that direct investigation of financial reporting issues has been virtually nonexistent in mainstream BRIA in the past decade [Choo, 1989; Davis and Solomon, 1989; Libby and Lewis, 1982]. Based on the predominance of financial reporting topics in Table 2, it appears that BRIGNA has yet to make a similar transition from applied to basic research. Therefore, BRIGNA is still subject to the criticisms of early mainstream BRIA. A shift from policy-oriented research toward more basic research will be necessary if BRIGNA is to mature into a well-developed and accepted subset of contemporary accounting research.[3]

Early BRIA was also criticized for having so much diversity in its topics that synergy could not be achieved in any one research issue [Hofstedt and Kinard, 1970; Lord, 1989]. However, since the lens-model was introduced into accounting research in the mid 1970s, a tremendous body of research devoted to human information processing issues has evolved (see Libby and Lewis [1977, 1982] for a comprehensive review of the evolution of this literature). The profound impact of this change in direction toward a more unified research agenda (with stronger theoretical bases) is well documented in the accounting literature [Birnberg and Shields, 1989; Lord, 1989] and is evidenced by the ability of reviewers to integrate the results across studies and reach (at least tentative) conclusions. To determine whether a similar synergy has occurred within BRIGNA to date, the topics in Table 2 were subdivided based on the specific research issues explored. The subdivision resulted in the identification of 13 separate research issues.

Breaking down the general topics into specific issues reveals that, particularly with regard to the general topic of financial reporting, a great deal of diversity still exists in BRIGNA. The 11 papers dealing with financial reporting topics actually investigated seven different financial reporting issues. These issues include service efforts and accomplishments [Reed, 1986; Reed and Koch, 1989], pensions [Robbins, 1988; Wardlow and Godfrey, 1989; Willets, Clancy, and Freeman, 1988], depreciation [F. Carpenter, 1988], alternative types of financial reports [Gaffney, 1986; Green, 1990], entity inclusion criteria [Shoulders, 1987], basis of accounting [Bokemeier, 1988] and states' decisions whether or not to adopt GAAP for external reporting [Carpenter and Feroz, 1990]. Given that seven very different reporting issues were explored, it would seem that there is significant breadth in BRIGNA. What is troubling, however, is that there is less depth than Table 2 depicts. As only three of the seven specific financial reporting issues had more than a single study devoted to the issue (service efforts and accomplishments, pensions, and alternative types of financial reports), it does not appear that much synergy has yet occurred, even within the most thoroughly researched topic in published BRIGNA.

Although auditing also appears to have received a reasonable amount of focused attention from BRIGNA researchers (four studies), closer inspection of the cited studies also revealed that such was not the case. As the subdivisions within Table 2 indicate, the four studies dealt with three different auditing issues: Berry, Harwood, and Katz [1987] investigated the magnitude of false sign-offs by governmental auditors; Meixner and Welker [1988] were concerned with the relationship between auditing experience and judgment consensus; and Herhold-Baskin [1986] and Lynn and Gaffney [1990] examined the importance of the audit report to users of governmental financial reports. As was the case with financial reporting topics, there was significantly more breadth than depth in the auditing area. Again, the lack of depth limited the potential for synergy within BRIGNA.

In their 1987 review, Herhold, Parry, and Patton advocated the use of two strategies that could have added depth, and thus resulted in synergy, within BRIGNA. The recommended strategies consisted of: (1) replication, and (2) triangulation. Replication would be evidenced by multiple studies utilizing the same methodology to explore a specific research issue. On the other hand, triangulation would be evidenced by multiple methodologies utilized to explore a specific issue. The extent to which BRIGNA published between 1986 and 1990 utilized the recommended strategies is assessed below.

1. Replication

Herhold, Parry, and Patton noted in their review that only one of the nine experimental studies conducted prior to 1986 was a replication [Howard, 1979] and concluded that, partially due to the lack of replications, "there is a need for more research" [Herhold, Parry, and Patton, 1987, p. 88]. Only three of the 13 specific issues identified in Table 2 (23%) contain studies that would constitute either a replication or moderate extension of prior research: Reed and Koch [1989] extended Reed [1986] on the issue of service efforts and accomplishments reporting; Green [1990] extended the work of Gaffney [1986] on the issue of alternative types of financial reports; and Lynn and Gaffney [1990] extended Herhold-Baskin's [1986] assessment of the importance of the audit report to other users. However, when integrated with experimental studies published prior to 1986, the issue of alternative types of financial reports has had more replications and/or extensions than any other BRIGNA issue as the current studies of Gaffney and Green represent extensions of the earlier experimental studies of Patton [1978], Howard [1979–80], and Ramanathan and Weis [1981].

Unfortunately, no replications or extensions were undertaken for the remaining 77 percent of the research issues as each was represented by a single publication. One possible explanation for this lack of replications might be the reluctance of journals to publish replications [Burgstahler and Sundem, 1989]. However, there are at least two potential types of outlets for such studies. First, some journals invite replications and/or moderate extensions as Research Notes (e.g., *The Accounting Review, Research in Governmental and Nonprofit Accounting*). Regional and/or national meetings of the American Accounting Association offer a second potential outlet for such studies.

Replications and/or extensions will be necessary if BRIGNA is ever to obtain the synergy necessary to develop into a cohesive body of literature. Given the relative lack of such studies during the 1986 to 1990 period, it appears that a significant need for replications still exists within BRIGNA.

2. *Triangulation*

Herhold, Parry, and Patton [1987, p. 105] also noted that "since no single study can truly answer a research question, triangulation is necessary." Triangulation requires multiple methodological approaches to address a single research issue [Abdel-khalik and Ajinkya, 1979]. Multiple methodological approaches make it possible to compare results across methodologies within a specific topic area. To the extent that the results are similar, confidence in the validity of the results of any single study can be increased. Thus, evidence of triangulation could also be a sign that synergy had taken place within BRIGNA during the period. As can be seen in Table 2, however, multiple methodologies were utilized for only four of the 13 specific research issues (31%)[4].

Given that the topic of financial reporting constituted the majority of the research conducted during the period, it should not be surprising that this topic shows the most evidence of behavioral research triangulation. Three of the four research issues in which there is some evidence of behavioral research triangulation relate to financial reporting topics: one experimental [Willets et al., 1988] and two survey [Robbins, 1988; Wardlow and Godfrey, 1989] methodologies were utilized to explore pension reporting; one experiment [F. Carpenter, 1988] and one survey [Robbins, 1988] addressed issues related to recording of depreciation; and the experimental work of Gaffney [1986] and Green [1990] on the issue of alternative types of financial reports was also explored in the Robbins [1988] survey. Taken together, the results of these studies provide additional evidence supporting the 1987 observations of Herhold, Parry, and Patton that "survey responses tend to support the status quo" [1987, p. 104], and that the "links between [preferences] and actual behavior have [yet to be] established unambiguously" [p. 103].

Clearly, however, there is not strong evidence that Herhold, Parry, and Patton's recommendation for triangulation within BRIGNA was vigorously pursued between 1986 and 1990. As was the case with the arguments supporting replications, triangulation could have a significant impact on the development of BRIGNA into a mature and respected subset of BRIA.

Two conclusions can be drawn from the assessment of BRIGNA research topics. First, the predominance of studies exploring financial reporting topics and the lack of significant depth on any specific research issue indicate that the development of BRIGNA is lagging behind that of mainstream BRIA. The BRIGNA studies published between 1986 and 1990 show little evidence of either a change in direction from a policy orientation toward more basic research or the synergy that would have resulted from a concentrated stream of research on any one issue. Second, the relatively large number of topics on which BRIGNA researchers published during the period may indicate that the potential exists for such development to occur in the future. Successful development, however, will depend upon the willingness of BRIGNA researchers to adopt a more theoretical orientation and a more focused research agenda.

B. Methodologies Employed

Table 2 also categorizes each paper into one of the three behavioral methodologies outlined in Herhold, Parry, and Patton: (1) experimental, (2) survey, and (3) case study research. As Table 2 shows, experiments far outnumbered either surveys or case studies (61% for experiments compared to 28% for surveys and 11% for case studies). Further, although the number of case studies published during the period was relatively small (two), this is actually twice as many as identified by Herhold, Parry, and Patton prior to 1987. An examination of the papers in each methodological category was made to determine the extent to which the papers addressed the methodological issues raised by Herhold, Parry, and Patton. A discussion of the issues related to each methodology follows.

1. Experimental Research

Herhold, Parry, and Patton were able to identify only 9 BRIGNA experiments conducted in the 11-year period between 1975 and 1986, 4 of which had not been published at the time of the review (Herhold-Baskin [1986], Reed [1986], F.Carpenter [1988], and Meixner and Welker [1988]). As Table 2 indicates, 11 experimental studies were published in the subsequent 5-year period, including the 4 unpublished studies cited in Herhold, Parry, and Patton. As a result, only 7 experimental studies were actually conducted *and* published subsequent to their review.

The predominant role of experiments is encouraging as a shift from survey to experimental methodologies may be a sign of both methodological and theoretical maturation in BRIGNA. That is, survey techniques may have been more appropriate in the past when little was known about users' attitudes, preferences, and so forth. As Herhold, Parry, and Patton [1987, p. 104] noted, surveys are particularly appropriate for "exploratory research rather than critical test(s) of theory." As BRIGNA matures, however, less exploratory research should be needed. A shift can be made to more sophisticated research methodologies (including experiments) that are more suited for hypothesis testing in theory-driven research.

While the publication of experimental BRIGNA increased during the period (11 between 1986 and 1990 compared to only 5 between 1975 and 1985), there still exists a need for additional experiments, particularly for those research topics that currently are limited to either a survey or case study methodology. Otherwise, the triangulation necessary to increase confidence in the results of BRIGNA may never be achieved.

Herhold, Parry, and Patton [1987, p. 97] concluded that "little experimental and theory-building research exist[ed] in government accounting" prior to 1986. At the present time, the need for theory-building may be even more critical than the need for experiments. Although the number of published experimental studies increased during the period, a closer inspection of the theoretical foundations for the experiments indicates that the studies rarely developed new theory or refined existing theory. Rather, the typical BRIGNA experimental study simply applied one or more theories from the psychology literature in the governmental and nonprofit setting. The theory was provided primarily to offer reasons for expecting differences in decisions due to experimental manipulations. For example, Green [1990] used both the information processing theory of Schroder, Driver, and Streufert [1967] and heuristic information processing theories [Braunstein, 1976; Simon, 1956; Tversky and Kahneman, 1974] as theoretical bases for predicting that the accuracy of municipal analysts' bond rating predictions would be affected when the amount of data in a governmental financial report was altered. Similarly, Willets et al. [1988] cited the psychological construct of data fixity as a possible reason to expect that informed users would be unable to adapt their decision models to incorporate changes in actuarial assumptions in a PERS report.

There are two problems associated with simply applying well-developed and well-tested general theories in experimental BRIGNA. First, the contribution of such studies to either psychology or mainstream accounting literature is modest. At best, these studies constitute replications of established theories in somewhat different settings. This could account for the decrease in experimental BRIGNA appearing in mainstream accounting journals over the past five years.[5]

The second problem is more troubling to the development of BRIGNA as a legitimate subset of BRIA. As stated earlier, the objective of BRIGNA is to explore those aspects of human behavior that are relevant in governmental and nonprofit accounting contexts. Applying generic psychological and/or information processing theories fails to recognize that there are unique characteristics in governmental and nonprofit settings that could have different (and perhaps contradictory) influences on behavior in those settings. For example, the civil service system is unique to the governmental sector. This system imposes a significantly different organizational structure and reward system on governmental accountants and internal users of accounting reports. Failing to incorporate the influence of these unique characteristics into theories undermines the legitimacy of BRIGNA as a subfield of BRIA.

The policy orientation of most BRIGNA studies that was noted earlier most likely contributed to BRIGNA's focus on general theory during the period. Nearly two-thirds of the published studies (11 of 18) investigated topics of direct interest to the Governmental Accounting Standards Board. The problem with a policy-based motivation is that the emphasis is placed on empirically observing whether a change in a current reporting practice would have an impact on constituents of the policy-making body. Theoretical questions as to *why* differences might be observed are relegated to a secondary role. For example, Green [1990] observed that highly summarized financial statements had negative effects on the decision-making performance of experienced municipal analysts, even when the reports only supplemented fund-by-fund statements. While such findings may be interesting to policymakers, the lack of a clear theoretical basis to explain the findings limits the extent to which the study contributes to our understanding of human information processing. More carefully designed, theoretically driven research will be required in the future if BRIGNA is to provide the necessary explanations.

BRIGNA researchers should also respond to Herhold, Parry, and Patton's recommendation for more theory-building research by recognizing that the un-modified application of generally accepted theories makes only a limited contribu-tion to our understanding of behavior in governmental and nonprofit settings. Instead, BRIGNA researchers should concentrate on *refining* existing theories to incorporate those features of the governmental and nonprofit setting that would be expected to influence behavior and *developing* new theories when existing theories cannot be modified. Theory refinement and theory development, rather than the current emphasis on general theory application, could significantly enhance the contribution of BRIGNA research.

It is important to recognize that there were two notable attempts at theory development during the period covered by this review. Herhold-Baskin [1986] developed a deductive theory of the role of the audit report in governmental settings. Although the empirical evidence provided only limited support for her theory, given the design of the study (which stressed external validity), rejection of her theory would be premature. Additional research stressing internal validity is needed before any conclusions can be made about the theory's validity. In another innovative attempt at theory development in BRIGNA, Shoulders [1987] used the results of an experiment to develop an inductive theory about decisions to include/exclude related units into/from the governmental reporting entity. To date, however, no additional behavioral research has been published which tests his theory.

The lack of theory-building research noted by Herhold, Parry, and Patton in 1987 is still the most serious deficiency in BRIGNA at the present time. BRIGNA researchers need to recognize that the objective of BRIGNA is to predict, under-stand *and* explain human behavior in governmental and nonprofit accounting contexts. Researchers must begin to devote more time to theory refinement and theory development in order to meet these objectives. Unless this change in motivation is made, BRIGNA will remain subject to the criticisms made of BRIA 15 years ago. Without the ability to answer questions as to *why* specific behaviors occur in governmental and nonprofit accounting contexts, it is doubtful that BRIGNA will be able to make a significant contribution to our understanding of human behavior.

2. Survey Research

Herhold, Parry, and Patton [1987, p. 104] noted that although survey research often investigates interesting and timely topics, there are flaws inherent in such research that limit the amount of reliance that can be placed in the results. Traditionally, surveys have been used to obtain opinions about the usefulness of various pieces of accounting information without considering the cost of such information. This often leads to an overassessment of usefulness, as users generally prefer more information to less if it is costless. Herhold, Parry, and Patton [p. 104] concluded that "more sophisticated surveying techniques which present realistic benefit and cost descriptions of the alternatives are needed before reliance can be placed on such results."

The study by Gaffney [1986] represents a significant move in this direction.[6] By adapting a technique developed by Larcker and Lessig [1980] for private enterprise capital budgeting decisions, Gaffney was able to (at least partially) impose the cost of processing the information in different types of governmental financial reports upon her respondents. Cost of processing was imposed by including sample financial statements in addition to the customary preference survey instrument. Respondents were asked to consider the information provided in the financial reports before responding to questions about their perceptions of the usefulness of the reports. Imposing information processing costs on users led to significantly different opinions about the usefulness of consolidated statements than those obtained in previous surveys where such costs were not imposed.

Herhold, Parry, and Patton [1987, p. 103] also cited "the inability/unwillingness of respondents to honestly reveal information" as another significant weakness of survey research. To overcome this weakness when investigating the sensitive topic of false sign-offs by governmental auditors, Berry et al. [1987] used the randomized response technique developed by Warner [1965]. This technique is particularly useful for investigating sensitive topics as it offers anonymity to individual respondents and encourages truthful responses. Thus, the reliability of the Berry et al. survey results was increased.

Finally, Herhold, Parry, and Patton criticized previous survey research for being theoretically unmotivated and recommended a move toward a more legitimate use of survey methodology. They suggested that "[t]heory to guide such inquiries is available—the survey would provide data for a nonexperimental empirical test of the theories" [Herhold, Parry, and Patton, 1987, p. 105]. Of the five surveys listed in Table 2, four papers (80%) made at least some attempt to provide a theoretical basis for the study. Although not formally set forth as expectations, Wardlow and Godfrey [1989] provided a number of reasons for expecting that users' opinions on PERS reporting would differ depending upon the user group with which they were affiliated. Bokemeier [1988] developed propositions about the opinions of state officials on accrual versus cash basis accounting. Berry et al. [1987] postulated that the rate of false sign-offs by governmental auditors would differ depending upon level of government, organizational independence, civil service protection, and professional certification. Meixner and Welker [1988] formally tested hypotheses about the relationship between auditor experience and judgment consensus. The decline in the number of theoretically unmotivated surveys published during the period should serve as a signal to BRIGNA researchers that such work is no longer acceptable in academic research.

Two conclusions can be reached from the assessment of survey methodologies during the 1986 to 1990 period. First, the number of such studies published seems to be declining; surveys constituted only 28 percent of published BRIGNA. Second, the sophistication of survey techniques has improved. Attempts have been made to impose costs of information processing, to overcome problems of social desirability in response to sensitive questions and to move away from the "theoretically unmotivated opinion surveys" criticized by Herhold, Parry, and Patton [1987, p. 105]. Both the decline in the number of published opinion surveys and the increase in the sophistication of the survey techniques may be a welcomed sign of maturation in BRIGNA, at least in the use of survey methodologies.

3. Case Study Research

In their 1987 review, Herhold, Parry, and Patton identified only one published case study pertaining to governmental and nonprofit accounting issues [Jonsson, 1982]. In the subsequent five years, two additional studies were published in academic accounting journals [V. Carpenter, 1987; V. Carpenter and Feroz, 1990]. Although the absolute number of case studies published to date remains quite small, the increase may well be an indication that Herhold, Parry, and Patton's [1987, p. 98] observation that such studies "seem to have become more respectable and acceptable as research methods" was correct.

Herhold, Parry, and Patton [1987, p. 99] observed that, as a general rule, the output of case studies is "often a description of the environment and the actors in the environment" and that the "features included in the description of the measures (quantitative or qualitative) depend upon the tastes of the researcher." On a more critical note, they commented that case studies rarely involved systematic observation to test hypotheses derived from a theoretical model [p. 99]. It would seem, then, that the need for theory refinement and theory development extends across all three methodologies employed by BRIGNA researchers.

As was the case for both experiments and surveys, there is some limited evidence that case study research in BRIGNA may also be moving away from theoretically unmotivated, exploratory research. For example, V. Carpenter [1987] drew upon the Economic Interest Group theory developed by Peltzman [1976] to derive testable hypotheses about the behavior of political interest groups in an MIS funding decision in the state of Michigan before the research was undertaken. Data to test the hypotheses were then collected from interviews with the parties involved and analyzed with both univariate and multivariate statistical techniques.

As only two BRIGNA case studies were published in academic accounting journals over the 5-year period under review (and the fact that one researcher was involved in both), it is difficult to assess the development of this methodological approach during the period. The current trend toward theoretically driven hypothesis testing, however, suggests that case studies could help to fulfill the need for theory development and theory refinement in BRIGNA. Theoretically driven case studies could also help to provide the triangulation that is presently lacking if combined with survey and/or experimental methodologies to address a specific research issue. Thus, the potential exists for case studies to make a significant contribution to future BRIGNA.

C. Observations About Publication Outlets for BRIGNA

Another way to evaluate the development of BRIGNA is to examine the distribution of journals publishing BRIGNA studies. Figure 1 contains the distribution of the 18 articles published between 1986 and 1990.

Figure 1 reveals that five of the 19 accounting journals surveyed published BRIGNA studies during the period. Eleven of the studies (61%) were published in

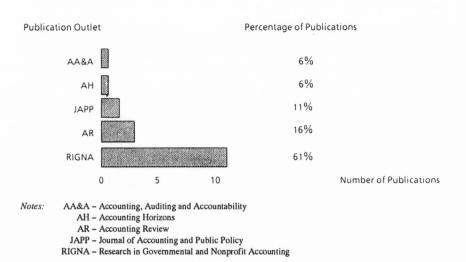

Figure 1.   Distribution of Publications by Publication Outlet

Research in Governmental and Nonprofit Accounting (RIGNA). *The Accounting Review* published three BRIGNA studies (17%) and the *Journal of Accounting and Public Policy* (JAPP) published two (11%). The remaining two BRIGNA studies appeared in *Accounting Horizons* and *Accounting, Auditing and Accountability*.

Several interesting observations can be made from this distribution. First, the vast majority of BRIGNA studies was published in specialized accounting journals. Together, RIGNA and JAPP published a total of 13 of the 18 studies (72%). This provides additional evidence about the validity of the earlier assertion that BRIG-NA which applies general theories to governmental and nonprofit settings makes a very limited contribution to mainstream accounting and psychological research.

On the other hand, three BRIGNA studies were published in the American Accounting Association's general purpose journal (*The Accounting Review*) over a recent 2-year period [Berry et al., 1987; Lewis, Patton, and Green, 1988; Meixner and Welker, 1988]. What distinguishes these studies from the majority of those published in the specialized governmental accounting journals is their emphasis on theory refinement and theory development rather than simple theory application.

Berry et al. [1987] were interested in the ways in which the *unique* characteristics of the governmental setting (e.g., levels within government and the civil service system) would influence the rate of false sign-offs by governmental auditors. By recognizing that the unique features of the governmental setting could have a significant impact on behavior *and* incorporating those characteristics into the design of the study, Berry et al. contributed to our understanding of the behavior of governmental auditors. In addition, they were able to identify a setting wherein the behavior of governmental auditors would be expected to be systematically different from that of other auditors. In doing so, Berry et al. also contributed to theory refinement in mainstream BRIA.

Lewis et al. [1988] and Meixner and Welker [1988] used a different approach to contribute to theory-building research. Unlike the setting explored by Berry et al. [1987], there was no clear theoretical basis for expecting that the unique features of the governmental setting would influence the specific type of behaviors under investigation. Lewis et al. were interested in generic issues related to information choice and information use. As there was no clear theoretical reason to expect that the information processing capabilities of municipal analysts would be systematically different from those of other individuals, Lewis et al. used subjects from the governmental sector to develop theory in mainstream BRIA. In fact, the work of Lewis et al. was a direct extension of the work of Abdel-khalik and El-Sheshai [1980] with bank loan officers as subjects, and has since been extended by Simnett and Trotman [1989] with auditors as subjects.

Similarly, Meixner and Welker [1988] were concerned with generic issues related to the effects of different types of experience (organizational and situational) on judgment consensus. The Audit Division of the State Auditor's Office in Texas offered an environment that was especially conducive to their research needs. As with the Lewis et al. [1988] study, Meixner and Welker used the governmental setting to extend our understanding of human behavior in settings where generic types of behavior were expected to occur.

There is a fundamental difference between these three studies and the financial reporting studies cited earlier. Rather than simply "borrowing" a general behavioral theory and applying the unmodified theory to issues in the governmental and nonprofit sectors, Berry et al., Lewis et al. and Meixner and Welker used this setting to refine and develop basic behavioral research.

This suggests two ways in which BRIGNA could make a significant contribution in the future. Most importantly, BRIGNA researchers must be sensitive to the characteristics that make the governmental setting unique and determine whether these characteristics would or would not be expected to have a systematic influence on behavior. If there are theoretical reasons to expect that behavior *will* be affected by these characteristics, BRIGNA researchers should refine the theory to incorporate the effects of these characteristics. Second, if there is *no* theoretical reason to expect that behavior in the governmental sector would be different than behavior in other settings, BRIGNA researchers can use subjects in governmental and nonprofit settings to further develop (rather than simply apply) theories from mainstream BRIA. As the three studies outlined above demonstrate, either approach can contribute not only to our understanding of behavior in the governmental sector but to our understanding of behavior in general.

D. Assessment of Additional Issues

1. Subjects

In their 1987 paper, Herhold, Parry, and Patton noted that, "although much has been written about users' 'needs' in government accounting, little empirical research exists outside of studies which relate to users in the municipal bond market" [p. 95]. A significant proportion of the research published between 1986 and 1990 still focused primarily on municipal analysts [Green, 1990; Herhold-Baskin, 1986; Lewis et al., 1988; Robbins, 1988].

It appears, however, that some BRIGNA researchers have begun to recognize that other user groups exist and have expanded their samples to include informed members of citizens' groups [Gaffney, 1986; Wardlow and Godfrey, 1989], officials of federal, state and local governments [Bokemeier, 1988; F. Carpenter, 1988; Shoulders, 1987; Willets et al., 1988], governmental auditors [Reed, 1986; Berry et al., 1987] and resource allocators in charitable organizations [Reed and Koch, 1989]. It appears, therefore, that considerable progress has been made by BRIGNA researchers in expanding their sampling frames to encompass some of the many diverse user groups of governmental and nonprofit accounting information.

BRIGNA researchers should be aware that there is a potential problem with the number of BRIGNA studies that have utilized municipal analysts as subjects. It was noted earlier that the population of municipal analysts was sampled no fewer than four times in the past five years.[7] Successful completion of any behavioral research project requires a sufficient number of observations from the relevant population to perform reliable statistical tests. Unfortunately, in the governmental and nonprofit sector, many of the relevant populations are quite small. For example, there are only approximately 500 members listed in the membership roster of the National Federation of Municipal Analysts. BRIGNA researchers must be sensitive to the fact that oversampling of a population decreases the likelihood that subjects will be willing to participate in future research endeavors. The indiscriminate use of mass mailing techniques should be avoided when at all possible to mitigate the problems associated with oversampling. Carefully designed and theoretically driven research could substantially reduce the number of subjects necessary for statistically reliable results.

2. Research Support

The availability of funding to support BRIGNA research could have a significant impact on both the level of activity and the quality of research conducted. Good behavioral research can be a very expensive endeavor in terms of both time and money and a lack of adequate support can be a source of discouragement to researchers. Well-designed behavioral research is time consuming, as data collection instruments often need multiple pretests and data collection can extend over several months (e.g., Green [1990] reported that nearly three months elapsed from the time that experimental materials were mailed and the final responses had been returned).

Monetary expenses can also be high. In addition to the duplicating and mailing expenses incurred by most behavioral researchers, other significant costs associated with BRIGNA published during the period included: (1) telephone calls to secure participants and follow-up calls to nonrespondents [Green, 1990; Herhold-Baskin, 1986]; (2) monetary incentives for participants [Green, 1990]; and (3) travel expenses for on-site data collection [F. Carpenter, 1988; V. Carpenter, 1987; Reed and Koch, 1989].

To assess the extent of research support for BRIGNA between 1986 and 1990, the acknowledgements sections of the 18 published papers were inspected for references to research support. The results are exhibited in Figure 2. As Figure 2 indicates, only one-third of the BRIGNA papers published during the period acknowledged any type of support: four of the projects (22%) recognized nonfinancial support (endorsement of the project and/or cooperation of members of a professional organization), one project (6%) received financial support and one project (6%) received both financial and nonfinancial support.

There are at least three potential explanations for the lack of recognized research support for BRIGNA: (1) support is not presently available for such projects; (2) BRIGNA research is not of a sufficient quality to warrant such support; or (3)

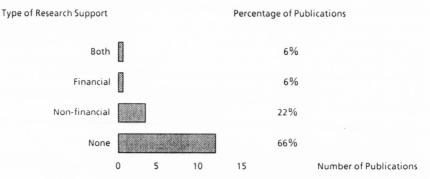

Type of Research Support   Percentage of Publications

Figure 2.   Distribution of Publications by Type of Research Support

BRIGNA researchers are not aware that sources of support exist or are not taking advantage of these sources. The fact that at least 6 of the 18 studies received some type of support suggests that the first two explanations are not the source of the problem. Sources acknowledged in these papers include the National Science Foundation [V. Carpenter and Feroz, 1990], the Association of Government Accountants [Berry et al., 1987], the Arthur Andersen Foundation and the Ford Foundation [V. Carpenter, 1987], the Governmental Accounting Standards Board and the National Federation of Municipal Analysts [Green, 1990], as well as support from the researcher's academic institution. BRIGNA researchers should be aware that other potential sources exist, including doctoral dissertation grants awarded by the Government and Nonprofit Section of the American Accounting Association and the recently announced grants sponsored by the Governmental Accounting Standards Board (see the Fall 1990 GNP newsletter or contact author for details). If BRIGNA researchers are aware of these sources and seek out support in the future, it is possible that more and better BRIGNA will result.

III.   SUGGESTIONS FOR THE FUTURE DEVELOPMENT OF BRIGNA

The ultimate objective of behavioral research has always been to understand, explain and predict human behavior [Ashton, 1982; Libby, 1981]. In seeking to meet this objective, BRIA has undergone some significant changes in direction in the past 25 years. As noted earlier, the focus of early BRIA shifted from policy-oriented, applied research toward more theoretically sound, basic research in the early to mid 1970s. This change in direction led BRIA researchers to focus on evaluating performance and identifying basic cognitive abilities and deficiencies that affected performance. To do so, the basic approach was to "borrow" theories from either psychology or sociology and apply those theories in simplistic accounting contexts.

As described by Libby [1989], another significant change in BRIA took place in the mid 1980s. BRIA researchers began to recognize that there were unique characteristics in accounting settings that *distinguished* them from those commonly examined by psychologists. Specifically, researchers began to explore the effects of: (1) task related knowledge [e.g., Bonner, 1990; Frederick and Libby, 1986; Libby, 1985] and (2) incentives and different types of market and organizational structures that exist in many accounting settings [e.g., Ashton, 1990; Camerer, 1987; Duh and Sunder, 1986]. This latest change in BRIA's direction has also had an impact on the development of basic psychological theories of decision making. For example, Ashton [1990] recognized that research on the effectiveness of decision aids in auditing contexts failed to incorporate many of the realistic features of the auditing environment. By including three such factors (incentives, feedback, and justification) into his experimental design, Ashton demonstrated that the positive effects of these factors that had been observed in simplistic settings were actually reversed when a decision aid was available. The result was that the underlying psychological theory was refined to incorporate these effects.

At least partially as a result of this recent change in direction, BRIA has regained the attention of accounting researchers and is becoming recognized by researchers from other academic disciplines as well (see Libby [1989] for a more complete discussion). The 1990 JAR Conference was devoted exclusively to behavioral issues. In addition, the Society for Judgment and Decision Making sponsored a symposium on decision making in competitive contexts. Thus, it appears that these changes have had a significant impact on the acceptance of BRIA as a legitimate subfield of behavioral research. The important question is whether BRIGNA researchers can benefit from being aware of what has happened in BRIA.

As a subset of BRIA, the ultimate objective of BRIGNA is to understand, explain and predict behavior in governmental and nonprofit settings. To date, the primary approach in BRIGNA has been to "borrow" theories of decision making from mainstream BRIA and apply those theories in simplistic governmental and nonprofit decision-making settings. It has been consistently argued in this paper that, while such an approach may help to provide partial answers to policy questions, such studies can make only a limited contribution to our understanding of human behavior in these settings.

Unlike BRIA, there is little evidence of a fundamental change in direction toward either more basic research or a focus on those characteristics that are unique to governmental and nonprofit settings. BRIGNA researchers can learn valuable lessons from the experiences of researchers in mainstream BRIA and can perhaps avoid some of the problems that have been encountered. Generally, the problems were associated with a policy orientation and the application of generally accepted behavioral theories in accounting settings. Changes in the direction of BRIGNA similar to those taken in mainstream BRIA over the last 25 years could have a similar impact on the contribution of BRIGNA to both mainstream accounting and psychological research.

In their 1987 review, Herhold, Parry, and Patton identified three significant deficiencies in BRIGNA prior to that date: (1) a lack of replications, (2) a lack of triangulation, and (3) a lack of theory-building research. The purpose of this paper was to assess how well BRIGNA published between 1986 and the present had addressed these deficiencies. Unfortunately, the review revealed that all three deficiencies remain. Two basic conclusions can be drawn from this review. First, significant progress has been made in both the quantity and quality of published BRIGNA research. Second, additional progress will be necessary if BRIGNA is to continue to contribute to our understanding of human behavior in the future. Although a wide variety of topics was researched during the period, the typical BRIGNA study: (1) applied an established generic behavioral theory to the governmental setting, (2) used an experimental methodology, (3) was published in a specialized governmental accounting journal, and (4) received no research support.

Replications and triangulation are needed to provide the synergy necessary for BRIGNA to evolve into a cohesive body of literature. Theory refinement and theory development, rather than the application of general behavioral theories to governmental and nonprofit accounting problems, are needed to provide answers to questions as to *why* specific behaviors occur. Two ways in which progress in theory refinement and theory development could be made are suggested in this section.

1. Additional Theoretical Bases

Identifying the unique characteristics of governmental and nonprofit settings that could be expected to influence behavior will not be an easy task. To do so, it may be necessary for BRIGNA researchers to look to other disciplines, in addition to the psychological and sociological theories traditionally defined as behavioral. Examples of instances in which the theory of other disciplines would be useful in explaining the effects of the unique features of governmental and nonprofit settings include[8]:

1. Accounting data generated in governmental and nonprofit settings are often used for political purposes. Would the presence of political incentives lead politicians to use the data differently than would be expected in a less political environment?
2. Politicians must be elected by voters to retain their positions. Civil service employees, on the other hand, are practically guaranteed continued employment once hired. Thus, users and producers of accounting data in governmental and nonprofit settings face very different economic incen-

tives than their counterparts in private enterprise. Would these different economic incentives be expected to influence behavior?

3. Accounting data generated in governmental and nonprofit settings report on the provision of public, rather than private, goods and services. Therefore, users and preparers in the governmental sector are held publicly accountable for their actions, whereas their counterparts in private enterprise are less subject to public scrutiny. Does being held publicly accountable for one's actions have an impact on the way in which accounting data are used?

Traditionally, behavioral researchers have relied almost exclusively on the literatures of psychology and/or sociology for theories from which to develop hypotheses. To answer questions such as those posed above, however, BRIGNA researchers may need to explore the literatures of other academic disciplines (e.g., economics, political science, and public administration) in addition to the traditional literatures. Given the political environment in which governmental and nonprofit accounting data are used, the literature pertaining to bargaining and negotiations may be particularly helpful to BRIGNA researchers.

Although such an approach will require a change in direction, BRIGNA researchers should recognize that they have the same type of competitive advantage that Libby [1989] attributes to mainstream BRIA researchers. That is, researchers in the governmental and nonprofit area are more knowledgeable about this environment than other researchers. Therefore, they can take advantage of this knowledge to identify the relevant characteristics of the environment and design their research to incorporate these characteristics. Although theory refinement and theory development will be more challenging for BRIGNA researchers than simple theory application, such a change could have a significant impact on behavioral research in general if this challenge is accepted.

2. Additional Methodological Approaches

If the direction of BRIGNA research shifts toward theory refinement and theory development in the future, it may also be necessary to adopt research methodologies more suited to testing these theories.[9] For example, a substantial amount of literature exists about the preferences and opinions of users of governmental financial information, yet virtually nothing is known about *how* this information is used. In addition, traditional experimental studies fail to recognize that individuals in governmental settings operate in political and economic "markets." Traditional behavioral methodologies (i.e., experiments, surveys, and case studies) may prove inadequate to explore these topics.

Two innovative methodologies, protocol analyses and laboratory markets, have recently been successfully published in mainstream BRIA (see Bouwman, Frishkoff, and Frishkoff [1987] and Schatzberg [1990] for examples of protocol and market studies, respectively). To date, however, there have been no BRIGNA studies published that utilized either methodological approach. To assist in the continued development of BRIGNA in the future, researchers must carefully select that methodological approach which is best suited to explore the research question. As more of the unique characteristics of governmental and nonprofit settings are incorporated into research questions, it will be necessary for BRIGNA researchers to also adopt innovative methodological techniques.

IV. CONCLUDING COMMENTS

Herhold, Parry, and Patton [1987, p. 98] noted that "behavioral research in accounting journals has gone through an interesting cycle." From the preceding assessment of BRIGNA published during the past five years, it appears that the same comment could be made about BRIGNA. Although considerable progress has been made in both the quantity and quality of BRIGNA, additional improvement will be necessary before BRIGNA will be recognized as a significant subfield of behavioral research.

It is recommended that BRIGNA researchers focus on developing a unified research agenda rather than exploring new issues. At the present time, there is so much diversity in the issues explored by BRIGNA researchers that it is not possible to reach even tentative conclusions about any one issue. Such a unified strategy, which would require replications and triangulation, would help to produce the synergy that is lacking at the present time.

It is also recommended that BRIGNA researchers focus on theory refinement and theory development rather than theory application. To do so, it may be necessary to expand the traditional definition of behavioral research to include additional theoretical bases and innovative research methodologies. Theory refinement and theory development could benefit from theories from economics, political science, and public administration in addition to the psychological and sociological theory bases that more traditionally characterize behavioral research. It may also be necessary to expand the methodological approach beyond the traditional experimental, survey, and case study methodologies to accommodate these characteristics. Although both recommendations will require a great deal of effort on the part of BRIGNA researchers, commitment to these strategies can make a significant contribution to the future development of BRIGNA.

ACKNOWLEDGMENTS

I would like to thank Jim Patton, an anonymous reviewer and participants in the Governmental and Nonprofit Research Workshop in Toronto for their helpful comments on earlier drafts of this paper.

NOTES

1.   Examples of other subsets of BRIA which combine a specific topic area with behavioral research methodologies include Behavioral Research in Auditing and Behavioral Research in Managerial Accounting.

2.   As the Herhold, Parry, and Patton review was not restricted to published research, some overlap exists between the experimental studies identified by Herhold, Parry, and Patton and those assessed in the present paper. Of the nine experimental studies identified by Herhold, Parry, and Patton, four had been conducted prior to 1986 but were published subsequent to that time. Therefore, those four studies are also included in the present review.

3.   Another useful way to compare the development of BRIGNA to that of mainstream BRIA might be to examine the contents of doctoral course outlines for both BRIGNA and BRIA seminars. In all likelihood, a BRIGNA seminar would be structured around the topics listed in Table 2, which would place considerable emphasis on financial reporting topics. If covered at all, only the early sessions in a BRIA seminar would most likely concentrate on financial reporting issues. The focus would then shift to more generic information processing issues, such as research on heuristic and biases which "borrow" and apply theories from the psychology literature. Later BRIA sessions would also reflect more basic research on issues related to the structure of memory and the effects of environmental factors on information processing.

4.   Note that the Robbins [1988] survey also covered topics related to depreciation, alternative types of financial reports, and the importance of the audit report.

5.   Note that this observation does not diminish the specific contribution of these studies. Each study investigated a topic of interest to policymakers and governmental and nonprofit researchers. The policy-oriented contribution of the studies is evidenced by the growing number of such papers being published in specialized accounting journals such as *Research in Governmental and Nonprofit Accounting.*

6.   Gaffney actually used an experimental methodology, as indicated in Table 2, since the type of financial report was manipulated between subjects. The data collection instrument is discussed in this section, however, as it would be equally relevant to surveys where this type of manipulation is not a factor.

7.   It is more likely that the actual number is considerably larger as this only represents studies published in academic accounting journals during the period.

8.   This should not be taken as an exhaustive list. Rather, the list is only meant to suggest a few of the many behavioral issues that arise in governmental and nonprofit accounting contexts.

9.   Obviously, BRIGNA researchers must also consider the willingness of academic accounting journals to publish studies utilizing such methodologies.

REFERENCES

Abdel-khalik, A.R., and B.B. Ajinkya, *Empirical Research in Accounting: A Methodological Viewpoint* Vol. 4, American Accounting Association, Accounting Education Series, [American Accounting Association, 1979].

Abdel-khalik, A.R., and K.M. El-Sheshai, "Information Choice and Utilization in an Experiment of Default Prediction," *Journal of Accounting Research* [Autumn 1980], pp. 325–342.

American Accounting Association, Committee on Accounting Practice for Not-for-Proft Organizations, "Report of the Committee on Accounting Practice of Not-for-Profit Organizations," *The Accounting Review,* Supplement to Vol. XLVI [1971], pp. 81–163.

American Accounting Association (AAA), "Report of the Committee on the Relationship of Behavioral Science and Accounting," *The Accounting Review* [Supplement, 1974], pp. 127–139.

————, *Statement on Accounting Theory and Theory Acceptance* [American Accounting Association, 1979].

Ashton, R.H., *Human Information Processing in Accounting* [American Accounting Association, 1982].

————, "Paradoxical Effects of Incentives, Feedback, and Justification in Accounting Decision Settings," Working paper. Duke University [1990].

Berry, L.E., G.B. Harwood, and J.L. Katz, "Performance of Auditing Procedures by Governmental Auditors," *The Accounting Review* [January 1987], pp. 14–28.

Birnberg, J.G., and J.F. Shields, "Three Decades of Behavioral Accounting Research: A Search for Order," *Behavioral Research in Accounting* 1 [1989], pp. 23–74.

Bokemeier, L.C., "Revenue Recognition Criteria for State and Local Governments," *Research in Governmental and Nonprofit Accounting* 4 [1988], pp. 129–157.

Bonner, S., "Experience Effects in Auditing: The Role of Task-Specific Knowledge," *The Accounting Review* [January 1990], pp. 72–92.

Bouwman, M., P.A. Frishkoff, and P. Frishkoff, "How Do Financial Analysts Make Decisions? A Process Model of the Investment Screening Decision," *Accounting, Organizations and Society* 12, 1 [1987], pp. 1–29.

Braunstein, M.L., *Depth Perception Through Motion* [Academic Press, 1976].

Bruns, W.J., Jr., "Comments on a Paper by David Green," in *Accounting Research 1960-1970: A Critical Evaluation*, edited by N. Dopuch and L. Revsine [University of Illinois Press, 1973], pp. 126–132.

Burgstahler, D., and G.L. Sundem, "The Evolution of Behavioral Accounting Research in the United States, 1968-1987," *Behavioral Research in Accounting* 1 [1989], pp. 75–108.

Camerer, C.F., "Do Biases in Probability Judgment Matter in Markets: Experimental Evidence," *American Economic Review* [December, 1987], pp. 981–997.

Carpenter, F.H., "The Impact of Financial Reporting Requirements on Municipal Officials' Fixed Asset Acquisition Decisions," *Research in Governmental and Nonprofit Accounting* 4 [1988], pp. 49–78.

Carpenter, V.L., "The Effects of Interest Group Competition on Funding Government Management Information Systems," *Research in Governmental and Nonprofit Accounting* 3, Part B [1987], pp. 67–105.

Carpenter, V.L., and E.H. Feroz, "The Decision to Adopt GAAP: A Case Study of the Commonwealth of Kentucky," *Accounting Horizons* [June, 1990], pp. 67–78.

Choo, F., "Expert-Novice Differences in Judgment/Decision Making Research," *Journal of Accounting Literature* 8 [1989], pp. 106–136.

Davis, J.S., and I. Solomon, "Experience, Expertise, and Expert-Performance Research in Public Accounting," *Journal of Accounting Literature* 8 [1989], pp. 150–164.

Duh, R.R., and S. Sunder, "Incentives, Learning and Processing of Information in a Market Environment: An Examination of the Base-Rate Fallacy," in *Laboratory Market Research*, edited by S. Moriarty [Center for Economic and Management Research, University of Oklahoma, 1986].

Dyckman, T.R., M. Gibbons, and R.J. Swieringa, "Experimental and Survey Research in Financial Accounting: A Review and Evaluation," in *The Impact of Accounting Research on Practice and Disclosure*, edited by A.R. Abdel-Khalik and T.F. Keller [Duke University Press, 1978], pp. 225–297.

Frederick, D.M., and R. Libby, "Expertise and Auditors' Judgments of Conjunctive Events," *Journal of Accounting Research* [Autumn 1986], pp. 270–290.

Gaffney, M.A., "Consolidated Versus Fund-Type Accounting Statements: The Perspectives of Constituents," *Journal of Accounting and Public Policy* 5 [1986], pp. 167–189.

Green, S.L., "The Effects of Altering the Amount of Data in Governmental Financial Reports on Analysts' Predictions of Bond Ratings," *Research in Governmental and Nonprofit Accounting* 6, [1990].

Herhold, S., R.W. Parry, Jr., and J.M. Patton, "Behavioral Research in Municipal Accounting," *Research in Governmental and Nonprofit Accounting* 3, Part B [1987], pp. 71–109.

Herhold-Baskin, S., "The Information Content of the Audit Report as Perceived by Municipal Analysts," *Research in Governmental and Nonprofit Accounting* 2 [1986], pp. 53–88.

Hofstedt, T.R., "Behavioral Accounting Research: Pathologies, Paradigms and Prescriptions," *Accounting, Organizations and Society* 1, 1 [1976], pp. 43–58.

Hofstedt, T.R., and J.C. Kinard, "A Strategy for Behavioral Accounting Research," *The Accounting Review* [January 1970], pp. 38–54.

Howard, T.P., "On the Role of Financial Statements in the Prediction of Interest Rates for Municipal Bonds," *Governmental Accountants Journal* [Winter 1979-80], pp. 58–62.

Jonsson, S., "Budgetary Behaviour in Local Government—A Case Study over Three Years," *Accounting, Organizations and Society* 7, 3 [1982], pp. 287–304.

Larcker, D., and V. Lessig, "Perceived Usefulness of Information: A Psychometric Examination," *Decision Sciences* [January 1980], pp. 121–134.

Lewis, B.L., J.M. Patton, and S.L. Green, "The Effects of Information Choice and Information Use on Analysts' Predictions of Municipal Bond Rating Changes," *The Accounting Review* [April 1988], pp. 270-282.

Libby, R., *Accounting and Human Information Processing: Theory and Application* [Prentice-Hall, 1981].

——, "Availability and the Generation of Hypotheses in Analytical Review," *Journal of Accounting Research* [Autumn 1985], pp. 648–667.

——, "Experimental Research and the Distinctive Features of Accounting Settings," Working paper. Cornell University [1989].

Libby, R., and B.L. Lewis, "Human Information Processing Research in Accounting: The State of the Art," *Accounting, Organizations and Society* 2, 3 [1977], pp. 245–268.

——, "Human Information Processing Research in Accounting: The State of the Art in 1982," *Accounting, Organizations and Society* 7, 3 [1982], pp. 231–285.

Lord, A.T., "The Development of Behavioral Thought in Accounting, 1952–1981," *Behavioral Research in Accounting* 1 [1989], pp. 124–149.

Lynn, S., and M.A. Gaffney, "Auditor Perceptions of Municipal Audit Report Messages," *Research in Governmental and Nonprofit Accounting* 6, [1990].

Meixner, W.F., and D.M. Bline, "Professional and Job-Related Attitudes and the Behaviours They Influence Among Governmental Accountants," *Accounting, Auditing and Accountability* 2, 1 [1989], pp. 8–20.

Meixner, W.F., and R.B. Welker, "Judgment Consensus and Auditor Experience: An Examination of Organizational Relations," *The Accounting Review* [July 1988], pp. 505–513.

Patton, J.M., "An Experimental Investigation of Some Effects of Consolidating Municipal Financial Reports," *The Accounting Review* [April 1978], pp. 402–414.

Peltzman, S., "Toward a More General Theory of Regulation," *Journal of Law and Economics* [August 1976], pp. 211–243.

Ramanathan, K.V., and W.L. Weis, "Supplementing Collegiate Financial Statements with Across-Fund Aggregations: An Experimental Inquiry," *Accounting, Organizations and Society* 6, 2 [1981], pp. 143–151.

Reed, S.A., "The Impact of Nonmonetary Performance Measures Upon Budgetary Decision Making in the Public Sector," *Journal of Accounting and Public Policy* 5 [1986], pp. 111–140.

Reed, S.A., and B.S. Koch, "Resource Allocation Decisions by Charitable Organizations: An Experiment," *Research in Governmental and Nonprofit Accounting* 5 [1989], pp. 99–122.

Robbins, W.A., "The Importance of Selected Information Items to Municipal Bond Analysts and Their Disclosure in Municipal Annual Reports: An Empirical Assessment," *Research in Governmental and Nonprofit Accounting* 4 [1988], pp. 103–128.

Schatzberg, J.W., "A Laboratory Market Investigation of Low Balling in Audit Pricing," *The Accounting Review* [April 1990], pp. 337–362.

Schroder, H.M., M.J. Driver, and S. Streufert, *Human Information Processing: Individuals and Groups Functioning in Complex Social Situations* [Holt, Rinehart and Winston, 1967].

Shoulders, C.D., "Criteria for Identifying the Municipal Organizational Reporting Entity," *Research in Governmental and Nonprofit Accounting* 3, Part A [1987], pp. 181–206.

Simnett, R., and K. Trotman, "Auditor Versus Model: Information Choice and Information Processing," *The Accounting Review* [July 1989], pp. 514–528.

Simon, H.A., "Rational Choice and the Structure of the Environment," *Psychological Bulletin* [1956], pp. 126–138.

Tversky, A., and D. Kahneman, "Judgment Under Uncertainty: Heuristics and Biases," *Science* [1974], pp. 1124–1131.

Wardlow, P.S., and J.T. Godfrey, "PERS Reports and Users' Information Needs," *Research in Governmental and Nonprofit Accounting* 5 [1989], pp. 71–98.

Warner, S.L., "Randomized Response: A Survey Technique for Eliminating Evasive Answer Bias," *Journal of the American Statistical Association* [March 1965], pp. 63–69.

Willets, S.D., D.K. Clancy, and R.J. Freeman, "Public Employee Retirement System Reports: A Study of Knowledgeable User Information Processing Ability," *Research in Governmental and Nonprofit Accounting* 4 [1988], pp. 3–48.

THE IMPACT OF THE WORK SETTING ON THE ORGANIZATIONAL AND PROFESSIONAL COMMITMENT OF ACCOUNTANTS

Dennis M. Bline, Wilda F. Meixner, and
Nissim Aranya

ABSTRACT

Accountants are traditionally employed in one of three work settings: public practice, governmental entities, or departments of large nonaccounting organizations. This study uses General Linear Models to investigate the effect of the work setting on the attitudinal variables of organizational commitment, professional commitment, and organizational-professional conflict of accountants. Work setting was observed to significantly affect the reported levels of organizational and professional commitment, but not the level of organizational-professional conflict.

Based on the results of this study, the current practice of categorizing accountants

Research in Governmental and Nonprofit Accounting, Vol. 7, pages 79–96.
Copyright © 1992 by JAI Press Inc.
All rights of reproduction in any form reserved.
ISBN: 1-55938-418-2

as professional/nonprofessional may not be fully warranted. The fact that similarities exist between professional and governmental accountants with regard to their professional commitment indicates that researchers should consider classifying governmental accountants with public accountants when professional attitudes are examined. On the other hand, the differences among professional, governmental, and departmental accountants with regard to their organizational commitment seems to indicate that accountants should be classified into three categories when investigating organizational attitudes.

I. INTRODUCTION

Organizational researchers have observed that job-related attitudes such as satisfaction and commitment affect employee behaviors such as absenteeism and turnover. A body of literature has evolved that examines these relationships in the context of accountants and their organizations. While most subjects in these studies have been employees of public accounting firms, a few studies have included groups of accountants employed in the public sector and in other entities such as manufacturing concerns, financial institutions, and retail organizations.

The purpose of this study is to investigate similarities and differences in job-related and professional attitudes among accountants employed in different work settings: public accounting organizations, governmental entities, and departments of large nonaccounting organizations. The attitudes investigated are organizational commitment, professional commitment, and organizational-professional conflict. The analyses use data gathered by Aranya and Ferris [1984], who classified their subjects as accountants employed in public practice (professional) and accountants employed in all other work settings (nonprofessional), and Meixner and Bline [1989], who surveyed governmental accountants.

The next two sections of this paper review the relevant literature and present the hypothesized relationships. Subsequent sections describe the research methodology and results. The final section presents discussion, conclusions, limitations, and suggestions for future research.

II. BACKGROUND

A. Work Settings

Scott [1965] described the work setting of a professional group as one in which professionals are central to the achievement of an organization's primary objectives. He investigated the employment of professionals in two work settings (autonomous and heteronomous) and distinguished between them based on the degree of control over professional activities that is retained by the administration. In an autonomous professional organization, much of the control over professional matters is delegated to the staff of professionals. Thus a high level of autonomy exists. In a heteronomous work setting, professional employees are subordinate to administrative rules and supervisory controls of the organization, that is, professional responsibility is retained by the administration [Scott, 1965]. As a result, professionals employed in a heteronomous work setting would be expected to receive more guidance on professional matters and have less autonomy than would professionals employed in an autonomous work setting.

Building on Scott's work-setting categorizations, Hall [1968] conducted an empirical study across a number of professions (including accounting) to examine differences in the degree of professionalization (the individual's internalization of professional norms and values) as a function of the extent of bureaucratization (structural control on professional tasks). He suggested that professionalization and degree of organizational bureaucracy within a profession may vary across work settings and proposed that one potential source of these variations is the degree to which the profession can be self regulating and autonomous. Although Scott's definitions of autonomous and heteronomous organizations were retained, Hall added a third work setting to include professional employees in departments of large organizations. Hall went on to propose that employees in professional departments of large organizations may be viewed as having little, if any, autonomy because the structure of the work environment is often controlled by the administrative structure of the organization. Based on this proposition, accounting departments in manufacturing organizations and universities were included in this category along with legal, engineering, and personnel departments.

Hall observed that autonomous professional organizations exhibited the highest level of professionalism and the lowest level of organizational bureaucracy. This was due to, among other things, the autonomy associated with the delegation of authority to the professionals. Physicians, law firms, advertising agencies, and CPA firms were identified as autonomous organizations. In the heteronomous professional organization, a lesser degree of both professionalism and autonomy, as well as a higher level of organizational bureaucracy, were found to exist when compared to the autonomous group. Public schools and libraries and other nonprofit agencies were identified as heteronomous organizations based on the fact that they are often subject to external or legislative structuring. Although the level of professionalism and autonomy in the departmental setting was observed to be less than that of the autonomous organization, Hall made no direct comparison between heteronomous and departmental work settings on this issue. In addition, while the level of organizational bureaucracy was observed to be higher in both the departmental and heteronomous work setting than in an autonomous work setting, the comparison between the heteronomous and departmental work settings was inconclusive. While Hall's investigation of the three work settings is somewhat limited, his work does generally support the existence of three separate work settings for professionals.

Hall's study investigated a wide variety of professions. However, all three work settings were not represented in any one profession. This makes it difficult to determine whether the observed differences result from differences across the work settings or differences across professions. The present study applies Hall's theory of three work settings in an examination of the accounting profession. The work settings investigated are: (1) public accounting firms (autonomous), (2) governmental entities (heteronomous), and (3) accounting departments in large organizations (departmental).

1.   Justification for the classification of CPA firms as autonomous is found not only in Hall [1968] but also in Scott's [1965] description of the association between professional officials and their subordinates in the autonomous work setting. Scott suggests that professional managers may have administrative authority but should only proffer advice on professional matters.

2.   The inclusion of governmental accountants in the heteronomous group may be supported by two factors. First, administrators in the governmental entity may not be trained in the same profession as the employees. Zimmerman [1977] described government officials as being agents of citizens and proposed that they may use their office for political gain. These officials may be more concerned with politics than with professional issues. Second, Hall's [1968] inclusion of nonprofit entities in the heteronomous category was based on the proposition that these organizations are subject to external or legislative structuring. This is manifested in the fact that controls are often designed to limit the negative behavior of politicians [Berry and Wallace, 1986]. In the governmental setting, rules attached to funding procedures act as an external authoritative force and may impose restrictions on the professional tasks performed by the professional accountants [Government Finance Officers Association, 1988]. Thus, autonomy may be inhibited.

3.   Although not subject to external or legislative control to the same extent as heteronomous organizations, accounting departments are still subject to control in the form of the organizational structure. While a heteronomous organization is an entity unto itself, a department is subject to the control of the entire organizational hierarchy. Accounting professionals in this work setting are subject to administrative controls. In addition, financial reports prepared for external users in many instances are not made public until they have been subjected to third party evaluation. Based on these concepts, Hall [1968] recognized accounting professionals employed in departments as part of this third group.

B. Commitment

Studies investigating the commitment of accounting professionals have examined both commitment to the employing organization and commitment to the profession [Aranya and Ferris, 1984; Aranya, Lachman, and Amernic, 1982; Harrell, Chewning, and Taylor, 1986; Lachman and Aranya, 1986; McGregor,

Killough, and Brown, 1989; Meixner and Bline, 1989]. These studies have been based on the definition of organizational commitment (OC) proposed by Porter, Steers, Mowday, and Boulian [1974, p. 604] as "the strength of an individual's identification with and involvement in a particular organization," that is, a strong belief in and acceptance of the organization's goals and values, a readiness to exert considerable effort on behalf of the organization, and a strong desire to remain a member of the organization. Researchers have established the importance of management's concern with the employee's OC by observing that higher levels of commitment are associated with increased job satisfaction [Porter et al., 1974], employee performance [Mowday, Porter, and Dubin 1974], and organizational effectiveness [Steers, 1977].

Professional commitment (PC) is commonly defined by replacing the term "organization" (in the previously stated definition) with the term "profession." Professional Commitment has been described as developing through the socialization process (formal education), which emphasizes basic professional values such as autonomy and conformity to standards [Larson, 1977; Volmer and Mills, 1966]. Lachman and Aranya [1986] proposed that employees with high PC will expect the organization to permit them to behave in accordance with professional norms (standards) in the achievement of the organization's goals, that is, professional autonomy.

In examining the relationship between OC and PC, researchers have discovered that the development of OC may be dependent on whether the organization permits the professional to achieve professional goals, thus realizing their expectations [Bartol, 1979b; Harrell et al., 1986; Kerr, VonGlinow, and Schriesheim, 1977; Lachman and Aranya, 1986; McGregor et al., 1989; Meixner and Bline, 1989]. In a study covering a wide variety of organizations, Bartol [1979b] investigated professionalism as a predictor of OC. In this effort, she included autonomy along with PC, ethics, professional identification and reward, and collegial maintenance of standards as attitudinal components of professionalism. She defined autonomy as "a perceived right to make decisions about both the means and goals associated with one's work" [Bartol, 1979b, p. 817]. Both autonomy and PC were found to positively affect OC. In addition, Aranya et al. [1982] observed autonomy to have a positive impact on both professionalization and PC. Thus, the work setting linkage to autonomy proposed by Hall [1968] can be extended to OC and PC through the research of Bartol [1979b] and Aranya et al. [1982].

C. Organizational-Professional Conflict

The potential for organizational-professional conflict (OPC) may exist when organizational goals and values are incompatible with professional goals and values [Sorensen, 1967]. This conflict is thought to occur when the control and authority of the organization subordinates standards of professional performance, thereby preventing the professional from exercising judgment under professional autonomy [McGregor et al., 1989]. This appears to indicate that high levels of professional structural control cannot exist simultaneously with high levels of organizational structural control. Early researchers presumed that a high level of commitment to either the profession or the organization precluded a high level of commitment to the other, that is, the existence of inherent incompatibility. Although some early studies supported the hypothesis of inherent conflict [Schroeder and Imdieke, 1977; Sorensen, 1967; Sorensen and Sorensen, 1974], other studies indicated that this incompatibility need not exist [Aranya and Ferris, 1984; Meixner and Bline, 1989; Montagna, 1968]. In departmental work settings, Harrell et al. [1986] and McGregor et al. [1989] observed that when OPC was found to exist, job satisfaction decreased and turnover intentions increased. In addition, these studies suggest that OPC may be affected by other factors including tenure and professional affiliation.

In summary, the literature appears to support the existence of three distinct work settings for professionals. In addition, it has been observed that the level of autonomy varies across these work settings. Although three work settings have been investigated, no study has analyzed the effect of the work setting within a single profession. Recent literature also suggests that the level of autonomy may be associated with the employee attitudes of OC, PC, and OPC. These relationships justify an investigation that examines the work setting of professionals in conjunction with both professional and organizational attitudes of employees. Accountants were chosen as subjects in this study because current practice categorizes them as professional/nonprofessional when in fact a third category may be justified.

III. HYPOTHESES

A. Organizational Commitment

Previous research has linked variations in some employee attitudes to differences in the work setting. Hall [1968] observed that the level of autonomy is greater in the autonomous work setting than either the heteronomous or departmental work setting and the levels of autonomy in the latter two are not significantly different. The link between autonomy and OC can be seen in Bartol's [1979a] observation that autonomy is positively associated with job satisfaction and the Porter et al. [1974] observation that job satisfaction is a predictor of OC. Based on the established relationships between autonomy and the work setting and between autonomy and OC, it is proposed that the level of OC in an autonomous work setting (public accountants) will be greater than the level of OC in either a heteronomous (governmental accountants) or a departmental work setting (departmental accountants) and that the level of OC between governmental and departmental accountants will not differ significantly. The research hypotheses are as follows:

H1: *The OC of public accountants is greater than the OC of governmental accountants.*

H2: *The OC of public accountants is greater than the OC of departmental accountants.*

H3: *The OC of governmental accountants is not significantly different from the OC of departmental accountants.*

B. Professional Commitment

Hall [1968] observed that the professional autonomy of the autonomous work setting was greater than either the heteronomous or departmental work setting; however, no tests of differences were made between the heteronomous and departmental work settings. In addition, Volmer and Mills [1966] and Larson [1977] propose that the process of socialization into the profession emphasizes professional autonomy and conformity to standards (professional self-regulation) and will lead to the development of PC. The relationships among autonomy, commitment, and the work setting from the perspective of the profession seem to mirror the relationships from the perspective of the organization. Thus, similar to OC, autonomy can be related to PC through the work setting. It is proposed that the level of PC for public accountants will be greater than the level of PC for either governmental or departmental accountants. Because Hall did not compare heteronomous and departmental work settings in terms of professional autonomy, no difference can be hypothesized in the level of PC between governmental and departmental accountants. The research hypotheses are as follows:

H4: *The PC of public accountants is greater than the PC of governmental accountants.*

H5: *The PC of public accountants is greater than the PC of departmental accountants.*

H6: *The PC of governmental accountants is not significantly different from the PC of departmental accountants.*

C. Organizational-Professional Conflict

Professionals in all work settings come to expect some level of autonomy in the work place because of the emphasis given to professional standards and the development of professional norms that result from a common socialization process [Larson, 1977]. However, the autonomy granted by different organizations has been observed to vary [Hall, 1968]. Autonomous professional organizations, managed by administrators trained in the same profession, can be expected to provide the greatest level of autonomy because of commonality in professional goals [McGregor et al., 1989]. When the professional goals of accountants are not in direct conflict with the goals of the organization, the professional accountant perceives the freedom to act according to his/her professional judgment, resulting in a low level of OPC [Sorensen, 1967]. On the other hand, a lower level of autonomy will occur when accountants are employed in governmental entities because external and legislative controls may tend to reduce the accountant's ability to achieve professional goals by exercising professional judgment. Thus, a greater level of OPC may occur. An even lower level of autonomy may exist when accountants are employed in departmental work settings because of increased administrative controls [McGregor et al., 1989]. As the level of autonomy decreases because of increased organizational control, the level of OPC would be expected to increase. Thus, the following research hypotheses are designed to investigate these proposed relationships.

H7:   *The OPC of public accountants is less than the OPC of governmental accountants.*

H8:   *The OPC of public accountants is less than the OPC of departmental accountants.*

H9:   *The OPC of governmental accountants is less than the OPC of departmental accountants.*

IV. RESEARCH METHODS

In separate studies, Aranya and Ferris [1984] and Meixner and Bline [1989] addressed the relationships among OC, PC, and OPC for accountants.[1] The respondents in Aranya and Ferris [1984] were categorized into two work settings, professional (public accounting firms) and nonprofessional (governmental and departmental). Meixner and Bline [1989] investigated job-related attitudes in a governmental work setting. The current study combines the two data sets to examine the impact of the work setting (independent variable) on the employee attitudes of commitment and conflict (dependent variables). The model will also control for potential confounding variables.[2] The general structure of the model examining these relationships is as follows:

(OC, PC, OPC) = f (confounding variables, work setting).

The two studies measured OC, PC, and OPC in a similar fashion. OC was measured using a 15-item, 7-point Likert scale (1 = Strongly Disagree, 7 = Strongly Agree) instrument [Porter et al., 1974] that has been used extensively in organizational research [Angle and Perry, 1981; Dubin et al., 1975; Mowday et al., 1974; Steers, 1977; Stone and Porter, 1975]. Consistent with other accounting studies [Aranya and Jacobson, 1975; Aranya et al., 1982; Aranya, Pollack, and Amernic, 1981; Harrell et al., 1986; Lachman and Aranya, 1986; McGregor et al., 1989], PC was measured by constructing similar questions based on the OC instrument (i.e., the term "organization" was replaced by the term "profession").[3]

Table 1. Sample Size, Means, and Standard Deviations of Organizational Commitment, Professional Commitment, and Organizational-Professional Conflict by Work Setting

	n	Mean	Std. Dev.
Organizational Commitment			
Public Accountants	1142	5.61	1.08
Governmental Accountants	632	5.19	1.03
Departmental Accountants	608	5.21	1.14
Professional Commitment			
Public Accountants	1126	5.30	0.83
Governmental Accountants	630	5.39	0.91
Departmental Accountants	581	5.07	0.83
Organizational-Professional Conflict			
Public Accountants	1154	2.30	1.31
Governmental Accountants	642	2.80	1.61
Departmental Accountants	606	2.79	1.38

Note: Greater values represent greater levels of the respective construct (organizational commitment, professional commitment, and organizational-professional conflict). The scales range from a low of 1 to a high of 7. Negatively worded questions are reverse scaled before the means are calculated.

OPC was measured using two 7-point Likert scale items. The two items, listed below, are commonly used in the literature [Aranya and Jacobson, 1975; Aranya et al., 1982; Aranya et al., 1981; Harrell et al., 1986; Lachman and Aranya, 1986; McGregor et al., 1989].

1. The type and structure of my employment framework gives me the opportunity to fully express myself as a professional.
2. In my organization there is a conflict between the work standards and procedures of the organization and my own ability to act according to my professional judgment.

The measures of OC and PC for each respondent were computed by averaging the responses to the 15 questions for each scale.[4] Similarly, the two OPC questions were averaged to obtain the measure of OPC used in the analyses. The means and standard deviations for each measure are presented in Table 1 for the three work settings. The means of the OC and PC scales are within the ranges reported by Mowday et al. [1979].

Selected items from the commonly measured variables in the instruments used by Aranya and Ferris [1984] and Meixner and Bline [1989] were used to control for potential confounding effects. Tenure, certification, and satisfaction were included as independent variables in the analysis of OC and PC because these variables have been observed to be related to commitment in previous studies [Harrell et al., 1986; Hrebiniak and Alutto, 1972; McGregor et al., 1989; Porter et al., 1974]. The previous employment work setting (public accounting, government, industry, or no previous experience) was also included in the analyses. If the level of autonomy varies between work settings as proposed by Hall [1968] and if the level of autonomy affects employee attitudes as proposed by Volmer and Mills [1966], Larson [1977] and Bartol [1979a], previous experience could be expected to influence the commitment of respondents with previous experience. In addition, Merz and Groebner [1982] found a continuing effect from a previous work setting in their investigation of OPC among management accountants. PC was included as an independent variable in the analysis of OC because of the Aranya et al. [1981] suggestion that PC will precede OC. In addition to the variables discussed above, OC and PC were included in the analysis of OPC as independent variables because the literature indicates a close relationship among these variables [e.g., Harrell et al., 1986; McGregor et al., 1989].

The data were analyzed using the General Linear Model procedure in SAS. This procedure was used because it provides tests for the significance of estimated regression coefficients for interval scale independent variables (satisfaction, commitment, and tenure) while testing for differences in regression coefficients across selected levels of categorical independent variables (work setting, previous employment, and certification) by means of the contrast option. This option accomplishes the comparison by establishing the regression line of one level of the categorical variable as a base and comparing the slope of the regression line for other levels to the base level. This option was used to test for differences in the levels of OC, PC, and OPC among the work settings. Three models tested were:

OC = f (work setting, PC, job satisfaction, tenure-firm, certification, previous employment)

PC = f (work setting, professional satisfaction, tenure-profession, certification, previous employment)

OPC = f (work setting, job satisfaction, professional satisfaction, OC, PC, tenure-firm, tenure-profession, certification, previous employment).

V. RESULTS

A. Organizational Commitment

With regard to OC, the results of the comparisons among work settings are presented in Table 2. Panel A discloses that the independent variables in the model explain 56.7 percent of the variability in the respondent's OC. Although it is not possible to directly test for differences in R^2 across studies, the R^2 observed here seems to compare favorably with the R^2 of .357 reported by Bartol [1979b] for her model that attempted to explain OC. While Panel B of Table 2 reveals that there is a significant difference (p < .0001) between all pairs of work settings

Table 2.   Results of GLM Analysis of Organizational Commitment Among
            Public, Governmental, and Departmental Accountants

Panel A			
Source	*df*	*Sum of Squares*	*Mean Square*
Model	9	1,474.720	163.858
Error	2,139	1,127.606	0.527
Total	2,148	2,602.326	
F Value	PR > F	R^2	
310.83	0.0	0.567	

Panel B		
Contrast	*F Value*	*Prob > T*
Public vs. Governmental	117.24	0.0001
Public vs. Departmental	49.72	0.0001
Governmental vs. Departmental	26.30	0.0001

Panel C			
Parameter	*Regression Estimate*	*T for H_o: Parameter=0*	*Prob > T*
Work Setting			
Public	0.287	7.05	0.0001
Governmental	−0.304	−5.13	0.0001
Departmental	0.000	—	—
Professional Commitment	0.166	8.38	0.0001
Job Satisfaction	0.478	43.31	0.0
Tenure-Firm	0.166	4.88	0.0001
Certification-CPA[1]	0.284	4.43	0.0001
Previous Position			
Public	0.194	4.34	0.0001
Industry	0.212	4.24	0.0001
Government	0.146	2.39	0.0170
None	0.000	—	—

Note: [1] 1 = Yes; 2 = No

(public/governmental, public/departmental, governmental/departmental), interpretation of the relationships must consider the sign of the regression estimates.
The estimates reported in Panel C reveal that being in a public accounting work
setting has a significant positive effect on OC (.287) when compared to a
departmental work setting. On the other hand , being in a governmental accounting
work setting has a significant negative effect on OC (−.304) when compared to a
departmental work setting. Public accountants exhibited a higher level of OC than
either governmental or departmental accountants; therefore, the research
hypotheses H1 and H2 are supported. In addition, while H3 proposed that
governmental accountants were not different from departmental accountants,
governmental accountants were observed to have significantly less OC than
departmental accountants; therefore, research hypothesis H3 was not supported.[5]

All potentially confounding variables in the model were observed to be sig-

Table 3.   Results of GLM Analysis of Professional Commitment Among
Public, Governmental, and Departmental Accountants

Panel A			
Source	df	Sum of Squares	Mean Square
Model	8	321.393	40.174
Error	1,028	447.414	0.435
Total	1,036	768.807	
F Value	PR > F	R^2	
92.31	0.0	0.418	
Panel B			
Contrast		F Value	Prob > T
Public vs. Governmental		1.04	0.3088
Public vs. Departmental		12.68	0.0004
Governmental vs. Departmental		10.06	0.0016
Panel C			
Parameter	Regression Estimate	T for H_o: Parameter = 0	Prob > T
Work Setting			
Public	0.205	3.56	0.0004
Governmental	0.288	3.17	0.0016
Departmental	0.000	—	—
Professional Satisfaction	0.510	25.74	0.0
Tenure-Profession	0.098	1.17	0.2417
Certification-CPA[1]	0.182	2.25	0.0246
Previous Position			
Public	−0.010	−0.17	0.8684
Industry	−0.026	−0.41	0.6825
Government	0.024	0.34	0.7346
None	0.000	—	—

Note: [1] = Yes; 2 = No

nificantly related to OC in a positive manner. Panel C reveals that higher levels of
job satisfaction and PC were related to higher levels of OC. In addition, it can be
seen that: (1) the longer the respondent had been a member of the organization, the
greater the level of OC; (2) certified respondents were observed to have less OC
than noncertified respondents; and (3) respondents having previous accounting
work experience, except governmental, were observed to have higher levels of OC
than respondents having no previous accounting work experience. Thus, each of
the potentially confounding variables was found to affect the respondents' commitment to their respective organization.

B. Professional Commitment

Table 3 presents the results of analysis of PC across the three work settings.
Panel A discloses that the independent variables in the model explain 41.8 percent

Table 4. Results of GLM Analysis of Organizational-Professional Conflict Among Public, Governmental, and Departmental Accountants

Panel A			
Source	*df*	*Sum of Squares*	*Mean Square*
Model	12	804.537	67.044
Error	1,003	1,256.707	1.253
Total	1,015	2,061.244	
F Value	PR > F	R^2	
53.51	0.0	0.390	

Panel B			
Contrast		*F Value*	*Prob >T*
Public vs. Governmental		0.10	0.7474
Public vs. Departmental		3.38	0.0661
Governmental vs. Departmental		0.81	0.3674

Panel C			
Parameter	*Regression Estimate*	*T for H_0:Parameter = 0*	*Prob T*
Work Setting			
Public	−0.186	−1.84	0.0661
Governmental	−0.141	−0.90	0.3674
Departmental	0.000	—	—
Job Satisfaction	−0.202	−5.41	0.0001
Professional Satisfaction	−0.007	−0.16	0.8735
Organizational Commitment	−0.523	−10.30	0.0001
Professional Commitment	−0.135	−2.47	0.0138
Tenure-Firm	0.117	1.43	0.1517
Tenure-Profession	−0.062	−0.42	0.6722
Certification-CPA[1]	0.320	2.31	0.0214
Previous Position			
Public	0.188	1.76	0.0781
Industry	0.206	1.88	0.0603
Government	−0.070	−0.57	0.5708
None	0.000	—	—

Note: [1] = Yes; 2 = No

of the variability in the respondent's PC. Although the PC model in Table 3 does not explain as well as the OC model presented in Table 2, the explanatory power of this model compares favorably with the amount of variability explained by Bartol's [1979b] OC model. Panel B of Table 3 reveals that public accountants did not have a significantly different level of PC than governmental accountants (p < .3088), thus research hypothesis H4 was not supported. Panel B also indicates that there is a significant difference between public and departmental (p < .0004) as well as between governmental and departmental (p < .0016) work settings. The regression estimates reported in Panel C of Table 3 reveal that being in a public accounting or governmental accounting work setting has a significant positive effect on PC (.205 and .288, respectively) when compared to a departmental work setting. Based on these results, the research hypothesis H5 was supported while the research hypothesis H6 was not supported.[5] The only control variable observed to be related to PC was professional satisfaction, a positive relationship. Thus, only one potentially confounding variable was found to affect the respondents' commitment to the accounting profession.

C. Organizational-Professional Conflict

Table 4 presents the results of the analysis related to OPC. Panel A discloses that the independent variables in the model explain 39 percent of the variability in the respondent's OPC. As with PC, the amount of variability explained by the OPC model appears to be an acceptable level of explanatory power. While significant differences in the levels of OPC across work settings were expected, Panel B reveals that no significant differences exist. Public accountants were not observed to have a significantly different level of OPC than either governmental (p < .7474) or departmental (p < .0661) accountants and the governmental accountants were not observed to have a significantly different level of OPC than departmental (p < .3674) accountants. Thus, research hypotheses H7, H8, and H9 were not supported. This model included eight control measures as independent variables; however, only job satisfaction and OC were found to be significantly associated with OPC, a negative relationship. This could be interpreted to indicate that organizational attitudes may impact OPC to a greater extent than professional attitudes.

VI. DISCUSSION AND CONCLUSIONS

This study found that the work setting in which professional accountants are employed affects the accountant's level of commitment (both organizational and professional) but not the level of organizational-professional conflict. The findings reported here generally support Scott's [1965] and Hall's [1968] proposition that organizational autonomy may differ across work settings based on Bartol's [1979b] proposed relationship between organizational autonomy and commitment. In concurrence with Hall, the autonomous work setting was observed to have a greater level of organizational commitment (autonomy) than either the heteronomous or departmental work settings. On the other hand, Hall's proposed relationship between the heteronomous and departmental work settings was not supported. Accountants employed in the departmental work setting were observed to have a greater level of organizational commitment than were accountants employed in the heteronomous work setting. One plausible reason for the difference in findings between this study and Hall [1968] is that Hall's study was broad based and did not investigate all three work settings in only one profession while the current study performs an in-depth investigation of the accounting profession. An explanation for the findings in the current study is the relationship between the department and the organization as discussed by McGregor et al. [1989]. Immediate supervisors within a professional department are likely to have been trained in the same profession as the employees and it is possible that these administrators may encourage more autonomy within the department than exists organization wide. In addition, the administrators may serve as a buffer from restrictive organizational controls and protect the autonomy of the department's professional employees. Therefore, if a strong departmental structure exists, the level of organizational autonomy in a professional department may be greater than expected.

Based on the assumption that professional commitment basically develops the same for all individuals during the socialization process prior to entering the organization [Larson, 1977; Volmer and Mills, 1966;], differences observed in the professional commitment of practicing accountants apparently result from circumstances encountered in the work place. The findings reported here indicate that professional commitment is similar between accountants employed in public practice and accountants employed by governmental entities, but that both are greater than the professional commitment of accountants employed in departments of large organizations. One major difference between work settings that may explain this is the presence of professional identity apart from the organization. While the public and governmental accountants may perceive themselves as accountants, the departmental accountants may be more inclined to perceive themselves as a member of their organization. If higher levels of commitment result in greater productivity [Mowday et al., 1974], organizational effectiveness could be increased by encouraging employees to strive for the attainment of professional identity and affiliation. Affiliation with organizations such as the Institute of Management Accountants and the Institute of Internal Auditors may serve to add a formal professional control structure to the departmental accountant's work environment.

From the results reported here, it cannot be concluded that the work setting, after controlling for potentially confounding variables, impacts the level of organizational-professional conflict. Conflict is proposed to occur when the professional's desire to exercise professional judgment is impeded by the organization's control structure [McGregor et al., 1989]. Previous discussion indicated that professional autonomy and organizational autonomy as represented by professional and organizational commitment differ across the work settings. Therefore, failure to observe a difference in the level of organizational-professional conflict across the work settings appears to indicate that the impact of professional and organizational autonomy on organizational-professional conflict is only indirect through the measures of professional and organizational commitment. These findings tend to support the existing literature where it has been observed that conflict is dependent on the levels of commitment [Harrell et al., 1986; McGregor et al., 1989].

The results reported here must be interpreted within the limitations of the study.

One limitation is that only one dimension of professionalism and bureaucratization was examined (autonomy). Future research should also consider the multidimensional aspects of these variables. Another limitation is that assumptions had to be made regarding the levels of organizational and professional autonomy based on existing literature. Future studies should directly measure these constructs along with commitment and conflict to more fully examine the impact of autonomy in the work place.

In conclusion, based on the results of the comparisons reported here, the current practice of categorizing accountants as professional/nonprofessional may not be fully warranted. The fact that similarities exist between public and governmental accountants in the level of professional commitment reported here appears to indicate that their professional orientations may be similar. Researchers should consider the possibility that governmental accountants should be categorized with public accountants when professional attitudes such as the elements of professionalization and their impact on commitment and conflict are examined. Further, based on the results of this study, the organizational attitudes of accountants appear to vary across three work settings. Therefore, when studying the organizational orientation of accountants, researchers should consider that differences across work settings may need to be included in studies investigating such constructs as the elements of bureaucratization and their relationship with the organizational control structure.

NOTES

1. Instruments will be made available by authors on request.
2. The potential for biased results from variables that co-vary with the items of interest necessitate controlling for such effects. This control reduces the likelihood of observing statistical significance resulting from random occurrence.
3. Modifying the OC questionnaire to construct the PC questionnaire has been shown to result in the measurement of two distinct constructs [Bline, Duchon, and Meixner, 1991].
4. Higher scores indicate greater levels of commitment and/or conflict. Because some questions are negatively worded, the scales of these questions were reversed before analyses were performed.
5. Failure to reject Hypotheses 3 and 6 would result in support for the theory presented in the literature section although the interpretation of this is not as strong as rejection of the alternative form of these hypotheses. This form of presentation and testing is used due to the inability to test for equality. The other hypotheses are tested in the standard way.

REFERENCES

Angle, H.L., and J.L. Perry, "An Empirical Assessment of Organizational Commitment and Organizational Effectiveness," *Administrative Science Quarterly* [March 1981], pp. 1–14.
Aranya, N., and K.R. Ferris, "A Reexamination of Accountant's Organizational-Professional Conflict," *The Accounting Review* [January 1984], pp. 1–15.
Aranya, N., and D. Jacobson, "An Empirical Study of Theories of Organizational and Occupational Commitment," *Journal of Social Psychology* [October 1975], pp. 15–22.

Aranya, N., R. Lachman, and J. Amernic, "Accountants' Job Satisfaction: A Path Analysis," *Accounting, Organizations and Society* 7 [1982], pp. 201–215.

Aranya, N., J. Pollock, and J. Amernic, "An Examination of Professional Commitment in Public Accounting," *Accounting, Organizations and Society* 6 [1981], pp. 271–280.

Bartol, K.M., "Individual versus Organizational Predictors of Job Satisfaction and Turnover among Professionals," *Journal of Vocational Behavior* 15 [1979a], pp. 55–67.

Bartol, K.M., "Professionalism as a Predictor of Organizational Commitment, Role Stress, and Turnover: A Multidimensional Approach," *Academy of Management Journal* 22 [1979b], pp. 815–821.

Berry, L.E., and W.A. Wallace, "Governmental Auditing Research: An Analytic Framework, Assessment of Past Work, and Future Directions," *Research in Governmental and Nonprofit Accounting* 2 [1986], pp. 89–115.

Bline, D.M., D. Duchon, and W.F. Meixner, "The Measurement of Organizational and Professional Commitment: A Test of the Psychometric Properties of Two Commonly Used Instruments," *Behavioral Research in Accounting* 3 [1991], pp. 1–12.

Dubin, R., J.E. Champoux, and L.W. Porter, "Central Life Interests and Organizational Commitment of Blue-Collar and Clerical Workers," *Administrative Science Quarterly* [September 1975], pp. 411–421.

Government Finance Officers Association, *Governmental Accounting, Auditing and Financial Reporting* [Chicago, 1988].

Hall, R.H., "Professionalization and Bureaucratization," *American Sociological Review* [February 1968], pp. 92–104.

Harrell, A., E. Chewning, and M. Taylor, "Organizational-Professional Conflict and the Job Satisfaction and Turnover Intentions of Internal Auditors," *Auditing: A Journal of Practice and Theory* [Spring 1986], pp. 109–121.

Hrebiniak, L., and J. Alutto, "Personal and Role-Related Factors in the Development of Organizational Commitment," *Administrative Science Quarterly* 17 [1972], pp. 555–573.

Kerr, S., M. A. Von Glinow, and J. Schriesheim, "Issues in the Study of 'Professionals' in Organizations: The Case of Scientists and Engineers," *Organizational Behavior and Human Performance* 18 [1977], pp. 329–345.

Lachman, R., and N. Aranya, "Job Attitudes and Turnover Intentions Among Professionals in Different Work Settings," *Organization Studies* 7 [1986], pp. 279–293.

Larson, M. S., *The Rise of Professionalism: A Sociological Analysis* [Berkeley, CA: University of California Press, 1977].

McGregor, C., L. Killough, and R. Brown, "An Investigation of Organizational-Professional Conflict in Management Accounting," *Journal of Management Accounting Research* 1 [1989], pp. 104–118.

Meixner, W.F., and D.M. Bline, "Professional and Job-Related Attitudes and the Behaviors They Influence Among Governmental Accountants," *Accounting, Auditing and Accountability Journal* 2 [1989].

Merz, C.M., and D.F. Groebner, "Ethics and the CPA in Industry," *Management Accounting* [September 1982], pp. 44–48.

Montagna, P.D., "Professionalization and Bureaucratization in Large Professional Organizations," *American Journal of Sociology* [September 1968], pp. 138–145.

Mowday, R.T., L.W. Porter, and R. Dubin, "Unit Performance, Situational Factors, and Employee Attitudes in Spatially Separated Work Units," *Organizational Behavior and Human Performance* [October 1974], pp. 231–248.

Mowday, R.T., R. Steers, and L. Porter, "The Measurement of Organizational Commitment," *Journal of Vocational Behavior* 14 [1979], pp. 224–247.

Porter, L.W., R.M. Steers, R.T. Mowday, and P.V. Boulian, "Organizational Commitment, Job Satisfaction and Turnover Among Psychiatric Technicians," *Journal of Applied Psychology* [October 1974], pp. 603–609.

Schroeder, R.G., and L.F. Imdieke, "Local-Cosmopolitan and Bureaucratic Perceptions in Public Accounting Firms," *Accounting, Organizations and Society* 2 [1977], pp. 39–45.

Scott, W. R., "Reactions to Supervision in a Heteronomous Professional Organization," *Administrative Science Quarterly* [June 1965], pp. 65–81.

Sorensen, J.E., "Professional and Bureaucratic Organizations in the Public Accounting Firm," *The Accounting Review* [July 1967], pp. 553–565.

Sorensen, J.E., and T.L. Sorensen, "The Conflict of Professionals in Bureaucratic Organizations," *Administrative Science Quarterly* [March 1974], pp. 98–106.

Steers, R.M., "Antecedents and Outcomes of Organizational Commitment," *Administrative Science Quarterly* [March 1977], pp. 46–56.

Stone, E.E., and L.W. Porter, "Job Characteristics and Job Attitudes: A Multivariate Study," *Journal of Applied Psychology* [February 1975], pp. 57–64.

Volmer, H.M., and D.L. Mills, (eds.), *Professionalization* [Englewood Cliffs, NJ: Prentice-Hall, 1966].

Zimmerman, J., "The Municipal Accounting Maze: An Analysis of Political Incentives," *The Journal of Accounting Research Supplement* 15 [1977], pp. 107–144.

PART II

PUBLIC CHOICE AND GOVERNMENTAL ACCOUNTING

_____

A CONTINGENCY MODEL OF GOVERNMENTAL ACCOUNTING INNOVATIONS IN THE POLITICAL-ADMINISTRATIVE ENVIRONMENT

Klaus G. Luder

ABSTRACT

This paper proposes a comprehensive contingency model of introducing accounting innovations in the public sector. Based on a comparative study of the United States, Canada, and several European countries, the model consists of four modules: stimuli, social structural variables about information users, structural variables describing the politico-administrative system, and implementation barriers. Whether a more informative accounting system is introduced depends on the specific combination of favorable and unfavorable conditions in these modules. Favorable conditions exist in Canada, Denmark, Sweden, the United States at the federal level, and those states that adopted GAAP. Conditions unfavorable to innovations prevail in Germany and France, and to a lesser extent in the United Kingdom and the European Community.

Research in Governmental and Nonprofit Accounting, Vol. 7, pages 99–127.
Copyright © 1992 by JAI Press Inc.
All rights of reproduction in any form reserved.
ISBN: 1-55938-418-2

I. REVIEW OF THE LITERATURE

A. A Classification of Recent Research

The first attempts to analyze and explain the similarities and differences between various public sector accounting systems in the light of the politico-administrative factors that condition them are found in the Anglo-Saxon literature on the subject from about the mid 1970s [e.g., Zimmerman, 1977]. The object of this research was primarily to investigate the causes and deciding factors responsible for the decision by the states and local governments in the United States to abide by governmental Generally Accepted Accounting Principles (GAAP) in preparing their annual financial reports [e.g., Baber and Sen, 1984; Evans and Patton, 1987; Ingram, 1983, 1984]. These principles, initially codified by the National Council on Governmental Accounting (NCGA), are now set by the Governmental Accounting Standards Board (GASB). The hypothesized influence of the conditioning factors was analyzed in subsequent research on the basis of various theoretical approaches, research methods and subjects. This body of literature may therefore be classified accordingly.

1. Theoretical Orientation

On the basis of theoretical approach, the studies may be approximately subdivided into (1) those that are influenced by political science, more particularly the economic theory of politics (public choice) or comparative political science, and (2) those that are predominantly oriented towards behavior theory. The two approaches cannot of course be separated with absolute precision, since they share certain basic assumptions. In particular they both adopt methodological individualism, emphasizing individual behavior as conditioned by specific inclinations (i.e., maximization of utility) and situations (i.e., social and/or institutional factors).

Those studies that draw their inspiration from political economy [e.g., Chan and Rubin, 1987] are based on traditional neoclassical principles of explanation. Starting from classical behavioral assumptions such as utility maximization and limited rationality of the individual, this approach uses market mechanisms for coordination to achieve equilibrium. Analysis of coordination via the "market" is not confined to a price system of supply and demand for public services. It also takes social forms of coordination, for example, the "market for electoral votes," into consideration. The principles of self-interest and the assumption of rational behavior are both taken as applicable to the state. That is, it is assumed that the protagonists in the fields of politics, government and administration pursue a form of self-interest [e.g., Buchanan, 1967; Chan and Rubin, 1987; Downs, 1957; Niskanen, 1971]. The possibility of being able to pursue one's self-interest presupposes a discretionary margin in decision-making, which, as an endogenous variable, can be accounted for on the basis of asymmetrical distribution of information between the participants. If the restrictive classical assumption of complete information is abandoned, information itself becomes the subject of investigation, and so does the government financial accounting system.

One line of research concerns how information influences individuals' decision-making processes. Other studies investigate how institutional arrangements (i.e., the political system and regulations) and changes to them shape the government's information instruments such as its financial accounting system, and vice versa. Typical research questions are: How, why, and to what extent are accounting systems affected by politico-administrative structures and processes? Are there any interactions between socioeconomic institutions and the government's financial reporting practices? If so, which interactions are significant? One consequence of such interactions is the further development of the government's accounting system [Ingram, 1984, pp. 127–131]. The hypotheses based on such an approach are logically predicted on institutional factors of influence.

Approaches that tend to be oriented towards behavior theory [Chan, 1989; Evans and Patton, 1987] address not so much the institutional factors of influence as the individual ones. Institutional factors are, of course, not ignored. But their influence is regarded as being peripheral or restricting on individual behavior. This line of research analyzes the configuration of individuals, their interests, situations and behavior. If we take the public accounts as the subject of inquiry, this means formulating hypotheses to explain what motivates individuals to demand information and to promote the development of particular accounting systems. The motivations are based on their interest as, for example, voters, taxpayers, recipients of services, or members of parliament.

2. Research Methods

Some studies test hypotheses by means of statistical or econometric techniques [Baber and Sen, 1984; Evans and Patton, 1987], while others examine the plausibility of hypotheses through a series of case studies of particular situations. The precision and accuracy of econometric methods undoubtedly contribute to their popular use in empirical studies. However, the nature of the data they use can often lead to questionable results. Statistical methods have minimum requirement for standardization of the subject of the investigation, especially as regards the quantification of variables. In view of the often purely qualitative nature of the variables to be tested, this requirement is not always assured. Exactitude of method does not exclude the possibility that a mathematical-statistical reshaping of the data will remain insignificant from the empirical point of view. Case studies, on the contrary, due to their flexibility, make it possible to describe a given situation closer to reality. The causal hypotheses underlying case studies are, however, not susceptible to statistical tests, although they could still meet plausibility tests.

B. Literature Analysis

This section analyzes a number of common themes and variables suggested in recent literature, followed by some concerns about research methods used.

1. *Themes and Variables*

Political Competition.   Political competition promotes the use of GAAP in government. This is one of the most frequently made assertions in the literature concerning the relationship between institutional conditions and innovations in governmental accounting [Baber and Sen, 1984; Evans and Patton, 1987; Ingram, 1984; and numerous recent conferences not available for quotation]. Surprisingly, despite the varying interpretations and measurements of this ambiguous concept, most of the studies show positive correlations between political competition and the adoption of GAAP.

The fundamental common assumption shared by these studies is that there exists a "market" consisting of exchange relationships between voters, interest groups, politicians, and administrators. In this "market for votes," politicians and parties are subject to a process of competition which, in order to maximize the number of votes, obliges them to satisfy the voters' needs. "Political competition" can assume several forms: the competition for electoral success between parties; competition within a party for nomination as a candidate; competition for the support of interest groups; or competition in the search for coalition partners.

Evans and Patton [1987, p. 137] expressed the relationship between political competition and the adoption of GAAP as follows: "the greater is the political competition, the weaker is the politician's position relative to the interest groups and, therefore, the better will be the monitoring information he must provide to obtain their support." Other studies posit that governments that are subject to "competitive pressures" have a stronger incentive to show that they have fulfilled their election promises—for example, distribution of budgetary resources over several policy areas, the repayment of debts, the soundness of the budgetary management. This line of thinking introduces public opinion as an influence on public sector accounting.

The connection between political competition and application of the GAAP generally corresponds to agency theory and it is done by marginal analysis [Baber and Sen, 1984]. In an agency model, the initial situation is characterized by the asymmetrical distribution of information between the principals (e.g., the voters) and their agents (e.g., elected politicians). This asymmetry is reduced by setting up a monitoring system, such as a system of financial reporting, which facilitates a *posteriori* control to ensure ensuring that the promises have been kept. Among the measures is the promise of better information resulting from the adoption of GAAP. It is commonly assumed that GAAP-based financial information is better and more economical to produce by virtue of standardization.

If the starting situation involves a high degree of political competition, for example, in a "neck to neck" race between the incumbent and opposition in an election, use of the GAAP (or, as appropriate, the promise to use it) increases the likelihood of an electoral victory for its advocate. This is because, at the margin, when other things (e.g., political preferences) are equal, an improvement in the starting situation will be achieved by compliance with GAAP. From this abstract description of the situation, we may derive the proposition: *ceteris paribus*, the intensity of political competition promotes the use of the GAAP.

Moving from this proposition to an empirically testable hypothesis creates considerable problems. On the one hand, the effect of the use or nonuse of the GAAP on specific voting decisions, in comparison with other factors that may have a decisive effect on election results, cannot be isolated and operationalized. On the other hand, suitable measurable surrogates must be found for unobservable political competition. To the extent, therefore, that a statistical test to measure the correlation between political competition and use of the GAAP was carried out in empirical research, the results appear to be questionable, at least from the methodological point of view.

The Method for Selecting Accounting Officials.   Alternatively, one might argue that the further development of public sector accounting is influenced by the way accounting officers are selected—by election or appointment [Ingram, 1984]. According to this view, an elected "monitoring agent" is directly subject to the competitive pressure of election and thus has a greater incentive, as compared with appointed (and in some cases tenured) public officials, to improve the accounting and reporting system. In addition, Ingram [1984, p. 17] comments, without any further justification, that "personal attributes (e.g., professional experience and training) may differ between elected and appointed administrators, and thus the extent of accounting disclosure may be affected by the administrative selection process itself." If the accounting officers are more efficiently recruited in the political market, rather than by appointment, Ingram's hypothesis acquires some plausibility from the extensive analyses of the economic theory of bureaucracy and the literature on public choice. Of course, in this specific expression the hypothesis is hardly capable of empirically testing. There also exists evidence to the contrary, that is, some jurisdictions that comply with GAAP have appointed accounting officials.

Size.   Another hypothesis that is similarly based on the monitoring agent theory postulate is that use of the GAAP is more likely as the size of the government increases [Baber, 1983; quoted by Evans and Patton, 1987]. Size is measured by the population in absolute terms or population density. The hypothesis goes as follows: the more populous the area governed, the higher the government's tax and other revenues tend to be, and the greater the amount of resources that may be badly managed. As the population increases, so does the number of persons who have an interest in the establishment of control systems. Monitoring costs as a proportion of the agency costs can be reduced in individual cases by standardized procedures (through the use of the GAAP). "Thus, cities with greater population are predicted to produce better reporting / more auditing because more resources are at stake" [Evans and Patton, 1987, p. 136]. This prediction, inspired by agency theory, is partly supported by empirical evidence from U.S. municipalities for the period from 1981 to 1984. Ironically, the Federal Government in the U.S., the largest of all in terms of the number of people under its jurisdiction, does not have a GAAP-based accounting system.

Capital Market and Rating Agency Influences. Another hypothesis suggests that the capital market generates incentives for GAAP adoption [Evans and Patton, 1987; Ingram 1984]. This is based on a policy statement issued in 1980 by Standard and Poor, one of the largest American rating agencies, that nonuse of the GAAP would count as a negative factor in assessing the creditworthiness of a government. The capital (more specifically, bond) market, according to this hypothesis, rewards the use of the GAAP as evidence of qualified financial management by granting borrowers lower interest rates. Ingram [1984] concludes from this that the incentive to adopt the GAAP must be high, especially in the case of governments that are heavily burdened with debt, provided that the savings on interest costs are greater than the cost of modifying the accounting system. This line of argument appears to be perfectly plausible in the case of the American situation on account of the system of bond rating of government debt. As financial reports are only one of several sources of information in arriving at a rating, the impact of the quality of information in these reports can be overridden by other factors (such as taxing capacity). Furthermore, this hypothesis has limited application in the international context, as government debts are not rated in all countries.

Financial Reports as a Signaling and Monitoring Tool. The hypotheses advanced in the research work analyzed so far are largely based on presumed individual attitudes. The accounting system, taken as a given and shaped by institutional conditions, is included in the analysis as a datum. The system of institutions provides the framework within which individuals are led to make conceptual changes to the public sector accounting system and financial reports. The institutional factors condition the attitudes of participants and those who are directly affected towards a definite reshaping of the accounting system. They also determine the demand for and the supply of financial information. In terms of agency theory, to quote Baber and Sen [1984, p. 92], "We view the political market as a nexus of contracting relationships between interest groups (principals) and public officials (public agents) and assume that the contracting parties are rational self-interested individuals." In such a model, the public officials as agents "signal" the principals, who in turn "monitor" the politicians. "Accounting practices evolve under the influence of politicians' attempts to maximize the benefits of office and voters' attempts to constrain the politicians' abilities to act to their detriment" [Ingram, 1984, p. 127].

Users' Socioeconomic Status. More recently, it is no longer assumed that individuals have identical demands for information, as they are not identical in the socioeconomic attributes relevant for predicting their demand for government financial information. The principal's (e.g., voter's) demand for information is related to one's socioeconomic status (SES) [Chan, 1989, p. 8]. As early as 1960, Downs [1960] posited that individuals find it easier to grasp the costs of state services than the benefit they derived from them—thus resulting in a kind of fiscal illusion. It is argued that the rising tax burden that accompanies a higher income is more acutely perceived than any increases in social service. This effect is reinforced by the fact that individuals whose incomes and tax burdens are rising ultimately become "net contributors" in respect to public services, whereas individuals with lower incomes and lower tax obligations are "net beneficiaries." For this reason, the level of demand for information goes up as one's socioeconomic status rises. It is therefore hypothesized that as one's SES improves, so does one's awareness of costs of government (i.e., government revenue and debt) increase relative to one's awareness of benefits of government (i.e., government expenditure). This line of reasoning leads to the following propositions about demand for specific information. "[Members of the public] of lower SES have greater demand for expenditure information. [Those] of higher SES have greater demand for information about revenues and liabilities" [Chan, 1989, p. 8].

Cost is a relevant consideration in the use of information, as it is in the adoption of GAAP. Demand for information is limited by the marginal benefit of additional information compared with the marginal cost of acquiring and evaluating information. The time needed to evaluate information is seen as an essential cost component. This leads to the complementary hypothesis that as socioeconomic status rises increased demands are made as regards the quality of the information. "Individuals of higher SES enjoy a higher cost-benefit ratio in investing their time in this activity on two accounts: (1) their higher educational level reduces the costs of analysis and evaluation; and (2) as they bear higher per capita tax burdens they have greater economic incentives to find tax savings or how their tax dollars are spent" [Chan, 1989, p. 12].

Professionalism. The existence of signalling incentives, which lead to the "voluntary" provision of financial information by the executive branch and the legislature, does not at first seem plausible because of the additional monitoring possibilities that are bound up with them. The fact that the signalling effects that stem from voluntary conformity with a system of rules such as the GAAP may be perfectly rational may, however, be explained in terms of the agency theory. In an initial situation that is characterized by intense political competition, for example, there is a need to demonstrate the qualifications and the quality of public management in order to increase the likelihood of reelection. One way of achieving that is to make use of an accounting system that is oriented towards the GAAP in order to signal a certain level of professionalism [Evans and Patton, 1984; Ingram, 1984]. Various topics were raised as test variables for such signalling incentives, for example, recourse to standard-setting bodies as advisers, the demands made on the account staff as regards qualifications and even the level of their salaries [Evans and Patton, 1984]. This latter approach rests on the assumption that governments that wish to indicate the level of professionalism of their financial management, for the purpose of obtaining highly qualified staff (e.g., auditors), must offer substantial financial incentives. In general, hypotheses that are formulated in this way exclude the possibility of their being clearly and neatly distinguished from others, such as, for example, the influence of political competition on use of the GAAP, so that the presumed influence of signalling incentives as compared with other influences cannot be singled out.

C. Comments

Inasmuch as an attempt is made in these studies to test the hypotheses with statistical procedures, reservations may be raised in at least three respects:

1.   The relationship between use of the GAAP as a dependent variable and the above-mentioned independent variables are not monocausal but multicausal. The independent variables may have an additional, mutual effect on each other. So it is conceivable (but so far barely demonstrated by the statistical tests) that, for example, the level and the growth of indebtedness, and the effect of professional organizations, do not favor the use of GAAP in isolation of each other but rather through a kind of synergy. Moreover, it is also conceivable that, as the growth of debt comes increasingly to be seen as "desperate," the need for competent advise from professional organizations will rise and become institutionalized. In the former case, instead of the usual simple regression, multiple regressions would have to be carried out. In the latter case, multicollinearity, which is statistically relevant, occurs. The doubtfulness of the statistical results of the studies being evaluated as regards multicausality and multicollinearity may presumably be applicable to an even higher degree in the concept of political competition, which is frequently tested as if it were an independent variable. If the use of GAAP is to be explained as dependent variable (with a decisive influence on election results), the existence of political competition (however defined and measured) as the only (independent) explanatory factor is probably not enough. Since the results of an election are decided by a "package" of political measures, it is doubtful that the use or nonuse of the GAAP would have such a decisive impact. As hypotheses are usually formulated independently of each other, their tests also tend to look for monocausal connections. The multicollinearity can be detected by observing correlation matrices. Multiple regression analysis, however, is only rarely carried out.

2.   The variables in the above-mentioned hypotheses are frequently difficult to measure directly. It is thus necessary to operationalize them by means of observable and measurable proxy variables. Valid surrogates are essential to avoid mistaken interpretation. Two examples may illustrate this point. "Interest costs of state debt" operationalize the capital market's rewards for the use of GAAP. On the other hand, salary of accountancy staff (used in Evans and Patton 1987, p. 131) is not an adequate reliable indicator of staff qualification, as salary is determined by many factors other than qualification. No account is taken, in this assumption, of other factors that also help to determine salary levels. In some cases other variables influence both use of the GAAP and salary levels. In such cases there is an apparent correlation, but it is *only apparent.*

Probably the most serious objection to statistical tests concerns the use of regression analysis. Regression analysis, in contrast to other multivariate methods (e.g., discrimination or contingency analysis), requires a metrical measurement of both dependent and independent variables. Of course, account may be taken of only nominally measured variables, by breaking them down into binary variables, but this is only applicable in the case of independent variables. This, however, is exactly what is *not* the case in the studies we are concerned with here: the use of a binarily defined dependent variable (use or non-use of GAAP). It is no more than the classification of a nominally measured, quantitative expression of qualities, for which it is only possible to calculate degrees of frequency, with which the categories of characteristics known as "use" and "nonuse" are filled out. For this same reason the forms taken by the characteristics in question can also not be subjected to the requisite accounting transformations without which a regression analysis is devoid of meaning.

3.   It also seems questionable whether the use or nonuse of the GAAP can really be conceived of as a binary variable at all. The extensive body of rules within which the GAAP are codified, with their numerous, intrinsic margins for maneuver on the basis of electoral legislation, ultimately does not make for any hard and fast decision as to when, in a particular case, it can be assumed that there is use or nonuse of the GAAP.

The present state of empirical research into the relationships between institutional conditions and the shaping of public accounting is characterized by the "incongruity" which Helmut Klages [1977] similarly found to exist in the case of organizational contingency theory, between "highly developed empirical instruments and manifold findings, on the one hand, and contradictory theoretical elements, on the other" [Kieser and Kubicek, 1983, p. 353, with reference to Klages, 1977, p. 61]. In this case, as in that of organizational contingency theory, this seems to be not least the consequence of a dominant paradigm of empirical social science research in the United States.

II. A CONTINGENCY MODEL OF GOVERNMENTAL ACCOUNTING INNOVATIONS

A. Overview and Assumptions

This section proposes a model that explains the transition from traditional government accounting to a more informative system. A more informative system performs two functions: it supplies comprehensive and reliable information on public finance, and it provides a basis for improved financial control of government activities. The transition assumes a specific starting point and final state for the public sector accounting system. The task of the model is to explain the innovation process that connects these two points. Unlike previous efforts that singled out individual background conditions, a conceptual overview is provided that would explain the process of innovation (or its absence) as fully as possible. Due to its high degree of complexity, the model currently may not be statistically testable.

The model seeks to integrate ideas from the literature as described earlier, along with observations made about the governmental accounting systems in Canada, the United States (the federal government and several states), and several European countries, including Denmark, France, Germany, Sweden, the United Kingdom, and the European Community. Interviews were conducted with knowledgeable persons to ascertain practices as well as innovations being contemplated or underway, if any. The politico-administrative environment in terms of the variables encompassed in the model was documented [Luder, 1989; Luder, et al., 1989]. After the model was described, these countries were compared along the various dimensions of the model on the basis of the empirical observations made in the empirical phase of the study (henceforth the "Comparative Study") in 1987–1988.

The structure of the model is similar to models of organizational contingency theory, extended, however, by behavioral components [Khandwalla, 1977, p. 270; Kieser and Kubicek, 1983, p. 355; Schreyogg, 1985]. Such a model can include both institutional background conditions and collective behavior as determinants of the innovation process. The contextual variables describing institutional conditions may be classified, according to their functions in the innovation process, into three categories:

1. Stimuli [Simon, 1981, p. 126]: events that occur at the initial stage of the innovation process and create a need for improved information on the part of the users of accounting information and increase the producers' readiness to supply such information.
2. Structural Variables: characteristics of the social and politico-administrative systems that influence the basic attitudes of users and producers of information towards the idea of a more informative form of public sector accounting.
3. Implementation Barriers: environmental conditions that inhibit the process

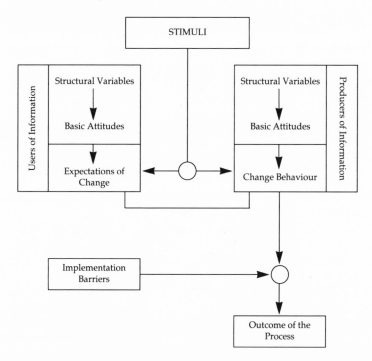

Figure 1.   Contingency Model of Public Sector Accounting Innovations –
Basic Model

of implementation, thus hindering, and in extreme cases preventing, the creation of a more informative accounting system which is in principle desirable.

The institutional part of the model thus consists of four modules: (1) the stimuli module, (2) the structural variables module of information producers, (3) the structural variables module of users of information, and (4) the implementation barriers module. Their posited relationships are described in Figure 1 (basic model).

In Figure 1, the arrows indicate the direction of postulated influence of the situational variables on the attitudes and behavior of the participants in the process and its outcome. The basic model rests on five assumptions about the process of innovation:

1.   There exist a number of stimuli, that individually or in combination, initially reveal a need for improved information.
2.   There are two sets of structural variables, describing the fundamental attitudes of information users and producers, respectively, toward the role

of information on government financial management and administrative efficiency.

3. Information users' expectations of change are influenced by their basic attitudes and by the stimuli that exist in the starting situation. The information producers' willingness to make changes is similarly affected by these two factors, and the effects of the information users' expectations of change.

4. The setting off of the process of innovation does not necessarily require the existence of a stimulus. Basic attitudes (that have been changed) can also raise the level of willingness to make change in such a way that the decision to do so is taken.

5. The decision to innovate is dependent not only of the information producer's willingness to change, but also the implementation barrier. Two extreme cases are conceivable. In the first case, if all the factors affecting implementation are neutral to the changes, the innovation decision is determined by the degree of willingness to accept change. In the second case, if all the factors affecting implementation inhibit change, a high degree of willingness to accept is required, or change may not be achievable at all.

In each case the complex of relationships between the specific form assumed by public sector accounting and the factors that affect it cannot be traced back like a monocausal concatenation of effects. Rather one must start from the assumption that a specific constellation of background conditions collectively affect the public sector accounting system (multicausal relationship).

As mentioned earlier, the specification of the basic model draws on the results of a number of empirical studies, primarily on the Comparative Study. However, the model has some speculative features, too, as the empirical relevance of the environmental conditions and their relationships with the accounting system are not definitely settled. Moreover, the model may not contain all conceivable and relevant independent variables. The contingency model therefore should be understood and interpreted as a first attempt to describe a complex innovation process by a set of hypotheses.

B. Description of the Model

The institutional part of the specific form of the model consists of the same four modules as the basic model. The components of the individual modules, the relationships between them and their effects on the results of the innovation process are set out in Figure 2. This section examines the institutional modules. It assumes, as does organizational contingency theory, that the specific configurations of institutional components influence the attitudes and behavior of the participants in public life, politics and administration. The mechanism by which this influence is exerted and its strength are not, however, examined in detail.

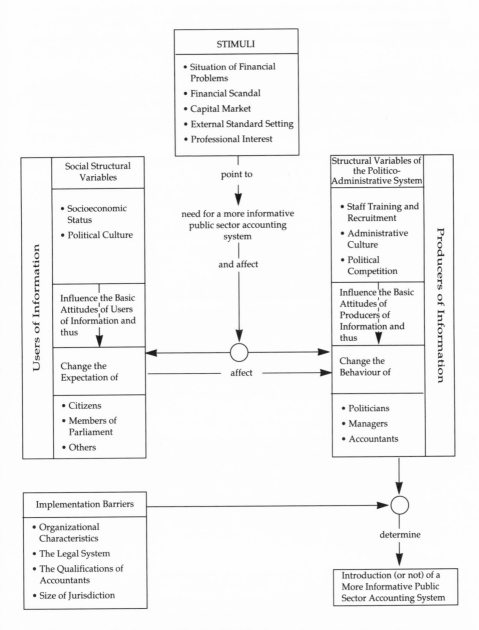

Figure 2. Contingency Model of Public Sector Accounting Innovations –
Detailed Model

1. Stimuli

Fiscal Stress. Financial difficulty arises when the increase in and/or the absolute level of public debt are considered to be no longer sustainable in terms of interest burden, interest rate or creditworthiness. In such a situation, comprehensive disclosure of the financial situation as well as financial management takes on enhanced importance. At the same time, however, the shortcomings of traditional public sector accounting systems are borne more strongly upon the consciousness of the participants, prompting demands for a more informative accounting system.

Research results have confirmed that financial problems serve to trigger reforms of public sector accounting systems. They regularly played a role in the case of governments that carried out conceptual changes to their accounting systems during the 1980s. This was true of Canada, Sweden, Denmark, the states of the United States, the Canadian provinces, and also Great Britain (which primarily reformed its internal accounting system to ensure better financial management of government departments and agencies). More recently, the budget deficits of the U.S. Government have, partially at least, contributed to the urgency of improving the federal Governments' accounting system [Carpenter and Feroz, 1990; GAO, 1989].

Financial Scandal. The term "financial scandal" refers to cases of negligent or deliberate waste in financial management by the public authorities with serious financial consequences for the taxpayers. In some cases such practices are connected to deliberate misleading information on the financial situation. Depending on a government's fiscal situation, and the scale and the timing of its revelation, a financial scandal may result in a situation of fiscal stress. Regardless of that, however, financial scandals draw the attention of the public and of those who are immediately involved, to shortcomings in the accounting system. This may trigger a reshaping of the system to make it more informative. For example, the poor quality of the fiscal information revealed in New York City's financial crisis helped to create an atmosphere conducive to the establishment of the Governmental Accounting Standards Board.

Capital Market. The capital market can be the source of incentives to create a more informative system of governmental accounting and financial reporting. However, this possibility rests on two premises: (1) bond issues are subject to formalized ratings; (2) the issue conditions, in particular the rate of interest, depend on the results of such ratings. The rating agencies mainly make use of annual reports, along with economic background data (such as expected tax revenues), as their sources of information. The other factor that affects the rating is the quality of the information in a government's annual report. If the generally accepted principles of accounting are not observed in describing the financial situation, the rating may be lower. This potential risk acts as a sanction for the distortion or concealment of information. It constitutes an incentive for the government in question to convert to GAAP, provided that the expected benefits exceed the costs.

Some evidence of the existence of such incentives can be found in particular in connection with issuing revenue bonds in the United States and Canada. However, the relevance of the capital market as a stimulus for the further development of public sector accounting, even in situations of this kind, has not been generally demonstrated by empirical research. In European countries, there does not exist formalized rating of government securities.

External Standard-Setting. External standard setting occurs when bodies external to governments are entrusted with the task of drafting and codifying the basic principles of accounting and financial reporting for the public sector. Such standard-setting bodies include: the Public Sector Accounting and Auditing Committee of Canadian Institute of Chartered Accountants, which has standard-setting responsibility for all three levels of Canadian governments; the Governmental Accounting Standards Board in the United States, which has standard-setting responsibility at local and state level. It is possible to speak of a weak form of external standard setting in cases where responsibility for setting standards is located within the government but there is also a permanent, independent advisory body involved. This is the case at the federal level in the United States in the form of the Federal Governmental Accounting Standards Advisory Board, and the "Conseil National de la Comptabilite" in France.

External standard-setting bodies concern themselves with introducing more informative accounting systems. Governmental financial managers are permanently forced to deal with and discuss the proposals of the standard-setting bodies. In such a situation of permanent discussion, it is much more difficult to defend and preserve the status quo in the absence of an external pressure body. Therefore, external standard-setting bodies have a stimulating effect on the development and the introduction of more informative governmental accounting systems. This thesis is supported by the following observations gathered in the comparative study:

1. Those countries where external standard-setting bodies exist belong to the group of countries that set about conceptual changes to their governmental accounting systems during the 1980s with the aim of achieving a higher degree of information content.
2. The number of states in the United States that have accounting systems that comply with the GAAP increased greatly during the 1980s, from two during the years prior to 1979 to 38 in 1988 [Van Daniker, et. al. 1986; Van Daniker, 1989].

Professional Bodies' Interest. There are two types of accountancy bodies which might be interested in governmental accounting: (1) professional associations such as the American Institute of Certified Public Accountants, the Canadian

Institute of Certified Accountants, the German "Institut der Wirtschaftspruefer", and (2) public accounting firms. Their interest is due to their members' need for guidance in technical matters (such as in auditing the public sector) and the amount of audit engagements available in the public sector. Usually these organizations are concerned with business accounting, however, certain circumstances may also result in the need to initiate reflections on ways to improve the public sector and particularly the governmental accounting system. These circumstances are present in North America. For example, the AICPA became an instrumental force in creating the GASB in part to protect its interests and that of the Financial Accounting Standards Board. If there is an interest of professional organizations in the public sector, a strong interest in the application of private-sector accounting in the public sector can be presumed as well. Proposals are frequently put forward for discussion at meetings of professional associations and within auditing firms [e.g., Arthur Anderson & Co., 1986]. In contrast, in the countries of Continental Europe covered by the comparative study, professional interest in public sector accounting is weak. Government and private-sector accountants do not belong to the same professional associations. Furthermore, there is also relatively little business potential for accounting firms in public sector audit engagements.

2. Social Structure Variables

Socioeconomic Status. Chan and Rubin [1987] introduced the notion of "socioeconomic status" (SES) as a means of explaining the influence of economic and social background conditions on the information content of public sector financial reports. Socioeconomic status is reflected by many variables, such as income and education levels. It is argued that voters' SES influence their tax burden and public services received. As one's SES rises, so does his share of the tax burden; however, SES is negatively correlated with the amount of public services received. Thus it is argued that higher SES individuals have a greater interest in disclosure of the public sector financial management. Socioeconomic status is therefore related to the basic attitude of information users toward more informative forms of public sector financial reporting. So far, this hypothesis has not been tested empirically; nor was it possible to obtain evidence of its validity during the comparative study.

Political Culture. "Political culture" in this context is to be understood as "patterns of political behavior" in which social value concepts are expressed. Political culture influences the basic attitudes of information users regarding the disclosure of information on public sector financial management, and thus also on their view of the need for a more informative accounting system. Political culture is revealed by the degree of openness and the participation by the citizenry in public decision-making processes. The more the political culture is open and disposed towards public participation, the greater the information users' expectations of financial information from the public sector. Active participants in the political system prefer comprehensive information on the government's financial management. An indication of the degree of openness and participation in political decision-making processes is the importance of referenda and other consultative procedures based on direct democracy (in particular, the direct election of the holders of the highest administrative offices).

To the extent that a relative high degree of openness and participation may be assumed in the countries included in the comparative study (Sweden, Switzerland, some states in the United States), innovation in the direction of a more informative system of governmental accounting may also be observed.

3. Structural Variables of the Politico-Administrative System

Staff Training and Recruitment. The training of administrative, especially accounting staff, and the recruitment of persons for top fiscal positions (e.g., financial controller, auditor) are factors that influence the basic attitudes (i.e., readiness to accept change) of these information producers to the further development of public sector accounting. Government accountants and auditors in different countries have rather diverse professional training and backgrounds. The United States and Canada have a large number of private-sector accounting specialists on their staffs in the public sector. This is due partly to formal legal requirements and partly to the customary practice of emphasizing the possession of professional accounting credentials, such as the CPA in the United States and the CA in Canada, for high level government accounting and auditing positions. On the other hand, in Germany, for example, the appointment to the position of the President of the Court of Auditors (federal and state) requires an education in law, but no education and practice as an accountant is required. The administrative staff in accounting and auditing in French government receive specialty training in public sector accounting. Whereas in some other countries (Germany, the United Kingdom) many governmental accounting staff have not had any accounting education at all and do get on-the-job training only.

Specialist training or qualifications as accountants, which cover knowledge and experience of private-sector accounting, give reason to expect a more positive basic attitude to the introduction of a more informative system. Such systems are regarded by some as more strongly oriented toward the private-sector approach. Those only trained in traditional public-sector accounting, on the other hand, often lack the incentive for suggesting innovations. A positive attitude toward improvements in governmental accounting does not only positively affect the accounting staff's willingness to implement changes but it even gives rise to initiating ideas for a more informative accounting system.

From the comparative study, it can be seen that in those countries with a form of staff training and recruitment that is strongly oriented towards the private-sector, as in the United States and Canada, further development of the public-sector system in the direction of a more informative type of accounting was observed.

Administrative Culture. Administrative culture is a part of the political culture. To the extent that the political culture is open and encourages participation, that will also be the case for administrative culture. Administrative culture has an effect on the basic attitude of administrative staff to openness and popular participation in the public policy process. In an open administrative culture, information producers themselves have a positive basic attitude to the idea of a more informative governmental accounting and financial reporting system.

Political Competition. The term "political competition" has two distinct meanings. The first is in the sense of competition in the "market for votes"; and the second refers to the competition between decision-making bodies (the executive and legislative branches of government) and the electorate. The first meaning is adopted in the above-mentioned American studies. The second meaning, however, seems to be more appropriate in the institutional module of a contingency model of governmental accounting. In both cases, however, the supposed connection between political competition and the form of accounting is rooted in agency theory considerations. Stronger political competition between users of information (i.e., the electorate and the legislature) and producers of information (i.e., executive) enables the former to assert their information interests more easily and thus to bring about a reduction in the asymmetrical distribution of information between users and producers.

Political competition in tendency causes an endeavor and readiness to achieve a more informative system of governmental accounting given the interest of users in additional or improved information. Under the institutional approach the strength of competition between producers and users of information is thought to be determined by the degree of symmetry in the distribution of power between the legislative, the executive branch, and electorate. A high degree of political competition may thus be assumed if the degree of division of power between the legislature and the executive is relatively symmetrical, for example, there exist extensive checks and balances. This criterion is supplemented by the extent to which elements of direct democracy are present in the political decision-making process. This situation is, for example, found in American federal and state governments. In contrast, there is a low degree of political competition if the division of power between the legislature and the executive is relatively asymmetrical and plebiscite-like aspects are entirely or mainly absent. France and the European Community (EC) can be named as examples for governments with a low degree of political competition. Figure 3 represents an attempt to binarily classify governments in terms of the degree of political competition.

It is hypothesized that vigorous political competition leads to information producers' positive basic attitude toward the introduction of a more informative governmental accounting system, whereas weak political competition is correlated

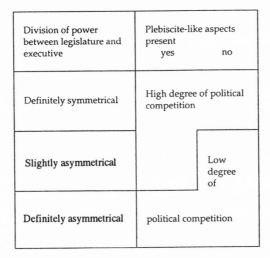

Figure 3. Political Competition

with a negative basic attitude. This hypothesis is largely borne out by the two extreme examples mentioned earlier, namely the United States and France. Political competition also acts as a mechanism whereby users of information are able to exert influence over producers of information.

4. Implementation Barriers

Organizational Characteristics. The decentralization of responsibility for changes of accounting practices in the government seem to be an important organizational implementation barrier. In a government with several organizational units exercising responsibility for the development of accounting procedures, there exists the risk that strongly diversified—and nonuniform—accounting systems will develop. Furthermore, those organizational units may have different ideas of what and how to change and thus get into conflict with each other. This was and still is the case at the Federal level in the United States: each agency, within the overall framework of the General Accounting Office's responsibility for issuing guidelines, is answerable for its own accounting. Even the GAO's authority to issue guidelines exists only on paper—it cannot be insisted on in face of the opposition of the executive branch: ". . . fragmentation of financial management functions has hindered development of a governmentwide financial reporting system" [Arthur Andersen & Co., 1986]. For this reason there has long been a call for the creation of the post of Chief Financial Officer, who would be responsible for the development of the conceptual bases for the federal accounting system and at the same time would have full powers to ensure their implementation.

Legal System. The legal systems of the countries included in the Comparative Study come either under the Roman-Germanic tradition or the English tradition. In the Roman-Germanic tradition—or civil law countries—a comprehensive and *detailed* system of statute law has been developed, whereas in the countries with English legal tradition—the common law countries—the statute law is limited in quantity and predominantly of the common law type. A country's legal tradition is also reflected in the extent of legal codification of the regulations for public sector accounting. In the countries with Roman-Germanic traditions, such as France and Germany, public sector accounting principles and procedures are laid down in details by law. On the other hand, in countries belonging to the English tradition such as the United Kingdom, the United States and Canada, there are only general legal prescriptions for the keeping of public sector accounts. The legal system thus influences the flexibility of the public sector accounting system. The tendency is for the system to be less flexible in countries that belong to the Roman-Germanic tradition than in countries with English legal tradition. As a result of its built-in inflexibility, the legal system of civil law countries offers greater impediment to changes to the public sector accounting system than the legal system of common law countries.

Qualification of Accountancy Staff. As described earlier, the accountancy staffs of some countries are dominated by individuals trained in private or public sector accounting, while in others the positions are occupied by nonspecialists, that is, not professional accountants or auditors, who learn specific accounting techniques on the job. The lack of certain general skills in the accounting field may create implementation barriers which cannot be eliminated in the short term and which may in certain circumstances mean that attempts to introduce more informative accounting will fail. This danger exists, for example, when accountancy techniques must be fundamentally altered in connection with the introduction of new accounting concepts (e.g., cameralistics, double-entry bookkeeping) and the accountancy staff lack the knowledge needed for the implementation of such new techniques.

Size of Jurisdiction. The size of a jurisdiction is expressed in terms of the population size and the number and size of government agencies, which are positively correlated. Understood in this sense, as the size of jurisdiction increases, technical and administrative problems of implementing a new accounting and financial reporting system multiply and cost of implementation rises. This may be an additional reason why innovations are more frequently seen in the smaller territorial units (smaller countries, such as Denmark, Sweden, and the member states of larger countries with federal constitutions) than in the larger ones.

III. SITUATIONAL PATTERNS

The environmental factors in a particular entity affecting accounting reforms may be described by a combination of the various manifestations of the institutional modules of the contingency model. For simplicity, it is assumed that each module exhibits just two different manifestations, one which is favorable (+) and the other one which is unfavorable (–) to accounting reforms. Since the model contains four modules a total of 16 (= 2^4) different patterns of environmental conditions can be derived which are differently favorable to the implementation of a more informative governmental accounting and financial reporting system. The two extreme patterns are characterized by only favorable manifestations and by only unfavorable manifestations of all the modules, respectively.

As each of the modules contains a set of variables, the following operational definitions of "favorable" and "unfavorable" are used.

- The stimulus module is favorable if at least one stimulus is present.
- The module of the social structural variables is favorable if the following conditions can be assumed to exist: a strong political competition; and either a relatively high socioeconomic status, or an "open" type of political culture, or both.
- The module of structural variables of the politico-administrative system is "favorable" if at the least either the contents of staff training are predominantly influenced by private-sector accounting, or the administrative culture may be regarded as open *and* the degree of political competition may be considered high. Here varying weights are attributed to the module components, mainly because political competition is effective only in conjunction with information users' expectations of change.
- The implementation barriers module is "favorable" if such barriers do not exist.

In Figure 4, the governmental accounting system of each of the jurisdictions included in the comparative study is assigned to the situation pattern it best fits. This assignment is based on either (1) the evidence of the respective politico-administrative background conditions as they were observed during the empirical investigations carried out in 1987 and 1988, or (2) if at that time an innovation process had already been initiated, the evidence of the politico-administrative situation existing prior to the commencement of the innovation process. As far as component states (U.S. states and Canadian provinces) of federations are concerned, the assignment is on a summary basis. The certainly observable differences between the politico-administrative settings of the states of a federation are neglected since the very broad classificatory approach does not seem to be sensitive to those differences. The overall assessment of a specific situational pattern as "favorable" or "unfavorable" to the implementation of a more informative

Module	SIGN	CAN (Federal & Provincial Gvts.)	D	DK	EC	F	S	UK	USA (Federal Gvt.)	USA (State Gvts.)
		JURISDICTION								
Stimuli	(+)	X		X	X		X	X	X	X
	(−)		X			X				
Social Structural Variables	(+)				X[1]				X	X
	(−)	X	X	X		X	X	X		
Structural Variables of Politico-Administrative System	(+)	X		X			X		X	X
	(−)		X		X	X		X		
Implementation Barriers	(+)	X		X			X			X
	(−)		X		X	X		X[2]	X	
Overall Assessment	(+)	X		X			X		X	X
	(−)		X		X	X		X		

Notes: (+): Favorable to the implementation of a more informative public sector accounting system
(−): Unfavorable
CAN = Canada; D = Germany; DK = Denmark; EC = European Community; F = France; S = Sweden; UK = United Kingdom; USA = United States of America
[1] The EC faces a particular situation: in the case of financial problems (which was under consideration here) the users of financial information (member countries) are able to considerably influence the behavior of the producers of the information (Commision).
[2] Relatively slight implementation barriers (only "qualifications," maybe size).

Figure 4. Classification of Jurisdictions

governmental accounting and financial reporting system may best be characterized, in the words of Khandwalla [1977, p. 279], as an assessment "on the basis of research results and/or informed speculation."

On the basis of the situation patterns observed for the various jurisdictions, the following hypotheses are proposed:

1. The politico-administrative background conditions for the introduction of a more informative system of governmental accounting are comparatively favorable in Canada, Denmark, Sweden, and the United States. In these countries, one may most readily expect innovations to have occurred, or will occur, in the system of public sector accounting.

2. The politico-administrative background conditions observed in Germany and France are comparatively unfavorable to the introduction of a more informative governmental accounting system. In the case of the EC (due to the stimulus and the influence of the users of information) and the United Kingdom (thanks to the presence of a stimulus and feeble implementation barriers) this is true only within certain restrictions. In all of those jurisdictions but particularly in France and Germany, innovations in governmental accounting and financial reporting are rather unlikely.

IV. EMPIRICAL OBSERVATIONS OF THE RELATIONSHIPS BETWEEN THE NATIONAL SITUATIONAL PATTERNS AND THE STATE OF THE ART IN GOVERNMENTAL ACCOUNTING

As to the state of the art in governmental accounting and financial reporting the jurisdiction that were included in the comparative study may be classified as "rather progressive" and "rather rooted in the tradition." "Rather progressive" entities are those which, during the 1980s, planned fundamental changes to their systems of governmental accounting and—in the meantime—at least initiated the implementation of these changes. In contrast, those entities that kept their systems of governmental accounting largely unchanged during the period in question, or carried out merely procedural (but not conceptual) changes, are classified as "rather rooted in tradition." The entities that were examined are assigned, as far as feasible, accordingly. In this way it can be established whether there are any common features that distinguish the entities in the two categories, in relation to the politico-administrative background conditions, and if so which.

A. Progressive Units

The "rather progressive" units include the Scandinavian countries of Denmark and Sweden, Canada, some Canadian provinces (in particular Alberta and British

Columbia) and those states in the United States that have adopted the GAAP. The characteristics of governmental accounting systems used in these entities are:

- Replacing the concept of net monetary debt with concept of net total debt or a near-net-total-debt approach.
- Expanding the recipients of government financial reports beyond Members of Parliament, in particular with the objective of making more and better information on the public financial management available to the general public.
- Making annual financial reports more "user-friendly" by means of improving their explanatory notes, producing summary reports, or otherwise improving the accessibility for those who do not belong to either the legislature or the executive branch of government.

As far as the politico-administrative background conditions are concerned, it is remarkable that the smaller territorial units that are covered by the comparative study are the progressive ones. The North American entities enjoy background conditions that are conducive to changes in the system of their public sector accounting. Using the notion of the contingency model described above, those conditions include:

- a relative strong political competition (with elements of direct democracy, competition between the executive branch and Parliament particularly on the state level of the United States);
- considerable influence exercised by external standard-setting bodies (i.e., the GASB in the United States and the CICA's Public Sector Accounting and Auditing Committee in Canada);
- accountancy staff trained in the techniques of private sector accounting;
- the existence of capital market incentives to produce informative financial statements; and
- a flexible legal system.

In the Scandinavian countries, the connection between the politico-administrative background conditions and the form of the public-sector accounting system is not so unambiguous. Both Denmark and Sweden are characterized in general by a particular orientation of the political process towards disclosure, with, as a consequence, specific attitudes on the part of politicians, administrators, and the public to the supply and demand for information. That means that the citizenry expect fundamentally candid information on the financial and economic situation of the state, and government agencies are fundamentally disposed to supply such information. In addition, in the first half of the 1980s, both Denmark and Sweden experienced critical financial situations, with rapid rises in the level of state indebtedness (by about 300% in Denmark between 1980 and 1985 and by more than 270% in Sweden). It may be assumed that this resulted in pressure on the government and administration to ensure administrative efficiency and to demonstrate sound financial management to the public. The device for being able to do that is an appropriate accounting and financial reporting system, for whose reshaping certain factors favorable to implementation existed: DP support for the system of public accounts and a legal system that was not too restrictive (this latter factor was even truer of Sweden than of Denmark). In contrast to the North American territorial units, Denmark and Sweden have built up and developed their management accounting systems ahead of, or at least in parallel with, their external systems. The reason for that may presumably be found in the external drive to improve governmental efficiency and the given economic and financial situation of the state.

B. Traditional Units

Germany, the United States at the federal level, and France may be considered "rather rooted in tradition." Their governmental accounting systems are:

- based on the net monetary debt concept or a near-monetary-debt approach;
- primarily, or exclusively, Parliament-oriented, and relatively user-unfriendly as regards explanatory notes to the annual reports and the availability of the revenue and expenditure accounts to the general public.

In respect to the politico-administrative background conditions, almost the only thing these three units have in common is their large population.

The federal government in the United States faces comparatively favorable institutional factors for the further development of its accounting system:

- there is a high level of political competition between the executive branch and the Congress;
- public sector accountancy staff are usually familiar with private-sector concepts and practice; and
- the growth of public debt points to a problematic financial situation and the need for demonstrating sound financial management.

The fact that there has, nevertheless, not yet been any fundamental change of the government's accounting practice may presumably be attributed to the existence of divergent values and attitudes as well as to the aggravating presence of implementation barriers:

- There exist different conceptions of the ideal situation in terms of supply of information between the legislature and the executive branch. The legislature is unable or unwilling so far to assert its more far-reaching conception.

- Pressure from the public to improve the information situation (e.g., as manifested in particular in the views expressed by professional organizations) is evidently not strong enough.
- The large number of diverse accounting practices in the huge federal government organization (i.e., degree of disharmonization) impedes the introduction of a more developed and uniform accounting system.

It is hypothesized that the relative inflexibility of the accounting system at the federal level in the United States is primarily due to values, attitudes, and implementation barriers, rather than structural background conditions. This is confirmed by the fact that numerous proposals for improving the federal government's accounting system have been suggested and as many meetings on this subject have been held. Thus, a lack of proposals and initiatives cannot be the reason for the present state of the art.

The situation has to be judged differently in the case of Germany and France: the combination of weak structural factors that promote change and the presence of factors inhibiting implementation create a context which is unfavorable for the further development of their governmental accounting systems. These two countries are characterized by the following:

- A low degree of political competition (No elements of direct democracy. An absence of competition between Parliament and the executive branch. The French constitution strongly emphasizes the role of the President. In Germany, the government and Parliamentary majority are closely identified with one party).
- Professional organizations having little influence on the governmental accounting system (with the sole exception in France via the Conseil National de la Comptabilite).
- Public-sector accounting staff having no or only limited experience of the concepts and practices of private sector accounting.
- No problematic financial situation.
- No capital market incentives.
- Relatively comprehensive and detailed legal prescriptions of governmental accounting systems (which in Germany are largely harmonized due to the Budgetary Principles Act).
- A lack of promotion by accounting professionals.

C. Special Cases

The United Kingdom and the EC occupy a rather special position—they cannot be assigned to either the "rather progressive" or "rather rooted in tradition" categories without some qualification.

In the United Kingdom, while it is true that its governmental accounting system is inclined to be "rooted in tradition," in the 1980s, however, great efforts were clearly made to develop and improve the management accounting system through the Financial Management Initiative. Similar to Denmark and Sweden, though to a lesser degree, the general economic situation and the situation of the government finance in the United Kingdom coincided with the appearance of a catalyst (in the person of Margaret Thatcher) to precipitate an initiative in favor of more effective, efficient, and economic administration and the creation of the necessary instruments to achieve that end. The fact that this initiative did not extend to the external system, unlike what happened in the Scandinavian countries, may be attributed to the following causes:

- The problem is purely one of time. The reform of the management system had priority. It may however be assumed that if the initiative had been spread out over a longer period of time a start would also have been made on the reform of the external accounting system. There is some evidence to support this interpretation.
- The restructuring of the external governmental accounting system rates lower in the hierarchy of priorities in the United Kingdom than in the Scandinavian countries due to a lower "openness" and "citizen-orientation" of British politics and government.
- The strength of the institutional factors promoting change in the United Kingdom is not great.

The EC, as a supranational entity, launched some early initiatives towards the end of the 1980s with a view to creating a management accounting system for the commission and made its own external accounting accessible to the public. More comprehensive conceptual changes did not, however, accompany these initiatives. The cause of the changes that took place was probably a temporarily critical financial situation in the EC in the mid 1980s and sharper criticism from the member states about the sound financial management aspect of the expenditure of Community resources by EC agencies. The changes that took place in the accounting system and in the accounts created the instrumental preconditions for improving the administrative efficiency and for demonstrating sound financial management. Fundamentally, however, the politico-administrative background conditions for the further development of the external accounting system are rather unfavorable:

- There is certainly political competition between Parliament on the one hand and the Council and/or the Commission on the other. But the European Parliament is of course even less able than the French one to influence the supply of information from the executive branch.
- There is no significant influence by professional organizations and even the

element of state debt or capital market incentives as factors precipitating change is absent.

- If those factors that are neutral as regards implementation are compared with those that inhibit it, the latter predominate, as reflected in the inflexibility of the legal system and the professional background of accountancy staff.

EDITORS' NOTE

This paper is based, in part, upon the "Comparative Government Accounting Study" recently completed by Professor Klaus G. Luder and his associates at the Postgraduate School of Administrative Sciences in Speyer, Germany. The Study's interim summary report is available in English, while the country studies cited in the References are in German only. Readers who wish to obtain copies of these publications may write to Professor Klaus G. Luder, c/o James L. Chan at the University of Illinois at Chicago. Readers interested in "comparative international governmental accounting research" (CIGAR) and the biennial CIGAR conference series may similarly communicate with James Chan, who will put them in touch with the appropriate parties.

REFERENCES

Arthur Andersen & Co., *Sound Financial Reporting in the U.S. Government* [Arthur Andersen & Co., 1986].

Baber, W.R., "Toward Understanding the Role of Auditing in the Public Sector," *Journal of Accounting and Economics* 5 [1983], pp. 213–227.

Baber, W.R., and P.K. Sen, "The Role of Generally Accepted Reporting Methods in The Public Sector: An Empirical Test," *Journal of Accounting and Public Policy* 3 [Summer 1984], pp. 91–106.

Buchanan, J.M., *Public Finance in A Democratic Process* [University of North Carolina Press, 1967].

Carpenter, V.L., and E. Feroz, "Fiscal Stress and State Government's Financial Reporting Practice: A Cross Case Analysis," paper presented to the Annual Conference of the American Accounting Association in Toronto, August 9–11, 1990.

Chan, J.L., "The Economics and Politics of Governmental Financial Information: Issues for Research," paper presented to the second CIGAR Conference in Speyer, April 3–4, 1989.

Chan, J.L., and M.A. Rubin, "The Role of Information in A Democracy and in Government Operations," *Research in Governmental and Nonprofit Accounting* 3, Part B [1987], pp. 3–27.

Downs, A., *An Economic Theory of Democracy* [Harper and Row, 1957].

Downs, A., "Why the Government's Budget Is Too Small in a Democracy," *World Politics* [July 1960], pp. 541–563.

Evans J.H., III and J.M. Patton, "Signalling and Monitoring in Public-sector Accounting," *Journal of Accounting Research* 25 [Supplement 1987], pp. 130–158.

Governmental Accounting Standards Board, "*Measurement Focus and Basis of Accounting— Governmental Fund Operating Statements,*" Proposed Statement of Governmental Accounting Concepts, [rev. ed.], Governmental Accounting Standards Series, No. 062-A [1989].

Ingram, R.W., "The Importance of State Accounting Practices for Credit Decisions," *Journal of Accounting and Public Policy* 2 [Spring 1983], pp. 5–19.

————, "Economic Incentives and the Choice of State Government Accounting Practice," *Journal of Accounting Research* [1984], pp. 26–134.

Ingram, R.W., and E.A. Wilson, "Governmental Capital Market Research in Accounting: A Review," *Research in Governmental and Nonprofit Accounting* 3, Part B [1987], pp. 111–126.

Khandwalla, P. N., *Design of Organizations* [Harcourt, Brace, Jovanovich, 1977].

Kieser, A., and H. Kubicek, *Organisation*, 2nd ed. [Berlin: De Gruyter, 1983].

Luder, K.G., "Comparative Government Accounting Study: Interim Summary Report," rev. ed. [Speyer: Speyerer Forschungsberichte, No. 76, 1989].

Luder, K.G., et al., "Vergleichende Analyse offentlicher Rechnungs systeme—Landerberichte." [Speyer: Speyerer Forschungsberichte, No. 73, 1989]:

Bd. 1: U.S.A.
Bd. 2: Kanada
Bd. 3: Frankreich und Grob Britannien
Bd. 4: Danemark
Bd. 5: Schweden
Bd. 6: Kommission der Europaischen Gemeinschaften

Niskanen, W., *Bureaucracy and Representative Government* [Aldine-Atherton, 1971].

Simon, H.A., *Entscheidungsverhalten in Organisationen* [Landsberg am Lech: Verlag Moderne Industrie, 1981], German translation of *Administrative Behavior*, 3rd ed.

U.S. General Accounting Office, *Proposed Framework for Establishing Federal Government Accounting Standards*, Exposure Draft [U.S. General Accounting Office, Washington, DC: May 1989].

Van Daniker, R.P., "Governmental Accounting in the U.S.—State Orientation," paper presented to the second CIGAR Conference in Speyer, April 3–4, 1989.

Van Daniker, R.P., et al., *State Comptrollers—Technical Activities and Functions* [National Association of State Auditors, Comptrollers and Treasurers, 1986].

Van Daniker, R.P., and T. Criswell, *State Comptrollers—Technical Activities and Functions* [National Association of State Auditors, Comptrollers and Treasurers, 1989].

Zimmerman, J.L., "The Municipal Accounting Maze: An Analysis of Political Incentives," *Journal of Accounting Research* 15 [Supplement 1977], pp. 107–144.

RECENT PUBLIC CHOICE RESEARCH RELEVANT TO GOVERNMENT ACCOUNTING AND AUDITING

Marc A. Rubin

ABSTRACT

The public choice literature offers a number of relevant and important insights into the operations of the public sector. Public choice pays specific attention to the incentives of voters, legislators, and bureaucrats, and interactions between these groups. This article reviews recent public choice literature that provide insights into the environment in which government accounting and auditing exist. Accounting researchers should consider the importance of this literature stream in conducting inquiries regarding government accounting and auditing.

Research in Governmental and Nonprofit Accounting, Vol. 7, pages 129–145.
Copyright © 1992 by JAI Press Inc.
All rights of reproduction in any form reserved.
ISBN: 1-55938-418-2

I. INTRODUCTION

Currently governmental accounting and auditing research does not have a well-developed theoretical foundation. Although recent research in governmental accounting and auditing issues and phenomena is helpful in forming a perception of the government environment, often an article only tests a single notion without examining the stream of political and/or economic research from which the theory or notion derives. If governmental accounting research is to develop in an organized and systematic manner, a common foundation is necessary for generating testable hypotheses and building a theory. The purpose of this paper is to provide a review of recent literature in the public choice discipline which is relevant for examining the role of accounting and auditing information in the public sector. Public choice is defined by Mueller [1989, p. 1] as "the economic study of nonmarket decision making, or simply the application of economics to political science." Public choice may provide insights for the development of a theory on the role of government accounting.

This article will be limited to reviewing recent contributions in public choice that deal with the role of information in the interactions among political executives, legislators, and bureaucrats. Additional areas of interest to government accountants, such as the role of information in credit markets, are not within the scope of this review.

This paper extends two previous review papers. In the mid 1980s Chan and Picur [1986] reviewed the state of governmental accounting research, focusing on mostly accounting publications. They urged that "the sophistication level of conceptual analysis . . . be raised to that of the basic discipline from which the ideas originate." That is, accounting researchers need to take the underlying disciplines of political science or public choice and extend (not just duplicate) it to develop a theory of government accounting. In order to know how to extend the underlying discipline, researchers first need to know the current state of that discipline. This paper is based on the belief that public choice is the discipline with the greatest potential relevancy to government accounting and auditing theory. This paper also extends Chan and Rubin [1987], which provides an initial review of public choice research applicable to the study of governmental accounting up to the mid 1980s. In that article, Chan and Rubin review several major public choice areas: median voter theorem, Tiebout hypothesis, voter rationale, fiscal illusion, and bureaucratic supply models. Over the last five years further developments have occurred in the public choice area that have increased the potential of that discipline helping accounting researchers formulate a theory of governmental accounting. This paper reviews these developments and suggests their implications for governmental accounting research.

In the second section of the paper , several overview papers are introduced. The third section reviews papers regarding formal models of government that relate to accounting and auditing issues. The fourth section reviews papers concerned with descriptive models of specific institutions. Concluding comments are offered in the final section of the paper.

II. OVERVIEW PAPERS

For those researchers who are becoming acquainted with public choice research for the first time, a number of resources are available that can introduce the basic concepts and notions of the public choice discipline. An older article by Ostrom and Ostrom [1971] is often overlooked. The Ostrom and Ostrom article introduces the public choice methodology with particular emphasis on articulating the differences between public choice and public administration. This article is particularly suitable for those researchers who are familiar with the traditional public administration literature and can appreciate the transition from Woodrow Wilson's concept of "good" public administration to "methodological individualism where the perspective of a representative individual is used for analytical purposes" [Ostrom and Ostrom, 1971, p. 205]. Public administration views the administrator or bureau head as the focal point of analysis and government accounting as a tool of good financial management. Public choice, however, expands the analysis of government to a variety of influential actors (voters, politicians, bureaucrats) all seeking to maximize their individual utility by whatever means available (including the possible use of governmental accounting).

Mitchell [1988] reviews the public choice developments accomplished at three major academic centers each representing a school of thought: Virginia, Rochester, and Bloomington. The Rochester school consists of positivists who primarily use mathematical methodologies (for example, game theory) to address political phenomena such as elections, party strategies, agenda setting, voting, and more recently, legislative institutions. A few of these phenomena (e.g., political competition and election strategies) have already been examined in selected accounting contexts [e.g., Baber, 1983; Zimmerman, 1977; Ingram and Copeland, 1981].

Virginia, the school of thought most often associated with the public choice discipline, is characterized by Mitchell as having a greater economic orientation. According to Mitchell [1988, p. 107] the basic economic tenet underlying the Virginia models is:

> In short, Virginia analyses emphasize properties of the democratic political process that are held to be inherent and universal. Unlike the private economy, the polity lacks an effective invisible hand which converts private selfishness into collective good. Accordingly, inequity, inefficiency, and coercion are the most general results of democratic policy formation.

Currently the Virginia school is primarily housed at George Mason University and is associated with a new journal reflecting its major focus of constitutional economics. Mitchell [1988, p. 107] summarizes the comparison between Rochester and Virginia as follows:

> Whereas Rochester has been led to investigate electoral politics Virginians focus on the lengthy periods between elections and institutions that exercise most of their influence during these time spans. Accordingly, a great deal of analysis is focused on bureaucracy, courts, regulation,

government employment, corruption, rent-seeking by interest groups, and constitutional
provisions, analyses leading, in turn, to theories of government growth.

The third school of public choice thought is Bloomington, specifically, the
Workshop on Political Theory and Policy Analysis led by Vincent and Elinor
Ostrom at Indiana University. This group comes from a more traditional political
science base. Mitchell [1988, p.111] states that:

Bloomington has concentrated upon actual problems involved in the delivery of public services
but it has not done so in any conspicuous manner suggesting the prior elaboration of deductive
models or even the explicit use of generalizations from Rochester and Virginia.

Mitchell also states that although Bloomington uses different research techniques,
it shares many of the same concerns as the Virginia school. The thrust of the
Bloomington school to rigorously model the delivery of government services will
benefit accountants examining cost functions and assessing the effectiveness and
efficiency of services. Mitchell's article is a good way for researchers to obtain a
brief macro-view of the three main literature streams that developed into the public
choice discipline.

Mueller's [1989] Public Choice II is a good starting place for developing a
general familiarity with the specific notions of the public choice discipline. As an
expanded version of his original book in 1979, Mueller [1989] includes six parts.
The subject matter for each of the six parts is as follows:

Part 1.   Origins of the state and the reasons for collective choice.
Part 2.   Public choice in a direct democracy—voting procedures, rules, and
          outcomes.
Part 3.   Representative democracy—two-party and multiparty competitive
          systems, rent seeking, and the supply of government output.
Part 4.   Applications of public choice—political competition, macroeconomic
          performance, size of government, and voting paradoxes.
Part 5.   Normative public choice—social welfare functions and social con-
          tracts.
Part 6.   Comparison of normative and positive public choice.

Chapter 14 (part 3) on supply of government output and chapter 17 (part 4) on
the size of government may be of most interest to government accounting researchers. The supply of government output deals with topics of information and
power and the ability for the bureaucracy to grow and be controlled. The chapter
relies heavily on the work of Niskanen [1971] and its extensions (see Chan and
Rubin [1987] for a detail review of Niskanen's research). Much of the research on
government outputs is applicable to accountants interested in management control
(particularly legislature control of the bureaucracy) including auditing. In this
literature, salient topics for accountants include the principal-agent relationships

in government, utility functions of the actors, and behavioral constraints (such as which actors have knowledge of cost functions and supply of outputs).

The chapter on size of government also covers some of the empirical research dealing with government and bureaucratic growth as well as the topic of fiscal illusion. These topics are of particular interest to accountants interested in how government grows and what drives revenue and expenditure patterns and the issuance of debt.

Bendor's [1990] review paper, unlike the previously mentioned literature, is more narrow in its focus. Bendor exclusively reviews the literature on formal models of bureaucracy. Formal models are particularly relevant to government accounting because they specify in a precise way the environment in which information games are played. Therefore, one can assess, under specified conditions, the role of accounting information in the control of bureaucracies. Bendor's work is further discussed in the next section of this paper.

III. FORMAL PUBLIC SECTOR INFORMATION MODELS

Formal models typically express economic or political theory by using mathematical or game theoretic techniques. These models are based on assumptions regarding the utility functions of the actors (such as legislators and bureaucrats) involved in the delivery of government services. Often the relationships examined in formal models are generic since they do not consider the structure of a specific institution. Building on the early work of Niskanen [1971], formal models represent a significant development relevant to accounting because they often directly address the information problems. The previously mentioned paper by Bendor [1990] is an excellent review of the developments in this area of public choice.

Bendor divides formal models of bureaucracy into four major categories. The first category of models consists of the Niskanen [1971] model of bureaucratic supply of output and its various extensions. The second category is concerned with political control and principal-agent analysis, including discussions of bureaucratic agents with multiple superiors and of the role of bureaucratic monitoring and oversight. The third category addresses the design of hierarchical institutions and the fourth category deals with models of bounded rationality. The first two categories are robust areas of research in formal models of bureaucracy and likely have the greatest significance to government accounting research. Next the research regarding Niskanen-type models of bureaucracy and principal-agent analysis is reviewed. This review will refer to Bendor's insights, along with a discussion of how Niskanen-type models may relate to government accounting research.

A. Niskanen Models

Niskanen and similar economic models of bureaucracy have been regarded as significant in the public choice discipline for a number of reasons. Bendor [1990, p. 380] states that,

> the techniques of formal modeling have certainly aided systematic inquiry. For example, because Niskanen laid bare his agenda-control assumptions in generating his oversupply result, later researchers could modify this model by dropping this postulate while retaining other features of the model.... Thus the process of trial and error became more rapid as the community of scholars discovered which assumptions were crucial for various conclusions.

Bendor further points out that the extensions of Niskanen have drawn a useful differentiation between authority-based and information-based agenda control. Agenda control refers to the power of determining which alternative proposals will be voted upon and the order of voting. Control of the agenda will have a significant influence on the final outcome of the voting process. Authority-based control is where responsibility for the voting agenda is explicitly invested in an individual or group. Information-based control stems from information asymmetries. The distinction between the two types of agenda control is of particular relevance to governmental accounting, since information-based agenda control may well have an impact on the role government accounting information plays in principal-agent relationships found in government. That is, the amount and type of information (including accounting information) generated by bureaus and made available to policymakers often influences the perception of the efficiency and effectiveness of a proposed policy, which in turn influences the voting agenda and outcome concerning the policy.

Bendor [1990, p. 380] makes the following warning about information-based agenda control research:

> the growing consensus to model asymmetric information as the foundation of bureaucratic influence will not be paralleled by a convergence on how to represent this asymmetry. Instead, we will see a proliferation of specialized models with different assumptions about what bureaucrats know that politicians do not (the set of feasible alternatives, the costs and benefits of a known set of alternatives, and so forth).

This comment by Bendor is reflected in a number of articles whose results concerning bureaucratic supply of output depend on the authors' assumptions. For example, Miller and Moe [1983], whose paper was one of the first to distinguish between authority-based and information-based agenda control, demonstrate that even a slight relaxation of the assumption of the bureaucracy having total control over information can change significantly the results of bureaucratic oversupply. Their results also suggest that the more the legislators keep the bureaucrats in the "dark" concerning legislative demand, the more likely bureaucrats will provide accurate cost information regarding output.

Further Niskanen extensions include Bendor, Taylor, and Van Gaalen [1985, 1987a, 1987b], Bendor and Moe [1985], Banks [1989] and Banks and Weingast [1989]. Bendor, Taylor, and Van Gaalen use a principal-agent mathematical modeling approach to derive results regarding agency output and the relative power of bureaucrats and legislators. The models assess the likely selection of a specific policy from a set of alternatives (for example, an agency budget amount) based on assumed utility function for both the principal and agent (for example, the politician desires the outcome with the greatest political benefits and the agent desires the greatest budget amount) and a specific information environment (for example, the agency head knows the cost function and demand for the output, while the principal only knows the demand).

In their initial [1985] article Bendor, Taylor and Van Gaalen demonstrate that under specified conditions, incentives (such as penalties) and monitoring can reduce the willingness of bureaucrats to deceive legislators. They also show that monitoring does not need to be perfect to have a disciplining effect on the bureau's propensity to seek excess budgets. In their follow-up article, Bendor et al. [1987b] extend their model by developing different assumptions. Their results suggest that more monitoring typically leads to better control. In a new model where uncertainty exists for both legislators and bureaucrats (in the initial model only the legislators are uncertain), the authors demonstrate conditions where the inducement of more uncertainty on the bureaucrat may produce better responses, but not necessarily under all conditions. Bendor et al. also demonstrate that the tougher the budget cuts, the less distorted the information provided by bureaucrats. In a related article, Bendor et al. [1987a] develop a model that suggests that control by legislators (over bureaucrats) can be obtained by review of policy decisions and appropriate incentives, although the incentive schemes can be very complex and expensive.

In the cases where a large number of parameters are analyzed, simulations may be used to ascertain outcomes even though results may be more difficult to generalize. For example, Bendor and Moe [1985] manipulate a variety of parameters including bureaucrat incentives, oversight, adaptation speed of bureau, and taxes. Due to tractability problems, they use simulation techniques. Results suggest that under certain conditions monitoring can check the power of bureaus. Additional models focusing specifically on oversight (monitoring) are reviewed in the next section.

Formal models of bureaucracy offer numerous insights for government accounting research. For example, they stress the importance of precise modeling. Model assumptions are provided leading to the development of conclusions. This allows the reader to assess the value of the model, and the generalizability of the model's results. In addition, formal models of the legislature-agency interaction provide results regarding the effect of information on bureaucratic supply, although the results are situation specific. Often the results of these models are not intuitively obvious. For example, Calvert's [1985] model of political decision making demonstrates a set of plausible conditions where decision makers will prefer to receive information from a biased rather than objective source. Also, formal models provide a clearer determination of how far we have advanced in understanding government. Formal models make it easier to assess the "state-of-the-art" and ascertain the progression of the research stream.

B. Political Oversight

The literature on political oversight, extending from the Niskanen models, mostly uses principal-agent analysis to examine the role of oversight in controlling bureaucratic output. The necessity for oversight stems from the differences in agenda between politicians (principals) and bureaucrats (agents). Oversight is exercised through two forms of control: administrative-based control and information-based control. Administrative-based control relies on laws, statues, regulation or rules. Information-based control is intended to overcome the information asymmetry that may exist between politicians and bureaucrats and among the different levels of government. For example, legislature-directed audits of agency output information may be considered an information-based control technique since it helps to reduce the information asymmetry between bureaucrats and legislators.

McCubbins and Schwartz's [1984] model of Congressional oversight covers two types of oversight policy—"police-patrol oversight" and "fire-alarm oversight." McCubbins and Schwartz [1984, p. 166] describe police-patrol oversight as "comparatively centralized, active direct...with the aim of detecting and remedying any violation of legislative goals and, by its surveillance, discouraging such violations." Fire-alarm oversight, on the other hand, is "less centralized and involves less active and direct intervention than police-patrol oversight." Fire-alarm oversight consists of rules and procedures set up by legislators to enable constituents to examine administrative decisions and seek remedies for those that are in conflict with legislative policy objectives.

McCubbins and Schwartz argue that fire-alarm oversight, an important but overlooked form of control, may be more efficient than police patrols. This classification of oversight raises a number of important issues to government accounting research: How does accounting and auditing fit into the model? Is accounting a form of police-patrol or fire-alarm oversight? Does accounting facilitate legislative control of bureaucrats? How, if at all, does accounting information facilitate fire-alarm oversight? How do different types of audits (pre-audits, post-audits, compliance audits, operational audits, financial audits) fit into a model of legislative oversight? Although the context of McCubbins and Schwartz's study is the federal government, it appears generalizable to most types of governments. Research into these issues may help further define the role of accounting information in government organizations.

Similarly, Weingast [1984] also suggests that indirect means of monitoring are important to Congress in its attempt to control the bureaucracy. Weingast describes a variety of methods that Congress can use to control the bureaucracy indirectly, including McCubbins and Schwartz's fire-alarms. Weingast [1984, p. 160] summarizes his model with the following observation:

> the congressional-bureaucratic system is a complex set of institutions designed to influence bureaucratic policy decisions without the direct and continuous participation of Congress in the day-to-day process of administration. The subtle nature of these mechanisms suggests that we study and interpret congressional-bureaucratic interactions from a different perspective than is usually taken in the traditional literature.

Weingast's observation indicates that accounting and auditing may be a subtle influence in the control of the bureaucracy. In addition, Weingast suggests that we must examine all controls (explicit and implicit) in order to assess the success of bureaucratic compliance.

Banks [1989] takes a further look at the legislature-agency interaction. He assumes a particular type of information asymmetry whereby only the agency has full knowledge of its cost for providing services. Banks specifically assesses the ability of the legislature to audit the agency, where audits are defined as a "costly means of verifying the agency's information" [Banks, 1989 p. 670]. Banks's conclusions regarding the usefulness of auditing depend on the specific environment in which the cost versus benefit of auditing is determined and the particular procedures used to determine the budget.

Banks's paper is significant to accountants because it is one of the first to assess the specific role and utility of auditing in the legislative-agency relationship. Banks recommends his model be extended to multiple time periods. Banks also assumes in his model that agencies know the cost of their output. Accountants realize the difficulty of identifying and measuring outputs, and of relating costs to such outputs. Thus a further refinement of the Banks model would be to relax the assumption of agency knowledge and extend the model to situations such as where agencies have imperfect cost and /or output information.

Following Banks [1989], Banks and Weingast [1989] similarly analyze the legislature-agency relationship where the agency has the informational advantage of knowing its own cost. They model the situation where politicians can use alternative sources of information (such as auditing) to overcome their informational disadvantage. Banks and Weingast's [1989, pp. 3-5] results suggest three significant insights:

> (1)   while an informational advantage potentially allows an agency to extract large amounts of the gains from politicians, agencies are likely to be created only in those areas where the advantage is minimal or low.
>
> (2)   the selection process by politicians will only create those agencies where the expected political gains are high and the agencies do not produce at too high a cost . . . . there may exist agencies which potentially provide valuable services to constituents that are not created because politicians have no means of preventing the agency from extracting a disproportionate share of

the rents. The politician therefore will prefer a less valuable agency with lower auditing costs, if the net return from this agency is greater.

(3)   agencies will be *observed* to serve interest groups because politicians are biased in favor of creating this type of agency. The source of the bias arises not because of the differential electoral rewards provided by the interest groups, but because the latter play an active role in the production process by providing an important, alternative source of information for politicians.

Banks and Weingast's research raises a number of questions related to the production and dissemination of accounting and auditing information. For example: What types of agencies have low-cost versus high-cost monitoring information available to politicians? What types of information might improve the ability of an agency to survive? What is the relationship between interest groups and the production of information? How is the decision to use auditing as an information source affected by the nature of interest groups? Research to address these questions may be within the domain of accounting.

Although the literature on information-based controls clearly impacts the way we perceive the role of government accounting and auditing, the administrative-based control literature should not be overlooked. In part, the two types of controls are not distinctly separable and both are important in determining success of bureaucratic compliance in a comprehensive model. In assessing the utility of administrative controls, McCubbins, Noll, and Weingast [1987, p. 244] state that:

> First, procedures can be used to mitigate informational disadvantages faced by politicians in dealing with agencies. Second, procedures can be used to enfranchise important constituents in agency decisionmaking processes, thereby assuring that agencies are responsive to their interests.

McCubbins et al. [1987, p. 253], after assessing the effectiveness of sanctions and monitoring as a method for bureaucratic control, conclude:

> by themselves, monitoring and sanctions do not comprise a perfect solution to the problem of bureaucratic compliance because they are costly, inexact, and subject to fundamental limitations. Thus, one would expect politicians to welcome other measures that may be available for altering the incentive structure of agencies, especially if these alternatives have relatively low cost. An optimal mix of the measures, where each measure complements the strengths of the other and substitutes for the other's weaknesses, will establish less costly and more effective control of the bureaucracy by political principals. Hence, the stage is set for analyzing administrative law as such a mechanism.

Calvert, McCubbins, and Weingast [1989] also assess the importance of administrative controls, along with the role of information-based control. They [1989, p. 589] develop a model of agency discretion, which "pits the ambitions of institutional actors against one another," and encompasses "the initial delegation of authority, the choice of policy alternatives, and opportunities for oversight and control." Their results suggest that,

Bureaucratic choice is embedded in a game in which the appointment power of the executive and legislature, together with the threat of sanctions, provides a potentially decisive influence over policy…. Thus even though the agency may be the sole active decision maker, policy outcomes are traceable to the preferences of all three institutions and to the constitutional process in which they act [p. 589].

The implications of their results are that "all else equal, the more important a policy area to politicians, the lower the amount of agency discretion" [Calvert et al., 1989, p. 589–590]. According to these authors, the important practical applications of their results include:

First, any attempt to improve policy outcomes systematically through structural or procedural reform depends on a sophisticated understanding of where the relevant policy decisions are made….Second, empirical analysis of the policymaking process, particularly using the case study approach, can be seriously misdirected if the analyst does not have the proper understanding of the nature of responsibility for policy outcomes [p. 590].

If the role of accounting as a monitoring device is to be completely understood, the administrative procedures that may impact the production and dissemination of accounting information must be assessed as well. Examples of other papers assessing the use of administrative controls to force agency compliance include McCubbins [1985], McCubbins, Noll and Weingast [1989], and Robbinson [1989]. Accounting researchers may ask: What are the objectives of an agency? Who has the most influence in the policy-making process? What types of controls are available to assure legislators that their desired policy outcomes are in fact being executed by bureaucrats?

IV. DESCRIPTIVE MODELS

Bendor [1990, p. 381] comments on Niskanen models as follows:

virtually none of the models in this tradition say anything about implementation. They are basically theories of exchange… . Implementation questions are finessed by positing that the agency knows that the political superior can perfectly and costlessly observe final output, so it will do whatever it must to generate that amount.

Bendor criticizes this aspect of Niskanen models by making the following observation:

as a generation of policy analysts has learned to its sorrow, measuring bureaucratic output is difficult. Output indicators are always imperfect; collecting them is always costly [p. 381].

These limitations of current bureaucracy models may be overcome by incorporating accounting systems into them. Devising appropriate output measures and especially determining their cost appears to be an area within the purview of governmental accounting research. Accounting's interest in estimating cost functions as well as the recent interest by the Governmental Accounting Standards Board [Hatry et al., 1990] concerning indicators of government's service efforts and accomplishments is such an acknowledgement.

Implementation gives rise to the importance of understanding the specific context in which models are constructed. That is, institution structure can no longer be overlooked since bureaucracies and legislatures are not generic. The political environment (for example, legislative constraints, judicial constraints, and political competition) and the decision-making environment (for example, the methods for obtaining resources) may differ considerably among governments and agencies. The differences may have a profound influence on the interactions and decisions occurring within the specific governmental unit.

In contrast to the Niskanen model and its derivatives, Wilson [1989] describes bureaucracies in great detail. He justifies his approach by saying:

> The details are not there simply to make the book long, but rather to persuade the reader that bureaucracy is not the simple, uniform phenomenon it is sometimes made out to be. Reality often does not conform to scholarly theories or popular prejudices [Wilson, 1989, preface].

Researchers who believe that institution structure is imperative to the study of bureaucracy (e.g., Wilson and Moe) may not be considered part of the mainstream in public choice literature. However, as Mitchell [1988, p. 116] states, "They might be labelled 'closet' public choice analysts." The remainder of this section will review recent literature on institutions.

Wilson [1989] approaches the study of politician-agency interaction with somewhat of a different set of biases than most of the authors of the recent public choice literature. Although he acknowledges the research attempting to find a theory of bureaucracies, Wilson [1989, p. xi] has

> come to have grave doubts that anything worth calling "organization theory" will ever exist. Theories will exist, but they will usually be so abstract or general as to explain rather little. Interesting explanations will exist, even some supported with facts, but these will be partial, place- and time-bound insights.

Wilson [1989, p. xii] justifies his approach to studying bureaucracy by stating that,

> I think it might be helpful to public discourse...if someone were to set forth what we now know about government agencies in all (or at least most) of their complexity, and to do so by sticking as close as possible to what actually happens in real bureaucracies.

Although Wilson's research is primarily descriptive, some of the aspects of organizations he identifies are relevant to accounting. He assesses bureaucracy by examining the key elements of an agency, such as the service providers, agency managers, agency executives, the context in which the agency operates and the methods of change in an agency. Wilson presents a number of ideas which are relevant to accounting. Examples of some of his insights are as follows:

Wilson classifies the agency environment in relation to outside interests as one of four types: client, entrepreneurial, interest-group and majoritarian. Understanding the differences in the environment in which an agency deals with outsiders, may offer important insights in the way the agency produces and disseminates information.

Wilson's suggestion that managers' action are constraint-driven as opposed to objectives-driven may also explain the way accounting and other information systems are often designed to provide information on compliance as opposed to the attainment of objectives.

He classifies agencies into one of four types: production, procedural, craft, and coping. These classifications reflect the manager's ability to observe the activity of an agency's service providers (outputs) and the results of the activities (outcomes). An agency's operations may be impacted by ability to observe and measure its outputs and outcomes. The more difficult it is to observe outputs or outcomes, the more difficult it is to enforce agency compliance with legislative objectives. Measurement difficulty is certainly a key concern to accountants.

Wilson classifies the decision-making strategy of executives as either: advocating, decision making, budget-cutting, or negotiating. The information requirements to execute each of these strategies may vary widely and needs to be considered in assessing the utility of government accounting information to the executive.

Wilson provides a number of examples of specific agencies and describes their environment, service providers, managers, and executives. He also offers a number of other insights, which may impact the way we perceive the role of accounting in a government agency. Most of Wilson's descriptions and examples come from the federal government, although they likely can be generalized to state and local government as well.

Public choice researchers, in addition to Wilson, also have concerned themselves with specific institutions. Ostrom, Bish, and Ostrom [1988], Advisory Commission on Intergovernmental Relations [1987], and Zodrow [1983] offer a number of insights into local government using a public choice approach. For example, Ostrom et al. [1988, p. 114] state:

> Once the "one-government, one-community" concept is abandoned, however, it is no longer necessary to use units of government as the only units of analysis appropriate for the study of local government in metropolitan areas.

This implies that the "entity" concept for preparing accounting reports may be an important issue in determining the appropriate way to assess the performance of local government services. There is evidence that accounting researchers have already been sensitive to this problem [e.g., Patton, 1987].

Ostrom et al. [1988] also suggest that management of government services depends on whether the activity is capital- or labor-intensive. They suggest that capital-intensive compared to labor-intensive activities have outputs that are comparatively easier to measure and manage. Therefore, capital-intensive activities (such as a utility) may be best served by a larger single producing organization, whereas, labor-intensive activities (such as police patrols) are best provided by a larger number of smaller organizations.

These insights may be significant to the way accounting information is reported. For example: How should accounting measures differ between capital-intensive and labor-intensive activities? Should accounting reports be prepared differently based on the type of government activity? Should different accounting entities be defined for different government services? In addition, the capital- versus labor-intensive dichotomy may be a consideration in determining cost functions of government services. That is, since capital-intensive activities are likely to have higher fixed costs, cost functions may be determined differently for labor and capital-intensive activities.

Ostrom, Bish, and Ostrom [1988] appear to have many views similar to Wilson [1989]. For example, both suggest governments are complex and unique and both stress the importance of structure in the study of government. Ostrom et al. [1988, p. 211] summarize their analysis by concluding:

> What we have found is that we cannot understand local government as a process by looking only at discrete individual units.... The system of local governance is not confined to formal units of government.

Moe [1989] also combines aspects of formal modeling with specific institutional characteristics to assess bureaucratic structure. Moe [1989, p. 268] specifically develops a model of bureaucracy which is based on "political choice and self-interest." He states that his interest is in determining

> what sorts of structures do the various political actors—interest groups, presidents, members of Congress, bureaucrats—find conducive to their own interests, and what kind of bureaucracy is therefore likely to emerge from their efforts to exercise power? In other words, why do they build the bureaucracy they do? [p. 268].

Moe suggests that both political uncertainty and compromise are the most significant issues motivating the structural design of bureaus. For example, Moe [1989, p. 276] asserts that interest groups opposing a particular agency may want a bureaucratic structure that allows "politicians to get at the agency." If this is the scenario, Moe claims that the opposition group will

> favor onerous requirements for the collection and reporting of information, the monitoring of agency operations, and the review of agency decisions—thus laying the basis for active, interventionist oversight by politicians [p. 276].

Moe has similar insights regarding how the interests of legislators, executives, and bureaucrats affect the structure of bureaucracies. He concludes that

> Bureaucratic structure emerges as a jerry-built fusion of congressional and presidential forms, their relative roles and particular features determined by the powers, priorities, and strategies of the various designers. The result is that each agency cannot help but begin life as a unique structural reflection of its own politics [Moe 1989, p. 282].

Moe further asserts that structural design of bureaus is a dynamic process and to understand the operations of the bureau is to understand its environment and how it changes.

Moe provides additional considerations for accounting research. His model of bureaucracy suggests that accounting and reporting policies in an agency is part of the structural design of the bureau. To understand the role of accounting and auditing in a bureau, we need to consider how the bureau developed: What players had the most influence in the development of the bureau? What are the interests of the significant players? How do the interests of the players affect the accounting and auditing policy of the bureau? How has the bureau changed and how has that affected accounting and auditing policies?

Wilson [1989], Moe [1989], Ostrom, Bish, and Ostrom [1988], and similar literature should be examined in analyzing the role of accounting information and auditing in the operations of bureaucracy. Although their approaches may not be as formal as the "mainstream" public choice literature, specific institution structure is important to the development of a complete model of government decision making and control.

V. CONCLUDING COMMENTS

Government accounting research can benefit by utilizing the current state-of-the-art in the underlying disciplines such as public choice, public finance and economics, political science, and public administration. This article reviews recent contributions in the public choice literature that are relevant to government accounting. For example, public choice research has already begun the process of modeling the interactions between voters, legislators, and bureaucrats. These models can increase our understanding of the government accounting environment. As suggested by the public choice literature, government accounting information production and utilization may be sensitive to a number of factors including: the utility functions of the producers and users, the types of decisions being made, and the environment in which the information is produced, organizational development and constraints, and technical feasibility. These factors need to be assessed in determining the role of information in government organizations. Some of the public choice models have already begun to look at the information and monitoring games that may be played in governments.

Accountants, who are information specialists, may want to extend the existing public choice models as well as attempt to validate them. To do this, accountants will need to be sensitive to the already mentioned factors. In addition, as Wilson, Moe, and others have stressed, government organizations are not generic and we need to focus on the structures of the particular institutions being studied and make sure we have an understanding of what decisions are being made, by who, why are they made, and what are the constraints on those decisions.

The research agenda for government accounting should include better models for the context in which accounting information is used. Public choice offers accountants both substantive insights as well as research methodologies that can be useful for obtaining a more complete understanding of the role of government accounting and auditing.

REFERENCES

Advisory Commission on Intergovernmental Relations, *The Organization of Local Public Economies* [Advisory Commission on Intergovernmental Relations, 1987].

Baber, W.R., "Toward Understanding the Role of Auditing in the Public Sector," *Journal of Accounting & Economics* [December, 1983], pp. 213–227.

Banks, J.S., "Agency Budgets, Cost Information, and Auditing," *American Journal of Political Science* 33, 3 [1989], pp. 670–699.

Banks, J.S., and B.R. Weingast, "The Political Control of Bureaucracies Under Asymmetric Information," Working paper [May 1989].

Bendor, J. "Formal Models of Bureaucracy: A Review," in *Public Administration The State of the Discipline*, edited by N. B. Lynn and A. Wildavsky [Chatham House Publishers, Inc., 1990], pp. 373–417.

Bendor, J. and T.M. Moe, "An Adaptive Model of Bureaucratic Politics," *The American Political Science Review* 79 [1985], pp. 755–774.

Bendor, J. , S. Taylor and R. Van Gaalen, "Bureaucratic Expertise versus Legislative Authority: A Model of Deception and Monitoring in Budgeting," *The American Political Science Review* 79 [1985], pp. 1041–1060.

———, "Stacking the Deck: Bureaucratic Missions and Policy Design," *The American Political Science Review* 81, 3 [1987a], pp. 873–896.

———, "Politicians, Bureaucrats, and Asymmetric Information," *American Journal of Political Science* 31 [1987b], pp. 796–828.

Calvert, R.L., "The Value of Biased Information: A Rational Choice Model of Political Advice," *Journal of Politics* 47 [1985], pp. 530–555.

Calvert, R.L., M.D. McCubbins, and B.R. Weingast, "A Theory of Political Control and Agency Discretion," *American Journal of Political Science* 33, 3 [1989], pp. 588–611.

Chan, J.L. and M.A. Rubin, "The Role of Information in a Democracy and in Government Operations: The Public Choice Methodology," *Research in Governmental and Nonprofit Accounting*, 3, Part B [1987], pp. 3–27.

Hatry, H.P., J.R. Fountain, Jr., J. M. Sullivan and L. Kremer, eds., *Service Efforts and Accomplishments Reporting: Its Time Has Come An Overview* [Governmental Accounting Standards Board, 1990].

Horn, M. J. and K. A. Shepsle, "Commentary on 'Administrative Arrangements and the Political Control of Agencies' Administrative Process and Organizational Form as Legislative Responses to Agency Costs," *Virginia Law Review* 75 [1989], pp. 499–507.

Ingram, R.W. and R.M. Copeland, "Municipal Accounting Information and Voting Behavior," *The Accounting Review* [October, 1981], pp. 830–843.

McCubbins, M.D., "The Legislative Design of Regulatory Structure," *American Journal of Political Science* 29, 4 [1985], pp. 721–748.

McCubbins, M.D., R.G. Noll, and B.R. Weingast, "Structure and Process, Politics and Policy: Administrative Arrangements and the Political Control of Agencies," *Virginia Law Review* 75 [1989], pp. 431–448.

———, "Administrative Procedures as Instruments of Political Control," *Journal of Law, Economics, and Organization* 3, 2 [1987], pp. 243–277.

McCubbins, M. D. and T. Schwartz, "Congressional Oversight Overlooked: Police Patrols versus Fire Alarms," *American Journal of Political Science* 28, 1 [1984], pp. 165–179.

Miller, G. and T. Moe, "Bureaucrats, Legislators, and the Size of Government," *The American Political Science Review* 77 [1983], pp. 297-322.

Mitchell, W.C., "Virginia, Rochester, and Bloomington: Twenty-five Years of Public Choice and Political Science, *Public Choice* 56 [1988], pp. 101–119.

Moe, T.M., "The Politics of Bureaucratic Structure," in *Can the Government Govern?* [The Brookings Institution, 1989], pp. 267–329.

Mueller, D.C., *Public Choice II* [Cambridge: Cambridge University Press, 1989].

Niskanen, W., *Bureaucracy and Representative Government* [Aldine-Atherton, 1971].

Ostrom, V., R. Bish and E. Ostrom, *Local Government in the United States* [ICS Press, 1988].

Ostrom, V. and E. Ostrom, "Public Choice: A Different Approach to the Study of Public Administration," *Public Administration Review* 31 [1971], pp. 203–216.

Patton, J.M. *An Empirical Study of Governmental Financial Reporting Entity Issues* [Governmental Accounting Standards Board, 1987].

Robbinson, G.O., "Commentary on 'Administrative Arrangements and the Political Control of Agencies':Political Uses of Structure and Process," *Virginia Law Review* 75 [1989], pp. 483–498.

Weingast, B.R., "The Congressional-Bureaucratic System: A Principal Agent Perspective (With Application to the SEC)," *Public Choice* 44 [1984], pp. 147–191.

Wilson, J.Q., *Bureaucracy: What Government Agencies Do and Why They Do It* [Basic Books, 1989].

Zimmerman, J.L., "The Municipal Accounting Maze: An Analysis of Political Incentives," *Journal of Accounting Research* 15 supplement [1977], pp. 107–144.

Zodrow, G.R., *Local Provision of Public Services: The Tiebout Model after Twenty-five Years* [Academic Press, 1983].

LEARNING FROM
JAMES M. BUCHANAN:
CHALLENGES FOR NATIONAL
GOVERNMENTAL ACCOUNTING

Rowan H. Jones

ABSTRACT

James M. Buchanan argues that budgeting and accounting for national governments should be used to force ourselves, as voters and politicians, to pay the cost, in current taxes, of our current public spending. This suggests a new and important direction for future research in governmental accounting.

In the citation that accompanied the award to James M. Buchanan of the 1986 Alfred Nobel Memorial Prize in Economic Sciences, it stated:

Buchanan's foremost achievement is that he has consistently and tenaciously emphasized the significance of fundamental rules and applied the concept of the political system as an exchange process for the achievement of mutual advantages. He has used his method with great success in the analysis of many specific problems and issues. Long before large budget deficits arose,

Research in Governmental and Nonprofit Accounting, Vol. 7, pages 147–157.
Copyright © 1992 by JAI Press Inc.
All rights of reproduction in any form reserved.
ISBN: 1-55938-418-2

for example, he showed how debt financing dissolves the relation between expenditures and
taxes in the decision-making process [Scandinavian Journal of Economics, 1987, p. 3].

The main purpose of this paper is to amplify this statement and in so doing to
provide governmental accounting with a perspective for learning from Buchanan,
emphasizing the specific issue of debt financing.[1]

The first section synthesizes Buchanan's views on the finance of national
governments, particularly those associated with his prescription of balanced
budgets. The second section identifies the challenges that these views raise for
governmental accounting in the national context, and includes a concomitant future
research direction for governmental accounting.

I. BALANCED BUDGETS FOR NATIONAL
GOVERNMENTS

It has been said that Buchanan's "The Pure Theory of Government Finance," a
paper published in 1949, "reads like a manifesto for his life's work" [Atkinson,
1987, p. 6]. The problem he addresses there is that the extant literature of public
finance concentrates too much on the income side to the virtual exclusion of the
expenditure side of government budgeting; but important though this is, the
manifesto lies not in this specific problem but in the way that he addresses it.

He offers "two separate and opposing theories of the state" [Buchanan, 1949,
p. 496]. The first he calls the "organismic theory," in which the state is viewed as
"a single organic entity," which "subsumes all individual interests," [p. 496]. The
second he calls the "individualistic" theory, in which "the state is represented as
the sum of its individual members acting in a collective capacity" [p. 496].

He argues that in both theories, the interdependence of the income side and the
expenditure side of government finance must be fully understood: for example,
how can we know whether a tax is regressive if we only take account of the
redistribution of income and ignore the effects of the expenditure? But he also
crucially concludes that although the "organismic framework gives a much more
complete normative behavior pattern for the fiscal authority... [t]he major
obstacles lie in the attempts at translation of the theoretical guides to action into a
realistic approach to practical policy" [Buchanan, 1949, p. 505]. This is essentially
because, in his opinion, terms like "social utility" and "social welfare" are "of little
use in the discussion of policy problems" [1949, p. 498].

His manifesto for the alternative to the organismic theory is offered in the final
paragraph of the paper:

In the individualistic approach the government represents only the collective will of individuals
and cannot be considered the originator of action in an abstract sense. The fisc cannot be assumed
to maximize anything. The fiscal system exists as one channel through which certain collective

desires may be accomplished. The content of theory becomes the setting-up of a structural framework to enable the results of policies to be evaluated [Buchanan, 1949, p. 505].

In a later book [Buchanan, 1958, p. 153], he develops his criticism by saying that the organismic approach to fiscal theory "neglects the most important problem of all, that is, the manner in which collective decisions actually are made." This provides one key to Buchanan's whole approach: economics cannot be divorced from politics.

Moreover, his perspective, as a founder and leading researcher in the field of public choice, is to apply economics to politics: thus man is seen as an "egoistic, rational, utility maximizer" [Mueller, 1976, p. 395], whether engaged in the voluntary exchange of goods [in a market] or whether engaged in voting, campaigning for political office or taking "collective" decisions in government. Yet there is an important self-acknowledged sense in which Buchanan's perspective departs from that of the "natural economist" [Buchanan, 1987a, chapter 2]. He defines such an economist as one who:

... views human beings as self-interested, utility—maximizing agents, basically independent one from another, and for whom social interchange is initiated and exists simply as a preferred alternative to isolated action .... To the economist who looks at persons in this way, there seems little room for moral or ethical precepts in either positive or normative exercises. Persons are observed to behave in certain patterns, and the economist's task is to offer an explanation-understanding of that behavior in terms of his model of self-interest utility maximization. And, because he considers himself successful in this positive aspect of his science, the economist offers normative guidance grounded on his own self-interest as a participating member of the inclusive political community [1987a, p. 9].

He applies this label to an early collaborator and colleague, Gordon Tullock. But he goes on to point out where he himself diverges from this view:

Independently of some emphasis on rules, on constitutional structures, straightforward extensions of economic models of behavior to politics ... offer no basis for constructive reform.... My own efforts have been toward the elaboration and development of what we now call "constitutional political economy," the analysis of alternative structures of rules which constrain man's self-seeking [1987a, p. 10].

To summarize Buchanan's methodological position, despite his central role in the development of public choice, he has never been aggressively positivist, as many of that school are. He has always concerned himself with "what ought to be." A prime example is that he thinks politicians ought to be constrained by a constitution. In the words of the Nobel citation "he has consistently and tenaciously emphasized the significance of fundamental rules and applied the concept of the political system as an exchange process for the achievement of mutual advantages" [Scandinavian Journal of Economics, 1987, p. 3].

If that serves as an outline of how Buchanan thinks about politics, where does the question of balanced budgets fit into his work? Reisman [1990, p. 136], in a major review of Buchanan's political economy, puts it clearly:

> The question of the national debt in particular is assigned by Buchanan a central position at the very crossroads of social experience—at the very spot, in fact, where ethics and economics happen to meet. Obsessive and even excessive though his concern with budgets and deficits may well be, one thing is certain: seldom if ever has so aridly technical a topic been invested with so much moral fervour…the story of public spending without public earning is … the story of how, thanks to "Keynesian apologetics" Victorian moral precepts and "traditional ethical considerations" have been swept aside by an insidious and short-sighted philosophy of "enjoy, enjoy" that is bound ultimately to leave the nation the poorer.

It can safely be taken that the question of balanced budgets has been central in Buchanan's work.

The first major statement of his position can be found in *The Public Principles of Public Debt* [Buchanan, 1958]. He demonstrates "the validity of three basic propositions which are diametrically opposed to those accepted currently by the great majority of economists" [1958, p. 151] namely that:

1.   The primary real burden of a public debt is shifted forward in time.
2.   The analogy between individual or private and public debt holds good in most essential respects.
3.   There is no important conceptual difference between internal and external debt.

The importance of demonstrating these propositions lay in the fact that their opposites had been offered by economists to promote, or to rationalize, the use of debt finance by national governments, as one part of Keynesian economics: public debt, as long as it is internal debt (that is, debt held within the country), only shifts the burden from current taxpayers to current lenders and therefore we are merely lending to ourselves; and public debt is different from individual's debt so that governments are not constrained by the traditional imperative for individuals to balance their budgets.

The essence of his argument is that "the real cost of public expenditure which is debt financed must rest on individuals *other* than those who participate in the social decisions made at the time of the approval or rejection of any proposed expenditure" [Buchanan, 1958, p. 156]. The reason for this is because "the tendency will be for future payments and returns in future periods to be too heavily discounted *in collective decisions*, although this will have *no effect on private decisions*" [p. 162]. However strongly individuals may feel about their living a long life or about their progeny being a part of themselves, they will have a shorter time horizon than required in social decisions, particularly given the absence of markets in individuals' claims on social assets.

As a result, in collective decisions, individuals would prefer to finance short-term projects by public loans because they receive the benefits but they shift the cost to future individuals and /or do not fully capitalize the future taxes payable by themselves. Therefore, according to Buchanan, "the public loan should not be considered to be an appropriate financing method for short-term public expenditure projects" [Buchanan, 1958, p. 158].

But what of long-term public expenditure projects? In principle, his analysis is no different. Individuals do not fully capitalize either the future costs of repaying public debt or the future benefits of the long-term project and we cannot merely assume that the miscalculation on one side offsets that on the other:

> In a very real sense, individuals choosing between a long-term project to be financed by a public loan and no project, are placed in the position of third parties. They are trying to assess the costs to future taxpayers and weigh these against the benefits to future taxpayers and arrive at some decision.... . The subjective evaluation which compares the individualized benefits with the real costs in the tax-expenditure decision is missing [Buchanan, 1958, p. 166–167].

However, he recognizes that:

> long-term public projects do present themselves and their financing cannot be ignored. The best that can be done is to insure that, insofar as individuals try to estimate accurately the future benefits in comparison with future costs, as much information as possible concerning the extent of these future income and payments streams be provided. It becomes essential that some method of financing the debt service and amortization be adopted at *the time of the initial decision* [Buchanan, 1958, p. 167].

Of course this prescription begs the question of how to define a "long-term project." Buchanan has no difficulty with debt financing for "projects which will directly yield to the government a money return sufficient to service and to amortize the debt" [Buchanan, 1958, p. 168]. However he accepts that limiting debt financing to these projects alone would be "overly restrictive" [1958, p. 168]. How could we extend the definition of long-term projects? He rejects the use of "physical form" to distinguish long-term projects from others by arguing that, in the case of a school, both the school building and teachers salaries are "investment" projects and merely by identifying the lasting physical form of the one does not help. Instead, he turns to whether expenditure is abnormal or whether it is recurring. The expenditure on the school building is abnormal because it will not recur; teachers salaries will recur. "Fiscal prudence would seem to suggest that borrowing is inappropriate for the latter type of expenditure but suitable for the former" [1958, pp. 169–170]. Moreover, he argues, borrowing for recurring expenditure would even be inappropriate for recurring capital expenditure because forcing this expenditure to be financed by taxes "will result in less of such expenditure over time than would be the case if such expenditure were to be debt financed, even with the requirement that future taxes must be earmarked for debt service at the time of issue" [1958, p. 170].

Over the years, the arguments offered in *The Public Principles of Public Debt*

[1958] have been reinforced, supplemented and in some cases changed, as might be expected: but throughout, the basic objection to public debt has remained. *Democracy in Deficit* [Buchanan and Wagner, 1977, p. 17] begins with a restatement of this basic objection:

> Resort to borrowing, to debt issue, should be limited to those situations in which spending needs are "bunched" in time owing either to such extraordinary circumstances as natural emergencies or disasters or to the lumpy requirements of a capital investment program. In either case, borrowing should be accompanied by a scheduled program of amortization. When debt is incurred because of the investment of funds in capital creation, amortization should be scheduled to coincide with the useful or productive life of the capital assets … such considerations as these provide the source for separating current and capital budgets in the accounts of governments, with the implication that principles of financing may differ as the type of outlay differs [p. 17].

They continue with an earlier argument that, as we have seen, Buchanan previously rejected:

> These norms incorporate the notion that only the prospect of benefits in periods subsequent to the outlay makes legitimate the postponing or putting off the costs of this outlay [Buchanan and Wagner, 1977, p. 17].

Having offered this restatement, the book concentrates on amplifying Keynesian economics and pointing out what they see as its central weaknesses. They also use the then-current U. S. experience of ever-increasing public budgets and public debt (presented as fundamental problems) to support their argument. What they term "the old-time fiscal religion" [Buchanan and Wagner, 1977, p. 21] of a government balancing its own budget was replaced by using the governmental budget to "balance the economy" [p. 147]. In other words, governmental budget balance or imbalance is determined by national macroeconomic management [p. 147]. This might broadly envisage governmental budget deficits during unemployment to be matched by governmental budget surpluses at full employment. Evidence in the United States at the time of writing was that these surpluses had not emerged. At which point Buchanan and Wagner [1977] can revert to their central argument that this is because individuals in one period, whether voters or politicians with a limited, and short, time horizon to the next election, have economic incentives to postpone the costs of collective decisions.

In the final chapter of the book, the authors offer their own proposals for reform in the U. S. federal government. These proposals differ from the theoretical position offered earlier, perhaps because the practical case being addressed is where public debt already exists and so the prescriptions would have to be tighter to force the ultimate redemption of that debt as well as to forbid deficit budgets.

But before we outline their proposals, it is perhaps worth reporting alternative visions of the future. The most sanguine position they identified is that politicians and voters would begin to behave "responsibly" [Buchanan and Wagner, 1977, p. 173]. Another hopeful position:

... embodies the conviction that the required structural-institutional reforms have been taken, that the Budget Reform Act 1974, when viewed from the vantage point of hindsight in, say, 1990, will be seen as having worked miracles [p. 174].

Buchanan and Wagner [1977] reject both views and instead argue that a "meaningful constitutional norm is required" which will act as "an external and "superior" rule that will allow them to forestall the persistent demands for an increased flow of public-spending benefits along with reduced levels of taxation" [p. 175]. This is essentially required because "[b]udgets cannot be left adrift in the sea of democratic politics" [p. 175].

This constitutional norm should have three qualities [Buchanan and Wagner, 1977, pp. 176].

1. It must be simple and straightforward
2. Politicians and the public must be able readily to discern when the rule is broken.
3. It must reflect and express values held by the citizenry.

This constitutional norm should be governmental budget balance, which should be included as an amendment to the U. S. Constitution [Buchanan and Wagner, 1977, pp. 176–177]. The amendment should take the following form:

1. The president shall be required to present annually to Congress a budget that projects federal outlays equivalent to federal revenues.
2. The Congress, both in its initial budgetary review, and in its subsequent approval, shall be required to act within the limits of a budget that projects federal outlays equivalent to federal revenues. (There is, of course, no requirement that the congressional budget be the same as that submitted by the president.)
3. In the event that projections prove in error, and a budget deficit beyond specified limits occurs, federal outlays shall be automatically adjusted downward to restore projected balance within a period of three months. If a budget surplus occurs, funds shall be utilized for retirement of national debt.
4. Provisions of this amendment shall be made fully effective within five years of its adoption. To achieve an orderly transition to full implementation, annual budget deficits shall be reduced by not less than 20 percent per year in each of the five years subsequent to the adoption of the amendment. Departure from this 20 percent rule for annual adjustment downward in the size of the deficit shall be treated in the same manner as departure from budget balance upon full implementation.
5. Provisions of this amendment may be waived only in times of national emergency, as declared by two-thirds of both houses of Congress, and

approved by the president. Declarations of national emergency shall expire automatically after one year. [Buchanan and Wagner, 1977, p. 180].

Liberty, Market and State [Buchanan, 1986] includes papers that develop this theme. In his paper "The Moral Dimension of Debt Financing," Buchanan adopts "the Hayekian differentiation between culturally evolved codes of conduct and biologically driven instincts" [Buchanan, 1986, p. 192]. The latter includes the instinct to destroy "national capital stock through the debt financing of public consumption" [p. 193] and only by recreating Victorian fiscal morality as an example of the former, can this be stopped. Further he argues that it is "not at all contradictory or inconsistent to recognize that the rules under which we choose may be non-optimal while at the same time behaving within those existing rules in accordance with rational, utility-maximizing norms" [pp. 193–194]. In "Public Debt and Capital Formation" Buchanan [1986] calls again for constitutionally restraining rules and in so doing returns to the problem of defining that part of public capital investment that he feels can legitimately be financed by borrowing. He argues that it is prudent to borrow "only if measurable and realizable income flows are anticipated" [1986, p. 201] on the ground that only then will money be available to pay off the debt. Thus, although a public monument may indeed yield utility throughout its existence, this utility cannot be used to pay off the associated debt. Moreover, he argues that since public investment that does yield measurable and realizable income flows is a relatively small proportion of government spending, "the analytical treatment of all public outlays as current consumption does not seem far off the mark" [1986, p. 201].

"Debt, Demos and the Welfare State" [Buchanan, 1986] similarly calls for constitutional constraints and "Economics on the Deficit" takes economists in general to task for not offering analyses that are relevant to the extant political economy, and calls for the same constitutional constraints; as he does in *The Reason of Rules* [Brennan and Buchanan, 1985, pp. 93–94].

Deficits [Buchanan, Rowley, and Tollison, 1987] is the most current and substantial manifestation of Buchanan's approach to public debt. A book of readings, it offers more than his own views but it is clearly descended from the literature that this paper has synthesized. It has a dedication:

> . . . to those future generations, as yet unborn, who may profit if our counsel is taken seriously and if the principle of budget balance is restored by the democracies.

The Buchanan paper of relevance here is called "Budgetary Bias in post-Keynesian Politics" [Buchanan et. al, 1987]. In this, he restates earlier positions. The reason why Keynesian notions prevailed was because the Victorian fiscal prudence was "aberrant" [p. 183]: it was "artificial and unnatural" [p. 184]. By returning to public profligacy, we were simply giving prominence to our biologically driven instincts. He also gives two sentences that capture his long-held, fundamental position:

The financing of current public consumption by debt issue is unjust because it shifts income from those who are not and cannot be beneficiaries of the outlay and also do not and cannot participate in complex political process that generates the observed results. "Taxation without representation" is literally descriptive of the plight of those who will face the debt-burden overhang in future periods [Buchanan, Rowley, and Tollison, 1987, pp. 188–189].

The blame for budget deficits in democracies since the 1930s is apportioned to Keynesian economics, the most important mistake of which was that it offered advice "to a benevolent despotism that acts always in the 'public interest,' as the latter is defined and formulated by the economists;" then and this serves as a summary of Buchanan's argument:

Public advocacy must always be placed squarely in a political setting, and it must be cognizant of the incentive structure that faces persons in their varying public choosing rules, as voters, as party leaders, as elected politicians, as bureaucrats. The most elementary prediction from public choice theory is that, in the absence of moral or constitutional constraints, democracies will finance some share of current public consumption from debt issue rather than from taxation and that, in consequence, spending rates will be higher than would accrue under budget balance [Buchanan, Rowley, and Tollison, 1987, p. 192].

II. CHALLENGES FOR NATIONAL GOVERNMENTAL ACCOUNTING

It is important, in learning from Buchanan's work, to understand just how radical his perspective is in relation to much of the economics literature. His work directly challenges neo-classical economics. His approach is the antithesis of welfare economics. Macroeconomics, at least when it presumes to offer policy advice, is politically naive. It is hardly surprising that he has remained outside the mainstream.

Moreover, Buchanan's perspective does not sit easily with the thrust of accounting research over the past twenty years or so, which has been primarily empirical. It is true that his work is built on testable propositions about people's behavior and what he would presumably take to be obvious evidence in support. However, not only has he not been concerned with formal testing of his propositions but more important he has always championed his value judgments about what ought to be done as a consequence of this evidence. And the work reviewed here is calling on the preparers of budgets and of budgetary accounts to implement a constitutional amendment whose purpose is to change people's behavior. Contemporary definitions do not see accounting playing this role, only providing information to be used in making decisions.

But it could be argued that it is the contemporary definitions of accounting that are misdirected and that accounting, especially governmental accounting, has always been used primarily to control people's behavior: to encourage them to do what they otherwise would not do or to prevent them from doing what they otherwise would. The last 150 years of local government accounting in the United Kingdom has been interpreted as a way of preventing local politicians postponing to future generations the costs of the programmes they offer to current citizens [Jones, forthcoming]. The accrual basis of accounting and a flow of financial resources measurement focus was used and is used to help to achieve it. The matching principle was and is irrelevant. The primary purpose of governmental accounting is to account for the financial consequences in the period, of the decisions taken during the period [Craner and Jones, 1989].

In other words, it could be argued that Buchanan is calling for accounting to play its traditional role, in the context of national governments. It is to be supposed that, without the constitutional amendment, he would have little faith in the accounting profession to achieve this. Leonard [1985, 1986], who sees the same problem with national governmental accounting as Buchanan, had no faith either. Perhaps it is time for government accountants to begin demonstrating that we can help.

The accounting literature, dominated as it is by the perspective of the accounting profession, has at best under-emphasized and often ignored national governmental accounting. Given the obvious importance of national governments this can seem surprising but it really is not. Professions and government are in competition and the power of the two is asymmetrical: this can most obviously be seen in that the former are products of the latter and what government creates, it can also dissolve.

Given that a national government will set its own "accounting standards," there is the possibility that these will be different, perhaps radically different, from the accounting profession's. With the domination of macroeconomics in a Keynesian setting, accounting for national governments has come to look very different, not least in that, as Buchanan puts it, it is the economy that is being "balanced" not the accounts of the government. Moreover, a macroeconomist would generally prefer cash flow data rather than "transformed" accrual accounting information. It is certainly likely that an accounting perspective would demand different information than the macroeconomist.

It must also be said, given the behavioral role suggested by Buchanan and despite the argument that this has traditionally been an important part of government accounting, there has been little discussion of what form of accrual accounting would best suit this primary purpose. Research is needed into this question.

Buchanan's indictment of deficit financing by national governments begs many important measurement questions that are familiar to accountants who have been concerned with state and local government accounting: the reporting entity, definition of capital, inflation accounting, the measurement focus, and so forth. The challenge Buchanan offers us is to bring our discussions into the context of national government and to reformulate our approaches so that we address a central question: how best to encourage us, as voters and politicians, to do what we otherwise would not do or not to do what we otherwise would.

NOTES

1.   Comprehensive Bibliographies of Buchanan's work are provided by Buchanan [1987b and 1992]. Atkinson [1987] provides a brief synthesis and Reisman [1990] is a fuller synthesis of his work.

REFERENCES

Atkinson, A.B., "James M. Buchanan's Contribution to Economics," *Scandinavian Journal of Economics* 89, 1 [1987], pp. 5–15.

Brennan, G., and J. M. Buchanan, *The Reason of Rules* [Cambridge University Press, 1985].

Buchanan, J. M., "The Pure Theory of Government Finance," *Journal of Political Economy* 57, 6 [1949], pp. 496–505.

———, *Public Principles of Public Debt* [Irwin, 1958].

———, *Liberty, Market and State* [Wheatsheaf, 1986].

———, "The Qualities of a Natural Economist," in *Democracy and Public Choice*, edited by C. K. Rowley [Basil Blackwell, 1987a].

———, "Bibliography of James M. Buchanan's Publications 1949–1986," *Scandinavian Journal of Economics* 89, 1 [1987b], pp. 17–37.

———, "Bibliography of Publications in Public Choice and Economics: 1949 to 1991," in *Research in Governmnetal and Nonprofit Accounting*, Vol. 7 [JAI Press, 1992], pp. 161–191.

Buchanan, J.M., and R.E. Wagner, *Democracy in Deficit* [Academic Press, 1977].

Buchanan, J.M., C.K. Rowley, and R.D. Tollison (eds.), *Deficits* [Basil Blackwell, 1987].

Craner, J., and R. Jones, "Accrual Accounting for National Governments: the Case of Developing Countries," *Research in Third World Accounting* 1 [1989], pp. 103–113.

Jones, R.H., *Scandinavian Journal of Economics* 89, 1 [1987], pp. 1–4. "The Nobel Memorial Prize in Economics 1986."

———, *"The History of the Financial Control of Local Government Accounting in the United Kingdom* [Garland, forthcoming, 1992].

Leonard, H. B., "Measuring and Reporting the Financial Conditions of Public Organisations," *Research in Governmental and Non-profit Accounting* 1 [1985], pp. 117–148.

———, *Checks Unbalanced: the Quiet side of Public Spending* [Basic Books, 1986].

Mueller, D.C., "Public Choice: a Survey," *Journal of Economic Literature* XIV, 2 [June 1976], pp. 395–433.

Reisman, D., *The Political Economy of James Buchanan* [MacMillan, 1990].

BIBLIOGRAPHY OF PUBLICATIONS ON PUBLIC CHOICE AND ECONOMICS: 1949–1991

James M. Buchanan

BOOKS

1. *Prices, Income, and Public Policy* (with C.L. Allen and M.R. Colberg) [New York: McGraw-Hill 1954]. Second edition (1959).
2. *Public Principles of Public Debt* [Homewood, IL: Irwin,1958].
3. *The Public Finances* [Homewood, IL: Irwin, 1960]. Second edition (1965). Translated into Spanish as *Hacienda Publica* (1968). Third edition (1970). Translated into Japanese (1972). Fourth edition (with Marilyn Flowers, 1975). Fifth edition (with M. Flowers, 1980). Sixth edition (with M. Flowers, 1986).
4. *Fiscal Theory and Political Economy* [Chapel Hill: University of North Carolina Press, 1960]. Translated into Turkish (1965). Translated into Japanese (1972).
5. *The Calculus of Consent: Logical Foundations and Constitutional Democracy* (with G. Tullock) [Ann Arbor: University of Michigan Press,

Research in Governmental and Nonprofit Accounting, Vol. 7, pages 159–189.
Copyright © 1992 by JAI Press Inc.
All rights of reproduction in any form reserved.
ISBN: 1-55938-418-2

1962]. Paperback Edition (1965). Translated into Japanese (1979). Translated into Spanish (1980).

6. *Public Finance in Democratic Process* [Chapel Hill: University of North Carolina Press, 1966]. Translated into Japanese (1971). Translated into Spanish (1973).

7. *Demand and Supply of Public Goods* [Chicago: Rand-McNally, 1968]. Translated into Italian (1968). Translated into Japanese (1974).

8. *Cost and Choice: An Inquiry in Economic Theory* [Chicago: Markham Publishing Co., October 1969] (Out of print). This book was reprinted by the University of Chicago Press, Midway Reprint, Chicago (1979). Translated into Japanese (1988).

9. *Academia in Anarchy: An Economic Diagnosis* (with N. Devletoglou) [Basic Books, 1970]. English edition (1971).

10. *Theory of Public Choice: Political Application of Economics* (edited with R. Tollison) [Ann Arbor: University of Michigan Press, 1972].

11. *LSE Essays on Cost* (edited with G.F. Thirlby) [London: Wiedenfeld and Nicholson, 1973]. This book was reprinted and republished by New York University Press for Institute for Human Studies, New York (1981).

12. *The Limits of Liberty: Between Anarchy and Leviathan* [Chicago: University of Chicago Press, 1975]. Translated into Japanese (1977). Translated into Italian (1979). Translated into German (1984).

13. *Democracy in Deficit: The Political Legacy of Lord Keynes* (with R.E. Wagner) [New York: Academic Press,1978]. Translated into Japanese (1979). Translated into Korean (1981).

14. *Freedom in Constitutional Contract: Perspectives of A Political Economist* [College Station: Texas A & M University Press, 1971]. Translated into Italian (1990).

15. *What Should Economists Do?* [Indianapolis, IN: Liberty Press, 1979].

16. *The Power to Tax: Analytical Foundations of a Fiscal Constitution* (with G. Brennan) [New York: Cambridge University Press, 1980]. Translated into German (1988).

17. *Toward a Theory of the Rent-Seeking Society* (edited by J.M. Buchanan, R.D. Tollison, and G. Tullock) [College Station: Texas A & M University Press, 1980].

18. *Theory of Public Choice, II* (edited with R.D. Tollison) [Ann Arbor: University of Michigan Press, 1984].

19. *Liberty, Market, and State: Political Economy in the 1980s* [Brighton, England: Wheatsheaf Books, 1985; New York: New York University Press, 1985].

20. *The Reason of Rules: Constitutional Political Economy* (with G. Brennan) [Cambridge: Cambridge University Press, 1985]. Translated into Japanese (1989).

21. El Analisis Economico De La Politico (with R. McCormick and R. Tollison,

and J.C. Pardo) [Madrid, Spain: Instituto de Estudios Economicos, 1985]. This is a Spanish translation of several previously published pieces incorporated in a single volume.

22. *Deficits* (edited with C. Rowley and R.D. Tollison) [Oxford: Basil Blackwell, 1987].

23. *Economics: Between Predictive Science and Moral Philosophy* (compiled and with a preface by R.D. Tollison and V.J. Vanberg) [College Station: Texas A & M University Press, 1987].

24. *Economica y Politica* [Valencia, Spain: University of Valencia, 1987].

25. *Maktens Graenser* [Stockholm, Sweden: A.B. Timbro, 1988]. Translation of previously published papers in English.

26. *Explorations into Constitutional Economics* (compiled and with a preface by R.D. Tollison and V.J. Vanberg) [College Station: Texas A & M University Press, 1989].

27. *Essays on the Political Economy* [Honolulu, HI: University of Hawaii Press, 1989].

28. *Stato, mercato, e liberta* [Bologna, Italy: Il Mulino, 1989]. This is a selected set of papers in an Italian translation.

29. *James M. Buchanan: Politische Okonomie als Verfassungstheorie* [Political Economy as Constitutional Theory], [Zurich: Bank Hofmann]. This is a special commemorative volume, including several papers in German translation.

30. *The Economics and the Ethics of Constitutional Order* [Ann Arbor: University of Michigan Press, 1991].

31. *Constitutional Economics*, IEA Masters of Modern Economics Series [Oxford: Basil Blackwell, 1991].

MONOGRAPHS

1. *The Inconsistencies of the National Health Service*, Occasional Paper No. 7 [London: Institute of Economic Affairs, 1965].

2. *Public Debt in Democratic Society* (with R.E. Wagner) [Washington, DC: American Enterprise Institute, 1966].

3. *The Organization and Financing of Medical Care in the United States* (with C.M. Lindsay), in *Health Service Financing* [London: British Medical Association, 1970].

4. *Academia in Anarchy: A Summary* [Center for Independent Education, 1970].

5. *The Bases for Collective Action* [New York: General Learning Corporation, 1971].

6. *Natural Liberty and Justice: Adam Smith and John Rawls*, published lecture in C.A. Moorman Series [Culver-Stockton College, 1976].

7. *Tax Reform in Constitutional Perspective* [Beta Gamma Sigma, 1977]. Reprinted in Congressional Record, No. 197, Pt.II [Washington DC: Government Printing Office, December 15, 1977], pp. S-19929–19933.

8. *The Consequences of Mr. Keynes* (with R. Wagner and J. Burton), Hobart Paper 78 [London: Institute of Economic Affairs, 1978]. Italian translation, "La Democrazia e le costituzioni Keynesiani," in *La Scuola di Public Choice*, edited by S. Carrubba and D. da Empoli [Rome: Fondazione Luigi Einaudi, 1979], pp. 217–251.

9. *Monopoly in Money and Inflation: The Case for a Constitution to Discipline Government* (with G. Brennan), Hobart Paper 88 [London: Institute of Economic Affairs, 1981]. Spanish translation, *Monopolio en la emision de dinero e inflacion* [Madrid, Centro de Estudios y Communicacion Economica, 1982].

10. *Constitutional Restrictions on the Power of Government*, the Frank M. Engle Lecture, 1981 [Bryn Mawr, PA: The American College, 1981].

11. *Moral Community, Moral Order, and Moral Anarchy*, the Abbott Memorial Lecture, No. 17 [Colorado Springs: Colorado College, 1981].

12. *Politiek Schuldbesef* [Political Debt Consciousness]. Rotterdamse Monetaries Studies, No. 16, 1984 (issued January 1985), 39 pages. Dutch translation of two unpublished draft papers. [Rotterdam: Erasmus University, 1985].

13. *Staatsschuld en Politiek* [Public Debt and Politics], Rotterdamse Monetaries Studies, No. 18, 1984 [Rotterdam: Erasmus University, 1985].

14. *Une Constitution pour l'Europe: Etats Unis 1787—Europe*, 1990 [Paris Euro 92, 1990]. This is a French translation of "Europe's Constitutional Opportunity" in *Europe's Constitutional Future* [London: Institute of Economic Affairs, 1990], pp. 1–20.

15. *Socialism Is Dead But Leviathan Lives On*, the J. Bonython Lecture. CIS Occasional Paper, 30 [Sydney, Australia: Center for Independent Studies, 1990]. Italian translation, "Il socialismo e finito il Leviatano vive," *Biblioteca della liberta 25* [luglio-settembre, 1990], pp. 3–12.

16. *Technological Determinism Despite the Reality of Scarcity: A Neglected Element in the Theory of Spending on Medical and Health Care* [Little Rock, AK: University of Arkansas Medical School, 1990].

17. *Analysis, Ideology and the Events of 1989* [Zurich: Bank Hofmann AG, 1991].

MAIN PAPERS

1. "Regional Implications of Marginal Cost Rate Making," *Southern Economic Journal* 16 [July 1949], pp. 53–61.

2. "The Pure Theory of Public Finance: A Suggested Approach," *Journal of Political Economy* 57 [December 1949], pp. 496–505.

3. "Federalism and Fiscal Equity," *American Economic Review* 40 [September 1950], pp. 583–599.

4. "Knut Wicksell on Marginal Cost Pricing," *Southern Economic Journal* 17 [October 1951], pp. 173–178.

5. "Federal Grants and Resource Allocation," *Journal of Political Economy* 60 [June 1952], pp. 208–217.

6. "The Pricing of Highway Services," *National Tax Journal* 5 [June 1952], pp. 97–106.

7. "The Theory of Monopolistic Quantity Discounts," *Review of Economic Studies* [June 1953], pp. 199–208.

8. "Social Choice, Democracy, and Free Markets," *Journal of Political Economy* 62 [April 1954], pp. 114–123.

9. "Individual Choice in Voting and the Market," *Journal of Political Economy* 62 [August 1954], pp. 334–343. Spanish translation, "La eleccion individual en las votaciones y en el mercado," in *Hacienda publica espanola* 77 [1982], pp. 322–330.

10. "La methodologie della teoria dell'incidenza: una rassegna critica di recenti contributi american," *Studi ecnomici* 10 [December 1955], pp. 1–25.

11. "Private Ownership and Common Usage: The Road Case Re-examined" *Southern Economic Journal* 22 [January 1956], pp. 305–316.

12. "Ceteris Paribus: Some Notes on Methodology," *Southern Economic Journal* 24 [January 1958], pp. 259–270.

13. "Positive Economics, Welfare Economics, and Political Economy," *Journal of Law and Economics* 2 [October 1959], pp. 124–138.

14. "The Theory of Public Finance," *Southern Economic Journal* 26 [January 1960], pp. 235–238.

15. "Politica economica, libere istituzioni e processo democratico," ["Economic Policy, Free Institutions and Democratic Process"], *Il Politico* 25 [1960], pp. 265–277.

16. "The Evaluation of Public Services" (with F. Forte), *Journal of Political Economy* 69 [April 1961], pp. 107–121.

17. "Simple Majority Voting, Game Theory, and Resource Use," *Canadian Journal of Economics and Political Science* 27 [August 1961], pp. 337–348.

18. "A Pricing Approach to Motor Vehicle Taxation," *Automobilissmo* [October 1961], pp. 1–19.

19. "Politics, Policy, and Pigovian Margins," *Economica* 29 [February 1962], pp. 17–28.

20. "The Relevance of Pareto Optimality," *Journal of Conflict Resolution* 6 [December 1962], pp. 341–354.

21. "Externality" (with W.C. Stubblebine), *Economica* 29 [November 1962], pp. 371–384.

164   JAMES M. BUCHANAN

22. "Perche gratis le strade?," *Mercurio* 5 [October 1962], pp. 32–37.
23. "Easy Budgets and Tight Money," *Lloyds Bank Review* 64 n.s. [April 1962], pp. 17–30. Spanish translation: "Presupuestos faciles y moneda dificil," *Rivista del banco de la republica* Bogota [December 1962], pp. 1411–1519.
24. "The Economics of Earmarked Taxes," *Journal of Political Economy* 71 [October 1963], pp. 457–469.
25. "What Should Economists Do?," *Southern Economic Journal* 30 [January 1964], pp. 213–222. Spanish translation: "Que deberian hacer los economistas?" *Libertas* 1 [October 1984], pp. 117–134.
26. "Are Rational Economic Policies Feasible in Western Democratic Countries?," *Il Politico* 29 [1964], pp. 801–808.
27. "Fiscal Institutions and Efficiency in Collective Outlay," *American Economic Review* 54 [May 1964], pp. 227–235.
28. "Fiscal Choice Through Time: A Case for Indirect Taxation" (with F. Forte), *National Tax Journal* 17 [June 1964], pp. 144–157.
29. "An Economic Theory of Clubs," *Economica* 32 [February 1965], pp. 1–14. *The Bobbs-Merrill Reprint Series in Economics* 68155 (Indianapolis: Bobbs-Merrill).
30. "Ethical Rules, Expected Values, and Large Numbers," *Ethics* 76 [October 1965], pp. 1–13.
31. "Externality in Tax Response," *Southern Economic Journal* 33 [July 1966], pp. 35–42.
32. "Joint Supply, Externality, and Optimality," *Economica* 33 [November 1966], pp. 405–415.
33. "Peak Loads and Efficient Pricing," *Quarterly Journal of Economics* 80 [August 1966], pp. 463–471.
34. "Monetary and Fiscal Policies for Economic Growth in a Free Society" *Il Politico* 31 [1966], pp. 801–807.
35. "Breton and Weldon on Public Goods," *Canadian Journal of Economics and Political Science* 33 [February 1967], pp. 111–115.
36. "Public Goods in Theory and Practice," *Journal of Law and Economics* 10 [1967], pp. 193–197.
37. "Cooperation and Conflict in Public Goods Interaction," *Western Economic Journal* 5 [March 1967], pp. 109–121.
38. "Politics and Science: Reflections on Knight's Critique of Polanyi," *Ethics* 77 [July 1967], pp. 303–310.
39. "Fiscal Policy and Fiscal Preference," *Papers on Non-Market Decision Making* 1 [March 1967], pp. 1–10.
40. "Democracy and Duopoly: A Comparison of Analytical Models," *American Economic Review* 58 [May 1968], pp. 322–331.
41. "A Behavioral Theory of Pollution," *Western Economic Journal* 6 [December 1968], pp. 347–348.

42. "A Public Choice Approach to Public Utility Pricing," *Public Choice* 5 [December 1968], pp. 1–17.
43. "Social Insurance in a Growing Economy," *National Tax Journal* 21 [December 1968], pp. 386–395.
44. "The 'Dead Head' of Monopoly" (with G. Tullock), *Antitrust Law and Economics Review* 1 [Summer 1968], pp. 85–96.
45. "Congestion on the Common," *Il Politico* 33 [December 1968], pp. 776–786.
46. "An Analytical Setting for a Taxpayers' Revolution" (with M. Flowers), *Western Economic Journal* 7 [December 1968], pp. 349–359.
47. "Pragmatic Reform and Constitutional Revolution" (with A. di Pierro), *Ethics* 79 [January 1969], pp. 95–104.
48. "Student Revolts, Academic Liberalism, and Constitutional Attitude," *Social Research* 35 [Winter 1969], pp. 666–680.
49. "A Future of Agricultural Economics," *American Journal of Agricultural Economics* 51 [December 1969], pp. 1027–1036.
50. "Notes on the Economic Theory of Socialism," *Public Choice* 8 [Spring 1970], pp. 29–43.
51. "On the Incidence of Tax Deductibility" (with M. Pauly), *National Tax Journal* 23 [June 1970], pp. 157–167.
52. "In Defense of Caveat Emptor," *University of Chicago Law Review* 38 [Fall 1970], pp. 74–83.
53. "The 'Social' Efficiency of Education," *Il Politico* 25 [Fall 1970], pp. 653–662.
54. "Equality as Fact and Norm," *Ethics* [April 1971], pp. 228–240.
55. "Principles of Urban Fiscal Strategy," *Public Choice* 11 [Fall 1971], pp. 1–16.
56. "The Backbending Supply Curve of Labor: An Example of Doctrinal Retrogression?," *History of Political Economy* 3 [Fall 1971], pp. 383–390.
57. "Violence, Law, and Equilibrium in the Universities," *Public Policy* 19 [Winter 1971], pp. 1–18.
58. "External Diseconomies in Competitive Supply" (with C. Goetz), *American Economic Review* 61 [December 1971], pp. 883–890.
59. "Public Finance and Academic Freedom," *AGB Reports* 14 [January 1972], pp. 9–18.
60. "Efficiency Limits of Fiscal Mobility" (with C. Goetz), *Journal of Public Economics* 1 [1972], pp. 25–43.
61. "Who 'Should' Pay for Common-Usage Facilities?," *Public Finance* 27, 1 [1972], pp. 1–9.
62. "Politics, Property and the Law: An Alternate Interpretation of Miller *et al.*, v. Schoene," *Journal of Law and Economics* 15 [October 1972], pp. 439–452.

63. "The Institutional Structure of Externality," *Public Choice* 14 [Spring 1973], pp. 69–82.
64. "Prospects for America's Third Century," *Atlantic Economic Journal* 1 [Fall 1973], pp. 3–13.
65. "The Coase Theorem and the Theory of the State," *Natural Resources Journal* 13 [October 1973], pp. 579–594.
66. "Good Economics—Bad Law," *Virginia Law Review* 60 [Spring 1974], pp. 483–492.
67. "Political Constraints on Contractual Redistribution," (with W. Bush), *American Economic Review* 64 [May 1974], pp. 153–157.
68. "Gasoline Rationing and Market Pricing: Public Choice in Political Economy" (with N. Tideman), *Atlantic Economic Journal* 2 [November 1974], pp. 15–26.
69. "On Some Fundamental Issues in Political Economy: An Exchange of Correspondence" (with W.J. Samuels), *Journal of Economic Issues* 9 [March 1975], pp. 15–35.
70. "Polluters' Profits and Political Response: Direct Control versus Taxes" (with G. Tullock), *American Economic Review* 65 [March 1975], pp. 139–147.
71. "A Contractarian Paradigm for Applying Economic Theory," *American Economic Review* 65 [May 1975], pp. 225–230.
72. "Utopia, the Minimal State, and Entitlement," *Public Choice* 23 [Fall 1975], pp. 121–126.
73. "Boundaries on Social Contract," *Reason Papers* 2 [Fall 1975], pp. 15–28.
74. "Public Finance and Public Choice," *National Tax Journal* 28 [December 1975], pp. 383–394.
75. "Taxation in Fiscal Exchange," *Journal of Public Economics* 6 [1976], pp. 17–29. Spanish translation: "La tributacion como intercambio fiscal" in *Hacienda Publica Espanola*, No. 56, Madrid, [1979], pp. 337–345.
76. "The Justice of Natural Liberty," *Journal of Legal Studies* 5 [January 1976], pp. 1–16.
77. "A Hobbesian Interpretation of the Rawlsian Difference Principle," *Kyklos* 29 [1976], pp. 5–25.
78. "The Expanding Public Sector: Wagner Squared" (with G. Tullock), *Public Choice* 31 [Fall 1977], pp. 147–150.
79. "Towards a Tax Constitution for Leviathan" (with G. Brennan), *Journal of Public Economics* 8 [December 1977], pp. 255–274. Spanish translation: "Hacia una constitucion fiscal frente al Leviathan," in *Hacienda Publica Espanola* 56 (Madrid) [1979], pp. 346–358.
80. "Markets, States, and the Extent of Morals," *American Economic Review* 68 [May 1978], pp. 364–368.
81. "Tax Instruments as Constraints on the Disposition of Public Revenues" (with G. Brennan), *Journal of Public Economics* 9 [June 1978], pp. 301–

318. Spanish translation: "Los instrumentos tributarios como restricciones sobre la disposicion de los Ingresos Publicos," in *Hacienda Publica Espanola* 56 (Madrid) [1979], pp. 358–369.

82. "Dialogues Concerning Fiscal Religion" (with R. Wagner), *Journal of Monetary Economics* 4 [July 1978], pp. 627–636.

83. "The Potential for Taxpayer Revolt in American Democracy," *Social Science Quarterly* 59 [March 1979], pp. 691–696.

84. "The Logic of Tax Limits: Alternative Constitutional Constraints on the Power to Tax" (with G. Brennan), *National Tax Journal* 32 [June 1979], pp. 11–22.

85. "Constitutional Design and Construction: An Economic Approach," *Economia* (Lisbon, Portugal) 2 [May 1979], pp. 292–314.

86. "Uncertainty, Subjective Probabilities, and Choice" (with A. di Pierro), in *Studi e Richerche*, Scuola Superiore "Enrico Mattei" [Torino: Gialichelli, 1979].

87. "Proportional and Progressive Income Taxation with Utility-Maximizing Governments" (with R. Congleton), *Public Choice* 34 [1979], pp. 217–230.

88. "Cognition, Choice, and Entrepreneurship" (with A. di Pierro), *Southern Economic Journal* 46 [January 1980], pp. 693–701.

89. "Subjective Elements in Rawlsian Agreement on Distributional Rules" (with R. Faith), *Economic Inquiry* 18 [January 1980], pp. 23–38.

90. "Politics Without Romance: A Sketch of Positive Public Choice Theory and Its Normative Implications," Inaugural Lecture, Institute for Advanced Studies, Vienna, Austria, *IHS Journal, Zeitschrift des Instituts für Hohere Studien* 3 [Wien, 1979], B1–B11.

91. "The Logic of the Ricardian Equivalence Theorem" (with G. Brennan), *Finanzarchiv* 38, 1 [1980], pp. 4–16.

92. "Convexity Constraints in Public Goods Theory" (with A. Barbosa), *Kyklos* 33, Fasc. 1, [1980], pp. 63–75.

93. "Resource Allocation and Entrepreneurship," *Statsvetenskaplig Tidskrift* 5 [1980], pp. 285–292.

94. "De las Preferencias Privado a una Filosofia del Sector Publico," *Libertad y Leviathan, Estudios Publico* 1 [December 1980], pp. 201–218. Spanish translation of "From Private Preferences to Public Philosophy: Notes on the Development of Public Choice" in *The Economics of Politics* (London) [1978], pp. 1–20.

95. "The Homogenization of Heterogeneous Inputs" (with R. Tollison), *American Economic Review* 71 [March 1981], pp. 28–38.

96. "Revenue Implications of Money Creation Under Leviathan," *American Economic Review, Proceedings*, 71 [May 1981], pp. 347–351.

97. "Entrepreneurship and the Internationalization of Externality" (with R. Faith), *Journal of Law and Economics* [March 1981], pp. 95–111.

168 JAMES M. BUCHANAN

98. "Der verteilende Staat: Ansaatze zu einer Theorie der Umverteilung" (with
    G. Brennan), *Zeitschrift fuer Wirtschaftspolitik* 30, 2 [1981], pp. 103–128.
99. "Towards a Theory of Yes-No Voting" (with R. Faith), *Public Choice* 37,
    2 [1981], pp. 231–245. Japanese translation, *Japanese Journal of Public
    Choice*, Inaugural Issue; Tokyo, Japan: Keio University, [1982].
100. "La Economia y sus Vecinos Cientificos," *Economia y Ciencia, Estudios
    Publicos* 2 [March 1981], pp. 9–32. Spanish translation of "Economics and
    Its Scientific Neighbors" in *The Structure of Economic Science* edited by S.
    Krupp [Englewood Cliffs: Prentice-Hall, 1966], pp. 166–183.
101. "The Normative Purpose of Economic 'Science': Rediscovery of an
    Eighteenth Century Method" (with G. Brennan), *International Journal of
    Law and Economics* 1 [December 1981], pp. 155–166.
102. "The Related but Distinct 'Sciences' of Economics and Political Economy,"
    British Journal of Social Psychology, Special Issue, *Social Psychology and
    Economics* 21, edited by W. Stroebe and W. Meyer [June 1982], pp. 97–106.
103. "Tax Rates and Tax Revenues in Political Equilibrium: Some Simple
    Analytics" (with D.R. Lee), *Economic Inquiry* 20 [July 1982], pp. 344–354.
104. "Politics, Time, and the Laffer Curve" (with D. Lee), *Journal of Political
    Economy* 90 [August 1982], pp. 816–819.
105. "Order Defined in the Process of Its Emergence," *Literature of Liberty* 5
    [Winter 1982], p. 5.
106. "The Political Ambiguity of Reagan Economics: Marginal Adjustments or
    Structural Shift?" *Journal of Monetary Economics* 10 [November 1982], pp.
    287–296.
107. "Interaccion publica y privada bajo externalidades reciprocas" (with G.
    Tullock), in *Hacienda publica espanola* 77 [1982], pp. 252–270. Spanish
    translation of "Public and Private Interaction Under Reciprocal Externality"
    in *The Public Economy and the Urban Community*, edited by J. Margolis,
    [Resources for the Future, 1965], pp. 52–73.
108. "Monetary Research, Monetary Rules, and Monetary Regimes," *CATO
    Journal* 3 [Spring 1983], pp. 143–146.
109. "Rent-Seeking, Non-Compensated Transfers, and Laws of Secession,"
    Journal of Law and Economics 26 [April 1983], pp. 71–86.
110. "Predictive Power and Choice Among Regimes" (with G. Brennan),
    Economic Journal 93 [March 1983], pp. 89–105.
111. "The Public Choice Perspective," *Economia delle scelte pubbliche* 1
    [January 1983], pp. 7–15.
112. "On Monopoly Price" (with G. Brennan and D. Lee), *Kyklos* 36 [December
    1983], pp. 531–547.
113. "Social Security Survival: A Public Choice Perspective," *CATO Journal* 3
    [Fall 1983], pp. 339–354.
114. "The Ethical Limits of Taxation," *Scandinavian Journal of Economics* 86
    [April 1984], pp. 102–114.

115. "Voter Choice: Evaluating Political Alternatives" (with G. Brennan), *American Behavioral Scientist* 29 [November/December 1984], pp. 185–201.

116. "The Matrix of Contractarian Justice" (with L. Lomasky), *Social Philosophy and Policy* 2 [Autumn 1984], pp. 12–32.

117. "The Moral Dimension of Debt Financing," *Economic Inquiry* 23 [January 1985], pp. 1–6.

118. "Constitutional Democracy, Individual Liberty, and Political Equality," *Jahrbuch fuer neue Politische Oekonomie*, Band 4, [1985], pp. 35–47.

119. "Vote Buying in a Stylized Setting" (with D.R. Lee), *Public Choice* 49, 1 [1986], pp. 3–16.

120. "Organization Theory and Fiscal Economics: Society, State, and Public Debt" (with V. Vanberg), *Journal of Law, Economics, and Organization* 2, 2 [Fall 1986], pp. 215–227.

121. "A Theory of Truth in Autobiography" (with R. Tollison), *Kyklos* 39, Fasc. 4 [1986], pp. 507–517.

122. "Better than Plowing," *Banca Nazionale del Lavoro Quarterly Review* 159 [December 1986], pp. 359–375.

123. "Bibliography," *Scelte Pubbliche* 4 [December 1986], pp. 125–148.

124. "The Economic Consequences of the Deficit," *Scelte Pubbliche* 4 [December 1986], pp. 149–156.

125. "La imposicion coativa en fase constitutiva," *Hacienda Publica Espanola* 100 [1986], pp. 41–55. Spanish translation of "Coercive Taxation in Constitutional Contract," *Explorations into Constitutional Economics*, edited by R. Tollison and V. Vanberg [College Station: Texas A & M University Press, 1989].

126. "Aproximacion de un Economista a la Politica como Ciencia," *Estudios Publicos* 25 [January 1987], pp. 5–16. Spanish translation of "An Economist's Approach to 'Scientific Politics'" in *Coursebook for Economics: Private and Public Choice*, R. Stroup, A. Studenmand, and J. Gwartney [New York: Academic Press, 1976], pp. 34–36.

127. "Towards the Simple Economics of Natural Liberty," *Kyklos* 40 [January 1987], pp. 3–20.

128. "The Incidence and Effects of Public Debt in the Absence of Fiscal Illusion" (with J. Roback), *Public Finance Quarterly* 15 [January 1987], pp. 5–25.

129. "The Constitution of Economic Policy," *American Economic Review* 77 [June 1987], pp. 243–250; and *Science* 236 [June 1987], pp. 1433–1439.

130. "Bibliography," *Scandinavian Journal of Economics* 89 [1987], pp. 17–38.

131. "Tax Reform as Political Choice," *Journal of Economic Perspectives* 1 [Summer 1, 1987], pp. 29–35.

132. "The Economizing Element in Knight's Ethical Critique of Capitalist Order," *Ethics* 98 [October 1987], pp. 61–75.

133. "Secession and Limits of Taxation: Towards a Theory of Internal Exit" (with R. Faith), *American Economic Review* 77, 5 [December 1987], pp. 1023–1031.

134. "Justification of the Compound Republic: The *Calculus in Retrospect*," *CATO Journal* 7 [Fall 1987], pp. 305–312. As "Retrospective on *The Calculus of Consent*," *Citation Classics* 11 [January 1988].

135. "The Gauthier Enterprise," *Social Philosophy and Policy* 5 [Spring 1988], pp. 75–94.

136. "Is Public Choice Immoral? The Case for the 'Nobel' Lie," *Virginia Law Review* 74 [March 1988], pp. 179–189.

137. "Contractarian Political Economy and Constitutional Interpretation," *AEA Papers and Proceedings* 78 [May 1988], pp. 135–139.

138. "Market Failure and Political Failure," *CATO Journal* 8 [Summer 1988], pp. 1–14.

139. "The Politicization of Market Failure" (with V. Vanberg), *Public Choice* 57 [May 1988], pp. 101–113. Translated into Galician as *Revista Galega de economia* (1990), pp. 193–213.

140. "Post-Reagan Political Economy," *Christian Perspectives in Business and Government* 2 [Summer 1988], pp. 1–13.

141. "Rational Choice and Moral Order" (with V. Vanberg), *Analyse & Kritik* 10 [December 1988], pp. 138–160.

142. "Economists and the Gains from Trade," *Managerial and Decision Economics* Special issue [Winter 1988], pp. 5–12.

143. "Interests and Theories in Constitutional Choice" (with V. Vanberg), *Journal of Theoretical Politics* 1 [January 1989], pp. 49–62.

144. "On the Structure of an Economy: A Re-Emphasis of Some Classical Foundations," *Business Economics* 24 [January 1989], pp. 6–12.

145. "A Theory of Leadership and Deference in Constitutional Construction" (with V. Vanberg), *Public Choice* 61 [April 1989], pp. 15–27.

146. "Cartels, Coalitions and Constitutional Politics" (with D. Lee), *Public Choice Studies* 13 [1989], pp. 5–20. (In Japanese).

147. "Reductionist Reflections on the Monetary Constitution," *CATO Journal* 9 [Fall 2, 1989], pp. 295–299.

148. "Nobelity," *Eastern Economic Journal* 15 [October-November 1989], pp. 339–348.

149. "The Domain of Constitutional Economics," *Constitutional Political Economy* 1 [Winter 1990], pp. 1–18.

150. "Economics in the Post-Socialist Century," *Economic Journal* 101 [January 1991], pp. 15-21.

CONTRIBUTIONS TO BOOKS

1. "On a Particular Aspect of Consumption Taxes," translated by J.M. Buchanan in *International Economic Papers* 6 [1956]. This is a translation of M. Fasiani, "Di un particolare aspetto delle imposte sul consumo."

2. "A New Principle of Just Taxation," translated by J.M. Buchanan in *Classics in the Theory of Public Finance*, edited by R.A. Musgrave and A.T. Peacock [London: Macmillan, 1958]. This is a translation of Knut Wicksell, *Finanztheoretische Untersuchungen*. "La scuola italiana di finanze pubblica," in *Il Pensiero Economico Italiano*, 1850–1950, edited by M. Finoia [Bologna: Cappelli, 1980], pp. 203–243. Italian translation of "The Italian Tradition in Public Finance Theory," initially published in *Fiscal Theory and Political Economy: Selected Essays* (Chapel Hill: The University of North Carolia Press, 1960), pp. 24–74. "La Scienza della finanze: The Italian Tradition in Fiscal Theory," in *Altro Polo: Italian Economics, Past and Present*, edited by P. Groenewegen and J. Halevi [Sydney: Frederick May Foundation for Italian Studies, University of Sydney, Australia, 1983], pp. 79–116.

3. "Introduction" to *Public Finances: Needs, Sources and Utilization*. A University-National Bureau of Economic Research Conference [Princeton, NJ: Princeton University Press, 1961], pp. xi–xiv.

4. "Comment on Musgrave and Tiebout Papers," in *Public Finances: Needs, Sources and Utilization* [Princeton, NJ: Princeton University Press, 1961], pp. 122–129.

5. "Predictability: The Criterion for a Monetary Constitution," in *In Search of a Monetary Constitution*, edited by L.B. Yeager [Cambridge, MA: Harvard University Press, 1963], pp. 155–183. Also published in *Money and Finance*, edited by D. Carson [New York: Wiley, 1966], pp. 52–57.

6. "Generalizations from the Experience of Local Communities in the United States Federalism." Paper delivered at Conference on Local Government and the Construction of European Unity (Stresa, Italy, 1961) and published in *Proceedings of Conference* [1963], pp. 375–381.

7. "Staatliche Souveraenitaet, nationale Planung und wirtschaftliche Freiheit" ["National Sovereignty, National Planning, and Economic Freedom"], *ORDO* Band XIV [Duesselldorf: Verlag Helmut Kupper, 1963], pp. 249–258.

8. "Federal Grants and Resource Allocation," in *Perspectives on the Economics of Education*, edited by C.S. Benson [New York: Houghton-Mifflin, 1963].

9. "'La Scienza delle Finanz': The Italian Tradition in Fiscal Theory," in *Public Debt and Future Generations*, edited by J.M. Ferguson [Chapel Hill: University of North Carolina Press, 1964], pp. 47–54.

10. "Concerning Future Generations," in *Public Debt and Future Generations*, edited by J.M. Ferguson [Chapel Hill: University of North Carolina Press, 1964], pp. 55–63.

11. "Public Debt, Cost Theory, and the Fiscal Illusion," in *Public Debt and Future Generations*, edited by J.M. Ferguson [Chapel Hill: University of North Carolina Press, 1964], pp. 150–162.

12. "Public and Private Interaction Under Reciprocal Externality," (with G. Tullock), in *The Public Economy and the Urban Community*, edited by J. Margolis [Resources for the Future, 1965], pp. 52–73.

13. "Foreword" to G. Tullock, *The Politics of Bureaucracy* [Washington, DC: Public Affairs Press, 1965], pp. 1–9.

14. "Critique of the Public Debt," in *Economic Issues and Policies*, edited by A.L. Grey and J.E. Elliott [New York: Houghton-Mifflin, 1965], pp. 185–190.

15. "An Individualistic Theory of Political Process," in *Varieties of Political Theory*, edited by D. Easton [Englewood Cliffs, NJ: Prentice-Hall, 1966], pp. 25–37.

16. "Economics and Its Scientific Neighbors," in *The Structure of Economic Science: Essays on Methodology*, edited by S. Krupp [Englewood Cliffs, NJ: Prentice-Hall, 1966], pp. 166–183.

17. "Social Choice, Democracy, and Free Markets," in *Public Finance: Selected Readings*, edited by H. Cameron and W. Henderson [New York: Random House, 1966], pp. 158–175.

18. "Easy Budgets and Tight Money," in *Monetary Theory and Policy*, edited by R. Ward [International Textbook Co, 1966], pp. 164–177; and in *Readings in Macroeconomics*, edited by Mitchell, Hand, and Walter [New York: McGraw-Hill, 1974] pp. 235–244.

19. "Las Contradicciones del Servicio Medico Nacional," ["The Inconsistencies of the National Health Service"], in *Orientacion Economica* [1966], pp. 22–31.

20. "Frank H. Knight" (biographical article), *International Encyclopedia of the Social Sciences* [1968], pp. 424–428.

21. "Public Debt" in *International Encyclopedia of the Social Sciences* 4 [1968], pp. 28–34; and in *The Federal Deficit*, edited by A.C. Kimmins, *The Reference Shelf* 57, 4 [New York: H.W. Wilson Co., 1985], pp. 11–23.

22. "An Economist's Approach to 'Scientific Politics'," in *Perspectives in the Study of Politics*, edited by M. Parsons [Chicago: Rand McNally, 1968], pp. 77–88.

23. "The Orthodox Model of Majority Rule," in *Public Finance in Canada: Selected Readings*, edited by A.J. Robinson and J. Cutt [Toronto: Methuen Publications, 1968], pp. 60–73.

24. "An Economic Theory of Clubs," in *Economic Theories of International Politics*, edited by B. Russett [Chicago: Markham Publishing Co., 1968], pp. 50–63; in *Readings in Microeconomics*, 2nd ed., edited by W. Breit and H. Hochman [New York: Holt, Rinehart and Winston, 1971], pp. 547–556; in *Externalities, Theoretical Dimensions of Political Economy*, edited by R. Staaf and F. Tannian [New York: Dunellen 1972], pp. 321–333; in *Municipal Expenditures, Revenues, and Services*, edited by W.P. Deatin [New Brunswick, NJ: Center for Urban Policy Research, Rutgers Univer-

sity, 1983], pp. 20–30; and in *The Theory of Market Failure*, edited by T. Cowen [Fairfax, VA: GMU Press, 1988], pp. 193–208.

25. "The Costs of Decision Making," in *Economic Theories of International Politics*, edited by B. Russett [Chicago: Markham Publishing Co., 1968], pp. 455–471.

26. "Can Federal Funds Save Our Cities," in *Our Cities in Crisis: Review and Appraisal*, Proceedings of the Fourth Annual Conference on Economic Affairs [Department of Economics, Georgia State College, Atlanta, Georgia, May 1968], pp. 29–36.

27. "Is Economics a Science of Choice?," in *Roads to Freedom, Essays in Honor of F.A. Hayek*, edited by E. Streissler [London: Routledge & Kegan Paul, 1969], pp. 47–64.

28. "Financing a Viable Federalism," in *State and Local Tax Problems*, edited by H. Johnson [University of Tennessee Press, 1969], pp. 3–19.

29. "Wachstrumsorientierte Geld-und Finanzpolitik in einer freien Gesellschaft" ["Growth Oriented Monetary and Fiscal Policies in a Free Society"], *ORDO* 18 [1969], pp. 299–310.

30. "In Defense of Advertizing Cartels," in *Pubblicita e Televisione* [Rome: RAI, 1969], pp. 84–93.

31. "Ueberfuellung der oeffentlichen Einrichtungen: Ein Argument fuer Staatseingriffe" ["Overcrowding of Public Facilities: An Argument for Political Intervention"], *ORDO* Band 20 [Duesseldorf: Verlag Helmut Kuepper, 1969], pp. 261–276.

32. "Die Bewertung oeffentlicher Leistungen" ["The Evaluation of Public Services"], (with F. Forte), in *Finanztheorie*, edited by C. Recktewold [Koeln, Kiepenheuer and Witsch, 1969], pp. 268–284.

33. "Externality" (with W.C. Stubblebine), in *A. E. A. Readings in Welfare Economics*, edited by K.J. Arrow and T. Scitovsky [Homewood, IL: Irwin, 1969], pp. 199–212; and in *Externalities: Theoretical Dimensions of Political Economy*, edited by R. Staaf and F. Tannian [New York: Dunellen, 1972], pp. 277–290.

34. "The Calculus of Consent," in *Law and the Behavioral Sciences*, edited by S. Macaulay and L.M. Friedman, [Indianapolis, IN: Bobbs-Merrill Co., 1969], pp. 56–75.

35. "Earmarked Taxes," in *Public Finances*, Penguin Book of Readings [London: Penguin, 1969], pp. 292–295.

36. "Internal and External Borrowing," in *Public Finances*, Penguin Book of Readings [London: Penguin, 1969], pp. 338–345.

37. "The Democratic Calculus," in *Frontiers of Democratic Theory*, edited by H.S. Kariel [New York: Random House, Inc., 1970], pp. 78–80.

38. "Public Goods and Public Bads," in *Financing the Metropolis*, edited by J. Crecine, *Urban Affairs Annual*, Vol. 4 [New York: Sage Publications, 1970], pp. 51–71.

39. "Taxpayer Constraints in Educational Finance," in *Economic Factors Affecting the Financing of Education*, edited by Johns-Goffman-Alexander-Stoller, National Education Finance Project, Vol. 2, [Gainesville, FL, 1970], pp. 265–290.

40. "How 'Should' Common-Access Facilities Be Financed?," in *Toward Liberty*, Vol. II, Essays in honor of von Mises [Menlo Park, 1971], pp. 75–87.

41. "Der 'Gesselschafts-politische' Nutzeffekt der Erziehung" ["The 'Sociopolitical' Utility of Education"], in *Der Unternehemer im Ansehen der Welt*, edited by G. Schmolders [Germany, 1971], pp. 57–68.

42. "Das Verhaltnis der Wirtschaftswissenschaft zu ihren Nachbardisziplinen" ["The Relation Between Economics and Its Scientific Neighbors"], in *Gegenstand und Methoden der Nationalokonomie*, edited by R. Jochimsen and H. Knobel [Koln: Kiepenheuer and Witsch, 1971], pp. 88–108.

43. "Ceteris Paribus: Einige Bemerkungen zur Methodologie" ["Ceteris Paribus: Some Remarks on Methodology"], in *Gegenstand und Methoden der Nationalokonomie*, edited by R. Jochimsen and H. Knobel [Koln: Kiepenheuer and Witsch, 1971], pp. 185–196.

44. "Economists, Government, and the Economy," in *Economic Policies in the 1970's. Michigan Business Papers*, No. 57, edited by A.K. Ho [Ann Arbor, MI: Bureau of Business Research, 1971], pp. 1–14.

45. "Politics, Policy and the Pigovian Margins," in *Externalities, Theoretical Dimensions of Political Economy*, edited by R. Staaf and F. Tannian [New York: Dunellen, 1972], pp. 179–190.

46. "External Diseconomies, Corrective Taxes and Market Structure," in *Externalities, Theoretical Dimensions of Political Economy*, edited by R. Staaf and F. Tannian [New York: Dunellen, 1972], pp. 269–272.

47. "External Diseconomies in Competitive Supply" (with C.J. Goetz), in *Kosoku Doro To Jidosha* [Japan, 1972].

48. "A Generalized Economic Theory of Constitutions," in *The Economic Approach to Politics*, edited by R. Frey and B. Frey [Tubingen, Germany: J.C.B. Mohr, 1972], pp. 63–84.

49. "Simple Majority Voting" (with G. Tullock), in *The Economic Approach to Politics*, edited by R. Frey and B. Frey [Tubingen, Germany: J.C.B. Mohr, 1972], pp. 131–145. Also published in *Economic Foundations of Property Law*, edited by B.A. Ackerman [Boston: Little, Brown, 1975], pp. 345–349.

50. "Preliminary Notes on the Samaritan's Dilemma," in *Economic Freedom, Growth, and Stability* [Kalamazoo: Western Michigan University Press, 1972], pp. 15–23.

51. "Laissez-Faire, Locational Patterns, Local Public Finance and National Policy," in *The Family and Rural Community Development*, edited by S.J. Richey [American Home Economics Association, 1972], pp. 13–22.

52. "Comment on Shoup," in *Public Expenditures and Taxation* [New York: National Bureau of Economic Research, 1972], pp. 62–66.

53. "Regole etiche, valori previsti e grandi numeri," in *Economia del benessere d democrazia*, edited by F. Forte and G.E. Mossetto [Milan: Franco Angeli Editore, 1972], pp. 393–410.

54. "Scelta sociale, democrazia, e mercati," in *Economia del benessere e democrazia*, edited by F. Forte and G.F. Mossetto [Milan: Franco Angeli Editore, 1972], pp. 285–300.

55. "Une teoria economica generalizzato delle scelta costituzionali" (with G. Tullock), in *Economia del benessere e democrazia*, edited by F. Forte and G.F. Mossetto [Milan, Franco Angeli Editore, 1972], pp. 617–638.

56. "Regolo di votazione a maggioranza qualificata, rappresentanza, e interdipendenza delle variabili costituzionali" (with G. Tullock), in *Economia del benessere e democrazia*, edited by F. Forte and G.F. Mossetto [Milan: Franco Angeli Editore, 1972], pp. 681–694.

57. "Notes on Irrelevant Externalities, Enforcement Costs and the Atrophy of Property Rights," in *Explorations in the Theory of Anarchy*, edited by G. Tullock [Blacksburg, VA: Center for Study of Public Choice, 1972], pp. 78–86.

58. "Before Public Choice," in *Explorations in the Theory of Anarchy*, edited by G. Tullock [Blacksburg, VA: Center for Study of Public Choice, 1972], pp. 27–37; and in *The Economics of Legal Relationships*, edited by H.B. Manne [St. Paul, MN: West Publishing Company, 1975], pp. 67–77.

59. "Social Choice and Freedom of Inquiry: The Internal and External Institutions for Decision-Making in Higher Education," in *Grenzen der Demokratie? Probleme und Konsequenzen der Demokratisierung von Politik, Wirtschaft und Gesellschaft*, edited by L. Erhard, K. Bruss, and B. Hagemeyer [Dusseldorf: Econ-Verlag GmbH, 1973], pp. 387–406.

60. "In Defense of Organized Crime," in *The Economics of Crime and Punishment*, edited by S. Rottenberg [Washington, DC: The American Enterprise Institute, 1973], pp. 119–132.

61. "Inflation, Progression and Politics," in *The Impact of Economic Growth on Taxation* [Spain, 1973], pp. 45–56.

62. "Public Choice and Public Policy," in *Increasing Understanding of Public Problems and Policies* [Farm Foundation, 1974], pp. 131–136.

63. "Ein Outside Okonom verteidigt Pesek und Saving" ["An Outside Economist Defends Pesek and Savings"], in *Geldtheorie*, edited by K. Brunner, H.G. Monissen, and M.J.M. Neumann [Koln: Kiepenheuer and Witsch, 1974], pp. 150–153.

64. "Who Should Distribute What in a Federal System?," in *Redistribution Through Public Choice*, edited by H. Hochman and G. Peterson [New York: Columbia University Press, 1974], pp. 20–42.

65. "Podatki od zatrudnienia i system uberzoieczen spoleczhych," in *Polityka*

Finansowa w Kapitalizmie, edited by J. Gluchowski [Torun, Poland, 1974], pp. 122–129.

66. "Federalne podatki akcyzowe i transfedowe," in *Polityka Finansowa w Kapitalizmie*, edited by J. Gluchowski [Torun, Poland, 1874], pp. 116–121.

67. "Eine allgemeine okonomische theorie der Verfassung" ["A Generalized Economic Theory of Constitutions"], in *Politische Okonomie des Wohlfahrsstaates: Eine kritische Darstellung der Neuen Politischen Okonomie*, edited by H.P. Widmaier [Frankfurt am Main: Athenaum Taschenbuch Verlag, 1974], pp. 68–87.

68. "The Samaritan's Dilemma," in *Altruism, Morality and Economic Theory*, edited by E.S. Phelps [New York: The Russell Sage Foundation, 1975], pp. 71–85.

69. "The Political Economy of Franchise in the Welfare State" in *Capitalism and Freedom: Problems and Prospects*, edited by R.T. Selden [Charlottesville: University Press of Virginia, 1975], pp. 52–77; and in *The Economics of Legal Relationships*, edited by H.B. Manne [St. Paul, MN: West Publishing Company, 1975], pp. 78–97.

70. "Local Government Expenditures: An Overview" (with M. Flowers), in *Management Policies in Local Government Finance*, edited by J.R. Aronson and E. Schwartz [Washington, DC: 1975], pp. 25–41; and in *Local Government Finance*, edited by J.R. Aranson and E. Schwartz [Washington, DC: International City Management Association, 1981], pp. 25–43.

71. "Inflation and Real Rates of Income Tax" (with J. Dean), in *Proceedings of the 67th Annual National Tax Association Conference on Taxation* [Columbus, OH, 1975], pp. 343–349.

72. "Consumerism and Public Utility Regulation," in *Telecommunications, Regulation and Public Choice* [Lexington, VA: Washington and Lee Press, 1975], pp. 1–22.

73. "Gold, Money, and the Law: The Limits of Governmental Monetary Authority" (with N. Tideman), in *Gold, Money, and the Law*, edited by H.G. Manne and R.L. Miller, [Chicago: Aldine, 1975], pp. 9–70. "Response to Comment," in *Gold, Money, and the Law*, edited by H.G. Manne and R.L. Miller [Chicago: Aldine, 1975], pp. 125–130.

74. "Sources of Government Growth," in *Fiscal Relations in the American Federal System*, Hearings Before Subcommittee of the Government Operations Committee, House of Representatives, 94th Cong., 1st Sess., July 1975 [Washington, DC: U.S. Government Printing Office, 1975], pp. 14–24.

75. "Preface" to *Essays on Unorthodox Economic Strategies: A Memorial Volume in Honor of Winston C. Bush*, edited by A. Denzau and R.J. Mackay [Blacksburg, VA: Center for Study of Public Choice, 1976.]

76. "Political Constraints on Contractual Redistribution" (with W. Bush), in *Essays on Unorthodox Economic Strategies: A Memorial Volume in Honor*

of Winston C. Bush, edited by A.T. Denzau and R.J. Mackay [Blacksburg, VA: Center for Study of Public Choice, 1976], pp. 57–64.

77. "School User Taxes and Economic Efficiency," in *Non-Public School Aid*, edited by E.G. West [Lexington, MA: Lexington Books, 1976], pp. 116–120.

78. "Methods and Morals in Economics: The Ayres-Knight Discussion" in *Science and Ceremony*, edited by W. Breit and W.P. Culberston [Austin: University of Texas Press, 1976], pp. 163–174.

79. "Government Transfer Spending," in *Government Controls and the Free Market: The U.S. Economy in the 1970s*, edited by S. Pejovich [College Station: Texas A & M University Press, 1976], pp. 122–140.

80. "An Economist's Approach to Scientific Politics," in R. Stroup, A. Studenmand, and J. Gwartney, *Coursebook of Economics: Private and Public Choice* [New York: Academic Press, 1976], pp. 34–36.

81. "Social Insurance in a Growing Economy," excerpts from this paper reprinted in *Poverty, Inequality, and the Law*, edited by B. Brudno [St. Paul, MN: West Publishing Co., 1976], pp. 557–558.

82. "Public Goods and Natural Liberty," in *The Market and the State: Essays in Honor of Adam Smith*, edited by T. Wilson and A. Skinner [Oxford: Oxford University Press, 1976], pp. 271–286.

83. "Law and the Invisible Hand," in *Interaction of Economics and Law*, edited by B. Siegan [Lexington, MA: D.C. Heath, 1977], pp. 127–138.

84. "Political Equality and Private Property: The Distributional Paradox," in *Markets and Morals*, edited by G. Dworkin, G. Berwent, and P. Brown [Washington: Hemisphere Publishing, 1977], pp. 69–84.

85. "Why Does Government Grow?," in *Budgets and Bureaucrats*, edited by T. Borcherding [Durham, NC: Duke University Press, 1977], pp. 3–18.

86. "Die Verfassung der Freiheit," in *Zu den Grenzen der Freiheit*, edited by O. Molden [Vienna: Fritz Molden, 1977], pp. 57–67. German translation of "The Constitution of Freedom," plenary lecture presented at Alpbach European Forum [September, 1976].

87. "A Contractarian Perspective on Anarchy," in *Anarchism, Nomos*, 19, edited by J.R. Pennock and J.W. Chapman [New York: New York University Press, 1978], pp. 28–42.

88. "The Political Biases of Keynesian Economics" (with R. Wagner), in *Fiscal Responsibility in Constitutional Democracy*, edited jointly with R. Wagner [Leiden/Boston: Martinus Nijhoff, 1978]. "Los segos politicos de la economia Keynesiana" (with R. Wagner), in *Teoria de la Politica Economica*, edited by A. Casahuga and J. Bacaria [Madrid: Instituto de estudios fiscales, 1984], pp. 735–764.

89. "Contemporary Democracy and the Prospect for Fiscal Control" (with R. Wagner), in *Fiscal Responsibility in Constitutional Democracy*, edited jointly with R. Wagner [Leiden/Boston: Martinus Nijhoff, 1978], pp. 1–9.

178   JAMES M. BUCHANAN

90. "The Justice of Natural Liberty," in *Adam Smith and the Wealth of Nations*, edited by F. Glahe [Boulder: Colorado Associated University Press, 1978], pp. 61–82; in *Adam Smith and Modern Political Economy*, edited by G. O'Driscoll [Ames: Iowa State University Press, 1979], pp. 117–131.

91. "From Private Preferences to Public Philosophy: Notes on the Development of Public Choice" in *The Economics of Politics* [London: Institute of Economic Affairs, 1978], pp. 1–20. "De Las Preferencias Privadas a una Filosofia del Sector Publico," in *Libertat y Leviathan*, edited by H.C. Douglas [Santiago: Estudios Publicos, No. 1, 1980]. "Dalle preference private alla filosofia pubblica," in *Scelte Pubbliche*, edited by S. Carruba and D. da Empoli [Florence: L. Monnier, 1984], pp. 13–36.

92. "Introduction" to W. Mitchell, *The Anatomy of Public Failure* [Los Angeles, CA: International Institute for Economic Research, 1978], pp. 1–3.

93. "Summing Up," in *The Economics of Politics* [London: Institute of Economic Affairs, 1978], pp. 155–158. "The Consequences of Mr. Keynes" (with R. Wagner), in *Solutions to Unemployment*, edited by D.C. Coplander [New York: Harcourt Brace, Jovanovich, 1981], pp. 27–31. "La democrazia e le costituzioni Keynesiane" (with R. Wagner), in *Scelte Pubbliche*, edited by S. Carrubba and D. da Empoli [Florence: L. Monnier, 1984], pp. 115–134.

94. "Tax Reform in Constitutional Perspective," in *Law and Economics*, edited by G. Skogh [Lund: Juridiska Foreningen, 1978], pp. 103–120.

95. "The Economic Constitution and the New Deal," in *Regulatory Change in an Atmosphere of Crisis*, edited by G. Walton [New York: Academic Press, 1979], pp. 13–26.

96. "Constitutional Constraints on Governmental Taxing Power," *ORDO* Band 30 [Stuttgart: Gustav Fischer Verlag, 1979], pp. 334–359; and in *Wirstchaftspolitische Blaetter* Heft, 2 [Vienna, Austria, 1989], pp. 183–193.

97. "A Hobbesian Interpretation of the Rawlsian Difference Principle," in *Economics and Social Institutions*, edited by K. Brunner [Boston: Martinus Nijhoff, 1979], pp. 59–78.

98. "In Defense of Budget Balance," *Congressional Report* 125, 30 [April 1979, No. 51], pp. S-4940–4944.

99. "Sector Publico versus Sector Privado" ["The Public Sector Versus the Private Sector"], in *El Sector Publico en Las Economias de Mercado* [Madrid: Espasa-Calpe, S.A., 1979], pp. 88–100.

100. "Public Choice and Public Finance," in *Public Choice and Public Finance*, edited by K. W. Roskamp [Paris: Editions CUJAS, 1980], pp. 11–18. Proceedings of 34th Congress, International Institute of Public Finance.

101. "Tax Reform Without Tears" (with G. Brennan), in *The Economics of Taxation*, edited by H. Aaron and M. Boskin, [Washington, DC: The Brookings Institution, 1980], pp. 33–54.

102. "Foreword" to T.L. Anderson and P.J. Hill, *The Birth of the Transfer Society* [Stanford, CA: Hoover Institution, 1980].

103. "Resource Allocation and Entrepreneurship," *Statsvetenskaplig Tidskrift*, No. 5 [Lund, Sweden, 1980].

104. "Procedural and Quantitative Constitutional Constraints on Fiscal Authority," in *The Constitution and the Budget*, edited by W.S. Moore and R.G. Penner [Washington, DC: American Enterprise Institute, 1980], pp. 80–84.

105. "Democracia y duopolia," in *Democracia y Economia Politica*, edited by A. Casahuga [Barcelona: Instituto de estudios fiscales, 1980]. (Translation of earlier paper.)

106. "Las Bases de la accion collectiva," in *Democracia y Economia Politica*, edited by A. Casahuga [Barcelona: Instituto de estudios fiscales, 1980].

107. "On Some Fundamental Issues in Political Economy: An Exchange of Correspondence" (with W. Samuels), in *The Methodology of Economic Thought*, edited by W. Samuels [New Brunswick: Transactions Books, 1980], pp. 517–540.

108. "A Governable Country," in *Japan Speaks* [Osaka, Japan: Suntory Foundation, 1981], pp. 1–12.

109. "Rent Seeking and Profit Seeking," in *Toward a Theory of the Rent-Seeking Society*, edited by J. Buchanan, R. Tollison, and G. Tullock [College Station: Texas A & M University Press, 1980], pp. 3–15.

110. "Rent Seeking Under External Diseconomies," in *Toward a Theory of the Rent-Seeking Society*, edited by J. Buchanan, R. Tollison, and G. Tullock [College Station: Texas A & M University Press, 1980], pp. 183–194.

111. "Reform in the Rent Seeking Society," in *Toward a Theory of the Rent-Seeking Society*, edited by J. Buchanan, R. Tollison, and G. Tullock [College Station: Texas A & M University Press, 1980], pp. 359–367.

112. "Federalism and Fiscal Equity," in *The Economics of Federalism*, edited by B.S. Grewal, G. Brennan, and R.L. Mathews [Canberra, Australia: Australian National University Press, 1980], pp. 183–200.

113. "Efficiency Limits of Fiscal Mobility," (with C. Goetz), in *The Economics of Federalism*, edited by B.S. Grewal, G. Brennan, and R.L. Mathews [Canberra, Australia: Australian National University Press, 1980], pp. 71–88.

114. "An Efficiency Basis for Federal Fiscal Equalization," in *The Economics of Federalism*, edited by B.S. Grewal, G. Brennan, and R.L. Mathews [Canberra, Australia: Australian National University Press, 1980], pp. 235–253. Originally published in *Analysis of Public Output*, edited by J. Margolis [New York: National Bureau of Economic Research, 1971], pp. 139–156.

115. "What If There Is No Majority Motion?," in *Toward a Science of Politics: Papers in Honor of Duncan Black*, edited by G. Tullock [Blacksburg, VA: Center for Study of Public Choice, 1981], pp. 79–90.

116. "An American Perspective: From Market to Public Choice" (with G. Tullock), in *The Emerging Consensus: 25 Years of IEA* [London: Institute of Economic Affairs, 1981], pp. 79–98.

117. "Equal Treatment and Reverse Discrimination," in *Social Justice*, edited by R.L. Braham [Boston: Martinus Nijhoff, 1981], pp. 79–94.

118. "Moglichkeiten institutioneller Reformen in Rahmen jultural geformter abstrakter Verhaltregeln" ["Possibilities for Institutional Reform Within Culturally Formed Abstract Rules of Conduct"], in *Evolutionismus oder vertragstheorietischer Konstitutionalismus?* edited by V. Vanberg [Tubingen: J.C.B. Mohr, 1981], pp. 45–48.

119. "The Limit of Taxation," in *The Constitutional Challenge*, edited by M. James [St. Leonards, N.S.W.: Center for Independent Study, 1982], pp. 113–130; in *Taxation: An International Perspective*, edited by W. Block and M. Walker [Vancouver, Canada: Fraser Institute, 1984], pp. 41–54.

120. "Kommentar" ["Commentary"], in *Ethik des Kapitalismus*, edited by P. Koslowski [Tubingen: Mohr, 1982], pp. 69–80.

121. "Democracia Limitada o Ilimitada," in *Conferencia Mont Pelerin, Estudios Publicos*, 6 [Santiago, Chile: Centro de Estudios Publicos, 1982], pp. 37–52.

122. "Foreword" to H. LePage, *Tomorrow, Capitalism* [Lasalle: Open Court, 1982], pp. vii–xi (English translation edition.)

123. "Foreword" to F.H. Knight, *Freedom and Reform* [Indianapolis, IN: Liberty Press, 1982], pp. ix–xiv.

124. "The Domain of Subjective Economics: Between Predictive Science and Moral Philosophy," in *Method, Process, and Austrian Economics: Essays in Honor of Ludwig von Mises*, edited by I. M. Kirzner [Lexington, MA: D.C. Heath, 1982], pp. 7–20.

125. "Barro y el teorema Ricardiano de la equivalencia" ["Barro on the Ricardian Equivalence Theorem"] in *La deuda publica* [Madrid: Instituto de estudios fiscales, 1982], pp. 713–721.

126. "The Tax System as Social Overhead Capital: A Public Choice Perspective on Fiscal Norms," (with G. Brennan), in *Public Finance and Economic Growth*, edited by K. Roskamp [Detroit, MI: Wayne State University Press, 1983], pp. 46–56. (proceedings of 37th Congress of the International Institute of Public Finance, Tokyo, 1981.)

127. "Where Are We on the Laffer Curve?: Some Political Considerations" (with D.R. Lee), in *Supply-Side Economics in the 1980s* [Westport, CT: Quorum Books, for Federal Reserve Bank of Atlanta and Emory University Law and Economics Center, 1982], pp. 193–196.

128. "I limiti alla fiscalita," in *La costituzione fiscale*, edited by A. Martino [Rome: CREA, 1983], pp. 17–34.

129. "The Logic of Tax Limits: Alternative Constitutional Constraints on the Power to Tax" (with G. Brennan), in *Municipal Expenditures, Revenues,*

and Services, edited by W.P. Deatin [New Brunswick: Center for Urban Policy Research, Rutgers University, 1983], pp. 91–111.

130. "Moral Community and Moral Order: The Intensive and Extensive Limits of Interaction," in *Ethics and Animals*, edited by H. Miller and W. Williams [Clifton, NJ: Humana Press, 1983], pp. 95–102.

131. "Constitutional Contract in Capitalism," in *Philosophical and Ethical Foundation of Capitalism*, edited by S. Pejovich [Lexington, MA: Lexington Books, 1983], pp. 65–69.

132. "Normative Tax Theory for a Federal Polity" (with G. Brennan), in *Tax Assignment in Federal Countries*, edited by C. McLure [Canberra: Australian National University Press, 1983], pp. 52–65.

133. "Fairness, Hope, and Justice," in *New Directions in Economic Justice*, edited by R. Skurski [South Bend, IN: University of Notre Dame Press, 1983], pp. 53–89.

134. "The Flat Rate and the Fiscal Appetite," in *New Directions in Federal Tax Policy for the 1980s*, edited by C. Walker and M. Bloomfield [Washington, DC: American Council on Capital Formation, 1983], pp. 314–316.

135. "The Achievement and Limits of Public Choice in Diagnosing Government Failure and in Offering Bases for Constructive Reform," in *Anatomy of Government Deficiencies*, edited by H. Hanusch, [Berlin: Springer-Verlag, 1983], pp. 15–26.

136. "Sources of Opposition to Constitutional Reform," in *Constitutional Economics*, edited by R. McKenzie [Lexington, MA: D. C. Heath, 1984], pp. 21–34.

137. "Rights, Efficiency, and Exchange: The Irrelevance of Transactions Cost," in *Anspruche, Eigentum und Verfugunsrechte* [Berlin: Duncker and Humblot, 1984], pp. 9–24.

138. "Dialogos sobre religion fiscal" ["Dialogues Concerning Fiscal Religion"], (with R. Wagner), in *La economia del deficit publico*, edited by J.J. Fernandex Cainzos [Madrid: Istudios de Estudios Fiscales, 1984], pp. 263–283.

139. "Un paradigma contractario para aplicar la teoria economica," in *Teoria de la Politica Economica*, edited by A. Casahuga and J. Bacaria [Madrid: Istituto de Estudios Fiscales, 1984], pp. 623–634.

140. "Some Simple Analytics of the Laffer Curve" (with D. Lee), in *Public Finance and the Quest for Efficiency*. Proceedings of the 38th Congress of the International Institute of Public Finance, Copenhagen, 1982 [Detroit, MI: Wayne State University Press, 1984], pp. 281–295.

141. "La ricerca di rendite parrassitarie e la ricerca di profitti" ["Rent Seeking and Profit Seeking"], in *Scelte Pubbliche*, edited by S. Carruba and D. da Empoli [Florence: L. Monnier, 1984], pp. 245–260.

142. "The Ethical Limits of Taxation," in *Limits and Problems of Taxation*, edited by F.R. Forsund and S. Honkapohja [London: Macmillan, 1985], pp. 4–16.

143. "Political Economy and Social Philosophy," in *Economics and Philosophy*,

edited by P. Koslowski [Tubingen: J.C.B. Mohr (Paul Siebeck), 1985], pp. 19–36.

144. "Politics and Meddlesome Preferences," in *Smoking and Society*, edited by R. Tollison [Lexington, MA: Lexington Books, 1985], pp. 335–342; and in *Clearing the Air*, edited by R. Tollison [Lexington, MA: D.C. Heath, 1988], pp. 107–116.

145. "First, the Academic Scribblers—Democracy in Deficit: The Political Legacy of Lord Keynes," in *The Federal Deficit*, edited by A.C. Kimmins, *The Reference Shelf*, Vol. 57, No. 4. [New York: H.W. Wilson Co., 1986], pp. 42–54.

146. "Our Times: Past, Present, and Future," in *The Unfinished Agenda* in honor of A. Seldon [London: Institute of Economic Affairs, 1986], pp. 29–38.

147. "The Economic Consequences of the Deficit," in *Symposium on Budget Balance*, edited by C. Cox [Washington, DC: Committee for a Responsible Federal Budget, 1986], pp. 11–18.

148. "Ideas, Institutions, and Political Economy: A Plea for Disestablishment," in *Carnegie-Rochester Series on Public Policy*, Vol. 25, edited by K. Brunner and A. Meltzer [Amsterdam: North Holland: Autumn 1986], pp. 245–258.

149. "Can Policy Activism Succeed?," in *The Monetary versus Fiscal Policy Debate*, edited by R.W. Hafer [Towota, NJ: Rownan and Allenfield, 1986], pp. 139–150.

150. "The Constitution of Economic Policy," Nobel Prize Lecture, 1986, in *Les Prix Nobel* [Stockholm: Almquist and Wicksell International, 1986], pp. 334–343; in *Public Choice Studies* 11 [Tokyo, 1988], pp. 5–12 (in Japanese) and in *Public Choice and Constitutional Economics*, edited by J. Gwartney and R. Wagner [Greenwich, CT: JAI Press, 1988], pp. 103–114.

151. "Government by Red Ink" (with C. Rowley and R. Tollison) in *Deficits*, edited by J. Buchanan, C. Rowley, and R. Tollison [Oxford: Basil Blackwell, 1987], pp. 3–8.

152. "The Ethics of Default," in *Deficits*, edited by J. Buchanan, C. Rowley, and R. Tollison [Oxford: Basil Blackwell, 1987], pp. 361–373.

153. "The Logic of the Ricardian Equivalence Theorem" (with G. Brennan), in *Deficits*, edited by J. Buchanan, C. Rowley, and R. Tollison [Oxford: Basil Blackwell, 1987], pp. 79–92.

154. "Budgetary Bias in Post-Keynesian Politics," in *Deficits*, edited by J. Buchanan, C. Rowley, and R. Tollison [Oxford: Basil Blackwell, 1987], pp. 180–198.

155. "Man and the State," in *Socialism: Institutional, Philosophical, and Economic Issues*, edited by S. Pejovich [Hingham, MA: Kluwer Academic Publishing, 1987] pp. 3–10.

156. "Constitutional Strategy and the Monetary Regime," in *The Search for*

Stable Money, edited by J. Dorn and A. Schwartz [Chicago, IL: University of Chicago Press, 1987], pp. 119–128.

157. "The Qualities of a Natural Economist," in *Democracy and Public Choice* edited by C. Rowley [Oxford: Basil Blackwell, 1987], pp. 9–19.

158. "The Fiscal Constitution," in *The Politics of American Economic Policy Making*, edited by P. Peretz [New York: M.E. Sharpe, 1987], pp. 225–228.

159. "Keynesian Follies," in *The Legacy of Keynes*, edited by D. Reese [New York: Harper and Row, 1987], pp. 130–145.

160. "Introduction" to *The Constitutional Convention*, by J. Bond, D. Engdahl, and H. Butler [Washington, DC: National Legal Center for the Public Interest, 1987], pp. v–vi.

161. "Konstitutionelle Demokratie, individuelle Freiheit, und politische Gleich-berechtigung" ["Constitutional Democracy, Individual Liberty, and Political Liberty"], in *Liberalism als Verjuengungskur*, edited by H. Buhofer [Zuerich: Orell Fussle, 1987], pp. 36–47.

162. "Reform in der Demokratie" [Reform in the Rent-Seeking Society], in *Liberalism als Verjuengungskur*, edited by H. Buhofer [Zuerich: Orell Fussle, 1987], pp. 185–195.

163. "Public Choice and Fiscal Theory," in *Collected Works of Nobel Prize Winners*, Vol. 16 [Seoul, Korea: Korea Economic Daily, 1987] (Korean translation).

164. "The Moral Dimensions of Debt Financing," in *A Nation in Debt*, edited by R. Fink and J. High [Frederick, MD: Maryland University Publication of America, 1987], pp. 102–107.

165. "Constructivism, Cognition, and Value," in *Erkenntnis und Entscheidung*, edited by O. Molden [Vienna: Europaeisches Forum Alpbach, 1987].

166. "Post Reagan Political Economy," in *Christian Perspectives in Business and Government* 2 [Summer 1988], pp. 1–13; also in *Reaganomics and After* [London: Institute of Economic Affairs, 1989], pp. 1–16; and *Constitutional Economics*, IEA Masters of Modern Economics Series [Oxford: Basil Blackwell, 1991], pp. 1–16.

167. "Political Economy: 1957–1982," in *Ideas, Their Origins, and Their Consequences*, Lectures to Commemorate G. Warren Nutter [Washington, DC: American Enterprise Institute, 1988], pp. 115–130.

168. "Justification of the Compound Republic," in *Public Choice and Constitutional Economics*, edited by J. Gwartney and R. Wagner [Greenwich, CT: JAI Press, 1988], pp. 131–138.

169. "Im Wandel begriffene Idee vom Staat" ["The Changing Concept of the State"], in *Wo Regeln Bremsen*, edited by G. Shwarz [Zuerich: Verlag Neue Zuericher Zeitung, 1988], pp. 115–119.

170. "Constitutional Imperatives for the 1990s," in *Thinking About America*, edited by A. Anderson and B. Bark [Stanford, CA: Hoover Press, 1988], pp. 253–264.

171. "The Simple Logic of Free Trade," in *Proceedings of the First Annual Symposium of the Institute for International Competitiveness* [Radford, VA: Radford University, 1988], pp. iii–x.

172. "Tax Reform as Political Choice," in *International Economic Perspectives* 13 [1988], pp. 29–35.

173. "The Work Ethic," in *Competing Through Productivity and Quality*, edited by Y.K. Shetty and V.M. Buehler [Cambridge, MA: Productivity Press, 1988], pp. 55–62.

174. "The Potential and the Limits of Socially Organized Humankind," in *Nobel Laureates Forum in Japan, 1988* [Tokyo: The Yomiuri Shimbun, 1989], pp. 85–94; and in *The Economics and the Ethics of Constitutional Order* [Ann Arbor: University of Michigan Press, 1991], pp. 239–251.

175. "The Simple Economics of the Work Ethic," in *Mt. Pelerin Special Meeting in Taiwan 31 August–2 September 1988, Conference Series, No. 9* [Taipei: Chung-Hua Institute for Economic Studies, 1989], pp. 185–190.

176. "Marktversagen und Politikversagen" ["Market Failure and Political Failure"], in *Individuelle Freiheit und Demokratische Entscheidung* [Tuebingen: J.C.B. Mohr, 1989], pp. 34–47.

177. "The State of Economic Science," in *The State of Economic Science: Views of Six Nobel Laureates*, edited by W. Sichel [Kalamazoo, MI: W. E. Upjohn Institute for Economic Research, 1989], pp. 79–96, and as "The Economy as a Constitutional Order," in *The Economics and the Ethics of Constitutional Order* [Ann Arbor: University of Michigan Press, 1991], pp. 29–41.

178. "Contractarian Presupposition and Democratic Governance," in *Politics and Process*, edited by G. Brennan and L. Lomasky [Cambridge: Cambridge University Press, 1989], pp. 172–182.

179. "Better Than Plowing," in *Recollections of Eminent Economists*, Vol. 2, edited by J.A. Kregel [London: Macmillan, 1989], pp. 279–296; and in *Essays on the Political Economy*, [Honolulu: University of Hawaii Press, 1989], pp. 67–85.

180. "The Potential for Politics After Socialism," in *Geschichte und Gesetz, Europaisches Forum Alpbach 1989*, edited by O. Molden [Vienna: Alpbach Europaisches Forum, 1989], pp. 240–256.

181. "Ricordo di un anno in Italia," introduction to Italian translation *Liberta nel contratto costituzionale* [Milano: Mondadori, 1989], pp. xiii–xxii.

182. "The Evaluation of Public Service" in *Explorations into Constitutional Eonomics*, edited by R.D. Tollison and V.J. Vanberg [College Station: Texas A & M University Press, 1989], pp. 176–193.

183. "A Note on Public Goods Supply," in *Explorations into Constitutional Economics*, edited by R.D. Tollison and V.J. Vanberg [College Station: Texas A & M University Press, 1989], pp. 194–207.

184. "Breton and Weldon on Public Goods," in *Explorations into Constitutional*

Economics, edited by R.D. Tollison and V.J. Vanberg [College Station: Texas A & M University Press, 1989], pp. 208–212.

185. "Fiscal Choice Through Time: A Case for Indirect Taxation?" (with F. Forte), in *Explorations into Constitutional Economics*, edited by R.D. Tollison and V.J. Vanberg [College Station: Texas A & M University Press, 1989], pp. 228–245.

186. "Private Ownership and Common Usage," in *Explorations into Constitutional Economics*, edited by R.D. Tollison and V.J. Vanberg [College Station: Texas A & M University Press, 1989], pp. 344–358.

187. "The Contractarian Logic of Classical Liberalism," in *Liberty, Property, and the Future of Constitutional Development*, edited by E. Paul and H. Dickman [Albany: State University of New York Press, 1990], pp. 9–22, and in *The Economics and the Ethics of Constitutional Order* [Ann Arbor: University of Michigan Press, 1991], pp. 125–135.

188. "Born Again Economist," in *Lives of the Laureates: Ten Nobel Economists*, edited by W. Breit [Cambridge, MA: MIT Press, 1990], pp. 163–180.

189. "Europe's Constitutional Opportunity," in *Europe's Constitutional Future*, [London: Institute of Economic Affairs, 1990], pp. 1–20.

190. "The Budgetary Politics of Social Security," in *Social Security's Looming Surplus: Prospects and Implicatons*, [Washington, DC: AEI Press, 1990], pp. 45–56.

191. "Rational Choice and Moral Order" (with V. Vanberg), *From Political Economy to Economics: And Back?*, edited by J.H. Nichols, Jr. and C. Wright [San Francisco, CA: Institute for Contemporary Studies, 1990], pp. 175–237.

192. "Belief, Choice, and Consequences: Reflections on Economics, Science, and Religion," in *Wege der Vernunft: Feschrift zum siebzigsten Geburtstag von Hans Albert*, edited by A. Bohnen and A. Musgrave [Tubingen: J.C.B. Mohr (Paul Siebeck), 1991], pp. 151–163.

MISCELLANEOUS

1. "A Note on the Different Controversy," *Southern Economic Journal* 17 [July 1950], pp. 59–60.

2. "Rejoinder to Mr. Jenkins," *Journal of Political Economy* 59 [August 1951], pp. 358–359.

3. "Criteria for Government Expenditures," *Journal of Finance* 6 [December 1951], pp. 440–442.

4. "Wicksell on Fiscal Reform," *American Economic Review* 42 [September 1952], pp. 599–602.

5. "Reply to Mr. Scott," *Journal of Political Economy* 60 [December 1952], pp. 536–538.

6.   "Decisions Affecting Economic Growth," *American Economic Review* 415 [May 1954], pp. 228–231.

7.   "Professor Maxwell on Fiscal Equity," *Journal of Finance* 10 [March 1955], pp. 70–71.

8.   "The Capitalization of a General Tax," *American Economic Review* 46 [December 1956], pp. 974–977.

9.   "Internal and External Debt," *American Economic Review* 47 [December 1957], pp. 995–1000.

10. "Saving and the Rate of Interest," *Journal of Political Economy* 67 [February 1959], pp. 79–82.

11. "The Real Debt," *Challenge* 7 [July, 1959], pp. 58–61.

12. "A Regional Countermeasure to National Wage Standardization" (with J. Moes), *American Economic Review* 1 [June 1960], pp. 434–438.

13. "A Note on Public Goods Supply" (with M. Kafoglis), *American Economic Review* 53 [June 1963], pp. 403–414.

14. "Taxation: The Other Side of the Budget," *Newsletter, Joint Council on Economic Education* [November 1963], pp. 1–2, 6.

15. "Economic Analogues to the Generalization Argument" (with G. Tullock), *Ethics* 71 [June 1964], pp. 300–301.

16. "Confessions of a Burden Monger," *Journal of Political Economy* 72 [October 1964], pp. 486–488.

17. "Marshall's Mathematical Note XIX" (with C. Plott), *Economic Journal* 75 [September 1965], pp. 618–620.

18. "A Note on Semantics," *The Exchange* 26 [November 1965], pp. 5–6.

19. "Gains-from-Trade in Votes" (with G. Tullock), *Ethics* 76 [July 1966], pp. 305–306.

20. "The Icons of Public Debt," *Journal of Finance* 21 [September 1966], pp. 544–546.

21. "Voluntary Social Security" (with C. Campbell), *Wall Street Journal* [December 20, 1966], p. 14.

22. "The Optimality of Pure Competition in the Capacity Problem: Comment," *Quarterly Journal of Economics* 80 [1967], pp. 703–705.

23. "What Kind of Redistribution Do We Want?," *Economica* [May 1968].

24. "External Diseconomies, Corrective Taxes, and Market Structure," *American Economic Review* 59 [March 1969].

25. "An Outside Economist's Defense of Pesek and Saving," *Journal of Economic Literature* 7 [September 1969], pp. 812–814.

26. "Political Economy and National Priorities," *Journal of Money, Credit, and Banking* 2 [November 1970], pp. 486–492.

27. "Pareto Optimality, Trade, and Gains-from-Trade: A Comment" (with W.C. Stubblebine), *Economica* 39 [May 1972], pp. 203–204.

28. "Rawls on Justice as Fairness," *Public Choice* 13 [Fall 1972], pp. 123–129.

29. "Reply to Leijonhufvud," *History of Political Economy* 5 [Spring 1973], pp. 266–267.

30. "External Diseconomies in Competitive Supply: Reply" (with C. Goetz), *American Economic Review* 63 [September 1973], pp. 745–748.

31. "Hegel on the Calculus of Voting," *Public Choice* 18 [Spring 1974], pp. 99–101.

32. "Comments on the Landes–Posner Paper," *Journal of Law and Economics* 18 [December 1975], pp. 903–905.

33. "Barro on the Ricardian Equivalence Theorem," *Journal of Political Economy* 83 [April 1976], pp. 337–342.

34. "Adam Smith on Public Choice" *Public Choice* 25 [Spring 1976], pp. 81–82.

35. "A Reply" (with G. Tullock), *American Economic Review* 66 [December 1976], pp. 983–984.

36. "Discussion of Feldstein Paper," in *Income Redistribution*, edited by C. Campbell [Washington, DC: American Enterprise Institute, 1977], pp. 99–101.

37. "Comment on Browning's Paper," in Financing Social Security, edited by C. Campbell [Washington, DC: American Enterprise Institute, 1977], pp. 208–212.

38. "Trying Again to Value a Life" (with R. Faith), *Journal of Public Economics* 12 [October 1979], pp. 245–248.

39. "The Budget Balance Amendment: Statement to the New Hampshire House of Representatives, 2 April 1979," *Congressional Record* [April 4, 1979], p. S–3858.

40. "Comment on Lindsay and McKean Papers," in *The Economics of Non–Proprietary Organizations*, Supplement No. 1, *Research in Law and Economics*, edited by R.O. Zerbe, Jr. [Greenwich, CT: JAI Press, 1980], pp. 234–237.

41. "Interview on Hutt's Role in Economics," *Manhattan Report* 3, 5 [December 1983], pp. 9–10.

42. "Alternative Perspectives on Economics and Public Policy," *Policy Report* 6 [January 1984], pp. 1–5.

43. "Democracy in Deficit," *Manhattan Report* 55 [1984], pp. 6–9.

44. "The Homogenization of Heterogeneous Inputs: Reply" (with R. Tollison), *American Economic Review* 74 [September 1984], p. 808.

45. "Schumpeter as Precursor to Non–Constitutional Public Choice," *Scelte Pubbliche* 1 [1984], pp. 51–53. (Published in 1985, dated 1984.)

46. "On Monopoly Price: Reply" (with D. Lee and G. Brennan), *Kyklos* 38 [1985], pp. 274–275.

47. "Review of R. Heilbroner, *The Nature and Logic Capitalism*," *Wall Street Journal* [October 16, 1985], p. 30.

48. "Review of Herbert Stein, *Presidential Economics*," *Public Choice* 47, 3 [1985], pp. 531–532.

49. "Il vero liberale e l'anti–protezionista," *Corriere della sera* [Milan, Italy] [October 17, 1986], p. 1.

50. "Quest for a Tempered Utopia," *Wall Street Journal* [November 14, 1986].

51. "Comments: The Relevance of Constitutional Strategy," *CATO Journal* 6 [Fall 1986], pp. 513–517.

52. "The Political Economy of the Deficit," *Florida Policy Review* 3 [Summer 1986], pp. 5–10.

53. "Some Remarks on Privatization," *Virginia Law Weekly* 40, 8 [October 1987], pp. 1–6.

54. "Debt–An Economic and Moral Crisis," *IPA Review* (Melbourne, Australia) [May-June 1987], pp. 56–57.

55. "Peut-on Approvoiser La Democratie," *Commentarie* (Paris), 9 [Winter 1986-1987], pp. 673–676.

56. "A Commentary: Liberty, Market, and State," *Economic Impact* 58 [February 1987], pp. 36–40.

57. "Interview," *The Margin* 2, 2 [February 2, 1987], pp. 9–11.

58. "The Deficit and Obligations to Future Generations," *Imprimis* 16 [January 1987], pp. 1–6.

59. "Im Wandel begriffene Idee vom Staat," *Neue Zuericher Zeitung* 29 [December 1987].

60. "Wolnosc ruek panstwo," *Res Publica* 5 (Warsaw: Poland), [1987], pp. 92–95. (In Polish).

61. "Retrospective on *The Calculus of Consent*," *Citation Classics* 11 [January 1988].

62. "The Economic Theory of Politics Reborn," *Challenge* 31 [March–April 1988].

63. "Economic Priorities for the Next President," *Policy Review* 44 [Spring 1988], p. 15.

64. "Reining in the Deficit," *The Owen Manager* 9 [Spring 1988], pp. 27–31.

65. "Interview," *Revista de Occodente* 83 (Madrid, Spain) [April 1988], pp. 120–135.

66. "Consecuencias economicas del estado benefactor," *Libertas* 8, 5 (Buenos Aires, Argentina) [May 1988], pp. 3–14.

67. "Review of R. Sugden, *The Economics of Rights, Cooperation, and Exchange*," in *Economics and Philosophy* 4 [1988], pp. 341–343.

68. "Public Choice Is New, Negligible, and Beyond Mainstream Economics," *Public Choice* 59 [December 1988], pp. 291–293.

69. "The Ethics of Work," *Scholar and Educator* 12 [Fall 1989], pp. 48–51.

70. "Review of Robert Higgs, *Crisis and Leviathan*," *Journal of Economic History* 48 [March 1989], pp. 226–227.

71. "Hayek and the Forces of History," *Humane Studies Review* [Winter 1988-1989], pp. 3–4.

72. "Camelot Will Not Return," *Reason* 20 [January 1989], pp. 36–38.

73. "Shackle and a Lecture in Pittsburgh," *Market Process* 7 [Spring 1989], pp. 2–3.

74. "Message to the Young People," in *Nobel Laureates Forum in Japan, 1988* [Tokyo: The Yomiuri Shimbun, 1989], pp. 130–131.

75. "Comment on Friedman," *National Review* 41 [June 16, 1989], p. 32.

76. "Richard Musgrave, Public Finance, and Public Choice," *Public Choice* 51 [June 1989], pp. 289–292.

77. "A Tale of Two Economies," *Durrell Journal of Money and Banking* 1 [August 1989], pp. 12–15.

78. "The Opportunity Cost of College Education," *Proceedings, AASCU* [1989], pp. 107–112.

79. "Hayek et les Forces de l'Historie" ["Hayek and the Forces of History"], *Journal des Economistes et des Etudes Humaines* [Winter 1989-1990], pp. 181–183.

80. "Hemmnisseund Hindernisse Marktwirtschaftlicher Reformen" ["Obstacles and Impediments to Market-Reform"], *Neue Zuricher Zeitung* [January 27–28, 1990], p. 97.

81. "Awakening the New Leviathan," *The Australian* (Sydney) [March 28, 1990], p. 11.

82. "Constitutional Manifesto," *Monetary Notes* 1 [May 1990], pp. 2–5.

83. "Socialism Is Dead But Leviathan Lives," *Wall Street Journal* [July 18, 1990], p. A8.

84. "L'Europe attend son James Madison," *Le Liberta* 14 (Paris), [July–August 1990], pp. 32–36.

85. "Democrazia e libero Mercato," *Impresa e State* 10 (Milan) [June 1990], pp. 8–13.

86. "Elements d'une constitution pour l'Europe," *Liberte economique, et progres social* 59 [October 1990], pp. 2–14.

87. "Review of S. Levinson, *Constitutional Faith* [Princeton: Princeton University Press, 1988]," *Public Choice* 66, 2 [1990], pp. 196–197.

88. "Review of Helen Boss, *Theories of Surplus and Transfer* [Boston: Unwin Hyman, 1990]," *Constitutional Political Economy* 1 [Spring/Summer 1990], pp. 92–93.

PART III

ABSTRACTS OF DOCTORAL DISSERTATIONS IN GOVERMENTAL AND NONPROFIT ACCOUNTING:

1986 TO 1990

ABSTRACTS

Pendlebury, Maurice Wilson, "An Investigation into the Role and Nature of Management Accounting in Local Government in England and Wales" (University of Wales, United Kingdom, 1986), 295 pp. [Order No. BRDX81187]

Local government is responsible for the provision of a wide range of services of major public importance. Whether measured in terms of total annual expenditure, share of gross domestic product, or number of people employed, it clearly constitutes a significant sector of our economy.

The primary objective of this thesis was to undertake a comprehensive examination of the present role and status of management accounting in providing information for the planning, control, decision-making and performance evaluation of local authorities in England and Wales. The thesis also examines whether changes in recent years in the economic and political climate facing local authorities have resulted in changes in the management accounting systems employed, and whether different management accounting systems are exhibited by different categories of local authority.

The thesis is based on two related research efforts. The first of these involved the use of a questionnaire survey aimed at obtaining a broad picture of current management accounting practices. The second stage was undertaken by means of a series of detailed interviews with the senior finance department staff of a sample of 25 local authorities.

The results of the research show that management accounting in local government is different from its mainstream accounting counterpart. The difficulty of measuring the output of many local authority activities means that the routine control techniques of management accounting are often inapplicable. In reality much of the management accounting emphasis in local government is directed at budget preparation and

Research in Governmental and Nonprofit Accounting, Vol. 7, pages 193–229.
JAI Press Inc.
ISBN: 1-55938-418-2

budgetary control, but even here the research revealed little evidence of a very direct contribution to the planning and control needs of a local authority. However, practices did vary from authority to authority and there was some evidence that changes were beginning to take place.

Nemeh, Ali G., "Operation Auditing Practices In Western Developed Countries: Implications for Government Audit in the State of Kuwait (Volumes I and II)" (University of Strathclyde, United Kingdom, 1986) 652 pp. [Order No. BRD83681]

This research aims at finding out to what extent the new audit techniques (operational auditing, value for money audit . . . etc.), which have been developed by western developed countries and used by their supreme audit institutions to review government activities, could be transferred to developing countries. To be more precise, this study attempts to achieve the following objectives: (1) To study the available literature on the nature and objectives of operational auditing [OA]. (2) To investigate how OA is performed in practice by some western countries (namely Canada, Sweden, the UK and the USA). (3) To determine whether there is a need for introducing OA techniques to the Kuwaiti Public Sector [KPS], and particularly to the Kuwaiti Audit Bureau [KAB]. (4) Finally, to draw-up conclusions and implications for the KAB.

Methods used for compiling and analyzing data have included: (1) Library research; (2) Review of government documents; (3) Fieldwork in UK local and health authorities and in the State of Kuwait; (4) Statistical analysis.

The study revealed that there is no generally accepted definition for operational auditing nor any general agreement on its main components. Furthermore, it confirmed the existence of differences of purpose and scope in the practice of OA investigations in the selected western developed countries (Canada, Sweden, the UK and the USA). The research concludes by identifying implications for the Kuwaiti Audit Bureau and any foreseeable obstacle which could hinder the introduction, or full adoption, of OA techniques in the Kuwaiti public sector. The researcher proposes suggestions and makes recommendations to overcome these impediments.

Babs, Islahudin, "The Role of Auditors in Information Systems Development Applied to the Malaysian Public Sector" (University of East Anglia, United Kingdom, 1988), 452 pp. [Order No. BRDX85342]

Internal auditors' involvement in systems development has been suggested as a means of overcoming control-related problems in computer based systems. One of the rationales given for such involvement is that auditors will ensure that controls are built-in to the applications rather than added on after installation. Thus the concept of internal auditor participation has been widely endorsed in the prescriptive literature. This thesis examines this concept in a specific setting—Malaysian public sector organizations.

This thesis examines the core concepts and issues relating to the idea, viewing them from the organizational perspective and to ascertain its appropriateness to a developing country's environment. It is also meant to complement the work done in the same area but focussing on the procedural and impact frameworks. The concepts and issues identified and clarified in the study as relevant to internal auditor participation are the degree of participation, the status of internal auditor vis-à-vis the systems development team, the role played by the internal auditor, controls and the design of controls, and the control areas to be focussed on by the internal auditors in the consultative participation in the systems development efforts. The organizational aspects of these issues and concepts are drawn out by viewing them in the light of organizational concepts such as status, role, objectives, organizational and management control. The organizational approach adopted allows the study to focus on factors that form the setting in which internal auditors function.

Two surveys and case studies of three organizations were carried out. The findings reveal that there was minimal participation by internal auditors in systems development activities or the overall computerization program in their respective organizations. There appears to be no one looking at control-related aspects of systems. Formal analysis and design of control were not considered as an integral part of the information systems development process. The reasons for this seem to be managerial and organizational in nature. Important issues were the awareness of the need to formally design controls as part of systems development; the need for explicit policies and objectives on controls related issues; the technical skill and experience of internal auditors; the appropriateness of the systems development approach; and the overall conduciveness of the organizational climate. Such issues were shown to be vital for the implementation of the concept of internal auditor participation to help mitigate if not overcome the problems caused by weaknesses in controls in computer-based applications.

Cassidy, Judith Helen, "A Study of the Impact of Medicare Prospective Payment System on Hospital Cost Containment Activities" (Texas Tech University, 1986), 169 pp. Chair: Lane K. Anderson. [Order No. DA8707902]

This study assessed the impact of changing Medicare payment method on hospital cost containment and revenue enhancing activities. The major objectives were to: (1) identify changes in the use of "good" management techniques resulting from changes in Medicare payment method, and (2) determine if Medicare and other hospital characteristics (size, ownership, affiliation with other hospitals, management, occupancy rate, nonpayment rate, and competition) influenced the use of "good" management techniques before and after enactment of the Medicare Prospective Payment System (PPS).

In 1980 the General Accounting Office (GAO) identified management techniques considered effective in controlling costs. This study incorporates those techniques and others the hospital literature suggested were effective in controlling costs and enhancing revenues. Techniques were grouped as: purchasing, energy conservation, general management, and revenue enhancement. The cost containment model suggested that Medicare payment method and other hospital characteristics determine usage of techniques within each category and influence the level of cost containment.

Community hospitals in Texas were studied. Administrators completed a questionnaire about techniques in use and when implemented. Demographic data came from questionnaires and the Texas Hospital Association. Tests of means and proportions identified changes in use of "good" management techniques subsequent to PPS. Discriminant analysis determined the influence of Medicare and other hospital characteristics on use of the techniques before enactment of PPS; regression analysis determined influence after PPS.

The model indicates that PPS provides incentives for cost containment while cost-based payments do not. Study results substantiate the model. The use of "good" management techniques increased significantly after enactment of PPS, but more so in hospitals with a high dependency on Medicare payments. Under cost-based payments, size and affiliation with other hospitals had a greater bearing on technique usage.

Fults, Gail Johnson, "How Participatory Evaluation Research Affects the Management Control Process of a Multinational Not-for-profit Organization" (Claremont Graduate School, 1987) 453 pp. Chairman: Joseph A. Maciariello. [Order No. DA8709291]

Problem. Eleemosynary organizations operate in a non-market environment where no single established indicator of performance, like profit, exist so other indicators of performance are needed. The Financial Accounting Standards Board asserts that service accomplishment elements, particularly measurement of program results, are generally underdeveloped and that research is needed to determine if measures can be developed for accounting information.

For this dissertation, initial research was conducted on one form of evaluation tool—participatory evaluations—to determine if it has the potential to function as a surrogate market and to report service accomplishment for non-for-profit organizations. Three questions were addressed. First, can host communities design and use their own project evaluation plan? Second, can evaluation findings be incorporated into the formal management control system of a multinational, non-for-profit organization? And third, does participatory evaluation provide the benefits attributed to management-by-objectives and self-control in a decentralized organization?

Methodology. A field study was conducted on one multinational, non-for-profit organization which was installing a participatory evaluation process into its development projects. Answers to all three questions were sought from survey data elicited from its employees in thirty-three countries.

Findings. First, the host community members were able to design and use their own project evaluation plan, thereby partially creating an open-system environment.

Second, the information provided by the participatory evaluation process served the needs of project-level management control system of the organization.

Third, the behavioral aspects of management-by-objectives and self-control in decentralized operations were present but the technical aspects were not.

Implication. Internal and external users aid accounting information need a service accomplishment measure to assess project performance. For external reporting, the Standards Board requires a good measure to be both relevant and reliable. This research suggests that participatory evaluation provides relevant data, but further development is needed for it to be considered a useful service accomplishment measure.

Michelman, Jeffrey Eliot, "The Development and Uses of Accounting Information for Managerial Reporting and Control: In a Healthcare Setting" (The University of Wisconsin–Madison, 1987), 408 pp.Supervisor: Mark Anthony Covaleski. [Order No. DA8714735]

This research study examines the interplay between accounting, the organization and the environment. In particular, this research helps to develop a more detailed contextual understanding of the accounting endeavor. The study explores the role of both accounting and accountants through the application of an interpretivist understanding and application of reality. From this perspective, the researcher became immersed in understanding the historical, political, and sociological underpinnings of accounting and healthcare organizational control. The research methods employed included both the examination of archival data and structured interviews. This research should offer new insight into better understanding accounting and the social. Moreover it should help to illuminate the role of accounting in teaching hospitals characterized by highly political environments.

Gupta, Parveen Parkash, "The Audit Process as a Function of Differentiated Environment: An Empirical Study" (The Pennsylvania State University, 1987), 339 pp. Adviser: Mark W. Dirsmith. [Order No. DA8714823]

Generally accepted auditing standards and a number of auditing standard-setting agencies have repeatedly emphasized the importance of proper planning and adequate supervision to the audit process. Planning and supervision, or more broadly, control and coordination have become increasingly important since the scope of auditing has expanded to include evaluation of an organization's operations.

The present study hypothesizes that planning and supervision or control and coordination in an operational audit are a function of four independent variables: audit task characteristics, or audit task complexity; size of the audit team; socio-political environment surrounding an audit, or visibility and political sensitivity of an audit; and cognitive style or tolerance-intolerance of ambiguity of audit team members. To study the impact of these variables on the planning and supervision processes contingency theory framework is used.

Empirical verification of these relationships was examined through a two-phase field study during which the U. S. General Accounting Office (GAO) was the main research site. In phase one of the research, preliminary interviews were conducted with several (GAO) management and staff members to gain a better understanding of the processes involved in an operational audit. Based on the results of phase one, phase two concentrated on developing a questionnaire and administering it to 355 GAO audit supervisors and staff auditors.

Research results indicate that planning and supervision, or control and coordination, in an audit team are indeed shaped by the various independent variables. The bureaucratic and group modes of control are significantly affected by changes in audit task complexity and the cognitive style of auditors. As the size of the audit team increases, the audit team moves more towards the bureaucratic mode of control, but does not change its use of the group mode. The personal mode of control is largely unaffected by changes in these variables and, therefore, is considered a pivotal coordination mechanism. The socio-political environment surrounding an audit does not lead to changes in the bureaucratic and group modes of control. However, further analysis on the components of bureaucratic mode of control reveals that increased visibility of an audit leads to increased reliance on the formal policies and procedures but not on the predetermined audit programs.

Calderon, Darryl Patrick, "The Use of a Formal Review Process on Prospective Financial Statements by Nonprofit Organizations as a Predictor of Effectiveness" (Nova University, 1987), 285 pp. Chairperson: William C. Wall. [Order No. DA8724418]

This study addresses the question of whether there is a benefit to organizations of formal planning/forecasting activities. The dependent variable was measured by the degree the organization changed during the past year, in specified operating dimensions, from the perspective/ perception of its policy-making leaders. The independent variable was measured by the degree of review on the prospective financial statements of the organization; viz, by the actions of the leadership in assuring proper preparation of plans/forecasts. The fundamental research question concerned the benefit of including an independent, objective perspective into the decision making process.

The study was modeled on the noted Grinyer and Norburn study; but, rather than an efficiency measure of performance/benefit, as used in most previous studies, this research study looked into the relationship between planning/forecasting and effectiveness. To do so it focused on the nonprofit sector. Responses were obtained by survey questionnaire from decision makers of 104 nonprofit organizations, including 21 personal interviews. A Spearman correlation analysis was performed to determine the nature of the relationship.

Findings: (1) A strong, positive relationship was found between planning/forecasting and organizational effectiveness, in the nonprofit sector (Rho = + .61). (2) A moderately strong, positive relationship was found between planning/forecasting experience and organizational effectiveness, and between comprehensiveness and complexity of the forecasting model used and organizational effectiveness, in the nonprofit sector. (3) Multiple regression analysis of all variables explained 53% of the total variation in effectiveness. (4) Indepth personal interviews with 21 nonprofit organizations reinforced these findings.

Chang, Stanley Yi, "A Study of the Basic Criteria and Standards by Internal Service Funds" (Texas Tech University, 1987), 200 pp.Chair: Robert J. Freeman. [Order No. DA8724425]

The use of Internal Service Funds in state and local governments is diverse. This precludes interperiod and intergovernmental comparisons, which are important for performance evaluation within and between governmental entities. Further, the lack of definitive standards provides loopholes for inappropriate IS Fund applications.

The purposes of this study were: (1) to evaluate the current "state of the art" of IS Fund practice; (2) to identify major basic "criteria"—factors usually considered by decision makers—for establishing IS Funds; (3) to identify and evaluate the differences in opinions and perceptions regarding the establishment and application of IS Funds among professionals; and (4) to identify, analyze, and support with research findings the important issues that need to be addressed in resolving IS Fund problems.

A research questionnaire was distributed nationally to collect needed information from the professionals. The research participants included 513 governmental accounting standard setters and key finance officers of major cities. Various approaches were used to analyze the data.

Seven "criteria" were found to have been weighted more important than the others in the research respondents' decision-making process. No significant disagreement in opinions was found between standard setters and municipal finance officers on criteria rank assignment or on the general answering pattern. Some demographic variables affected the responses within the municipal finance officers group, however. Several important IS Fund isssues were identified based on the literature analysis—including the review of municipal annual reports—and empirical study findings, and recommendation were made to the Governmental Accounting Standards Board.

Langston, Carolyn Ann Patti, "An Evaluation of the Cost Accounting Procedures for Outpatient Care at a VA Medical Center" (Louisiana Tech University, 1987), 229 pp. [Order No. DA8803377]

Outpatient care is an increasingly important part of the Veterans Administration's role in providing health care for the nation's veterans. The cost effectiveness of outpatient care can only be evaluated using reliable cost data which has been gathered and reported in a manner consistent with accepted cost accounting standards.

The purpose of this study was to increase the usefulness of the Veterans Administration's outpatient care cost information for management and research purposes. The cost accounting procedures used by the Veterans Administration at its Little Rock Medical Center were compared to those prescribed by acceptable cost accounting standards available in the literature. Their adherence to these standards was evaluated, and recommendations for improved allocating and reporting techniques were suggested.

In the first phase of the research, a search of the literature was conducted for cost studies in the health care industry to identify the elements of costs incurred and the problems encountered in using the cost data. The second phase of the research required a survey of the publications of known authoritative sources to assemble relevant cost accounting standards which could be used for evaluation purposes. In the third phase of the study, the flow of cost data through the Veterans Administration's accounting system was documented and the procedures used to gather and report the cost information were examined.

Finally, the procedures prescribed by the accepted standards were compared to those used by the Veterans Administration to asses the likely reliability of the total and unit costs reported for outpatient care.

From the evaluation of the Veterans Administration's application of accepted standards from authoritative sources to the procedures employed for determining the cost of care, it was concluded that the Veterans Administration applies many of the standards in an appropriate manner. Other procedures used by the Veterans Administration, however, seem likely to result in overallocations of costs to some cost centers and activities. When distortions appeared to occur, an attempt was made to suggest alternative procedures which more closely adhered to the accepted standards.

Forgione, Dana Anthony, "Incentives and Performance in the Health Care Industry: The Case of For/non-profit Multihospital Systems" (University of Massachusetts, 1987), 175 pp. Director: Ronald C.Mannino. [Order No. DA8805917]

This study provides improvements upon prior comparative research in assessing the association of real valued hospital financial and operating performance variables with for-profit/non-profit incentive structures, both within the population of multihospital systems and across system/independent hospitals.

A national sample of data under the first year of the Medicare Prospective Payment System was used, alone with a concurrent measure of Medicare case mix. Multivariate Factor Analysis was used to analyze the correlation structure of the variables and provided a 70% reduction in the data set. Twelve major factors of variation were extracted, accounting for 75.3% of the data variance. Multiple Discriminant Analysis was used to assess the marginal relative discriminatory power of both the factors and highest loading raw data variables.

Hospital service production, service volume, and multihospital system size and organizational related factors were found to be significantly associated with managerial incentive groups. The results have implications for assessment by policy makers of the relative merits of for/non profit incentive structures, by providing direction in the identification of managerial decision variables upon which benchmark standards may be established.

Ahn, Tae Sik, "Efficiency and Related Issues in Higher Education: A Data Envelopment Analysis Approach" (The University of Texas at Austin, 1987), 193 pp. Supervisor: Abraham Charnes; William W.Cooper. [Order No. DA8806287]

The purpose of this thesis is to examine Data Envelopment Analysis (DEA) as a potential tool for use in managerial accounting in comparison with other approaches for measuring the efficiency of not-for-profit entities. This study will compare DEA to other techniques in measuring the efficiency of Institutions of Higher Learning (IHLs) in the U. S.

The recent studies by the Select Committee on Higher Education in Texas (SCHE) provided an opportunity to examine different ways of evaluating such performances in a context of practical managerial decision making and policy formulation. By comparing DEA results with those secured from the ratio analysis of the SCHE, DEA was found to be superior not only in raising questions but also in supplying decision aids with accompanying supporting information.

When DEA was applied to doctoral-granting universities in the U. S., the results were compared with the scholarly literature that is now available on regression studies of educational activities. For purposes of our study IHLs were separated into those with and without medical schools. This distinction proved very important in uncovering substantial differences in behavior between the two groups. Contrary to hypotheses suggested in these regression studies, public universities proved more efficient than private universities "on the average." Using concepts from DEA a distinction was drawn between "managerial" and "program" efficiency. Here it turned out that when medical schools are not present private universities' programs are more efficient than public counterpart. In this way new distinctions were made in this study which were not heretofore present in the literature on IHL efficiency.

Another portion of our study dealt with returns-to-scale possibilities which differed markedly (even on the average) between IHLs with and without medical schools. Moreover, analyses by DEA showed marked ranges of variation for returns to scale possibilities for individual IHLs within each group that was concealed by the statistical averaging utilized in these econometric studies.

Recommendations for further research include uses of data for more than a single year and more elaborate tests of the different kinds of models that incorporate the methods and concepts of DEA.

Daniels, Janet DeLuca, "An Investigation of Municipal Financial Report Format, User Preference, and Decision Making" (Boston University, 1988) 282 pp. Major Professor: David Young. [Order No. DA8810224]

The adoption of corporate-style, consolidated financial statements has been advocated by critics of the current, fund-by-fund municipal reporting format. In the past, research to test format preferences had at least one of two limitations. In some cases, subjects were not representative of all users of municipal statements, but were familiar with, and biased toward, a particular practice. In other cases, statements, if included in the study at all, were hypothetical with less complexity than real statements.

This study included subjects from the three user groups identified by the Governmental Accounting Standards Board—citizens, investors/creditors, and legislative/oversight officials. They were given the general purpose financial statements of two, similar-size, Connecticut cities in either the fund-by-fund format (as published, but with names disguised) or the consolidated format. The accompanying survey instrument was tailored to the subject's user group.

Subjects were asked about (1) the usefulness of providing four types of information—compliance, viability, operating performance and cost of services—in statements; (2) the adequacy of the statements in presenting each of the four types of information and (3) the part of the statements most useful in making the decision about adequacy. Subjects also ranked the two cities in terms of financial condition. Since the cities had different bond ratings, the accuracy of the ranking could be determined. Finally, a mean usefulness score was calculated for each format.

Legislative/oversight subjects felt the consolidated format provided more adequate information on cost of services. This information was very useful to them. Also, the mean usefulness score showed the legislative/oversight group judged the consolidated format significantly more useful in assessing overall financial condition.

Format did not affect (1) the part of the statements used to determine adequacy of information, nor (2) the accuracy in ranking the cities for any user group.

Each user group prefers different changes in municipal reporting. Citizens consider neither format satisfactory. They prefer information presented in easy-to-understand written form. Investors/creditors find either format satisfactory. They want additional information included, such as five-year trends. Legislative/oversight officials would welcome a change in format, if a comparison of budget to actual is retained for judging compliance, performance and cost of services.

Surdick, John Joseph, Jr., "An Investigation of the Bond Ratings Assigned to Tax-exempt Hospital Revenue Bonds: An Empirical Model for Not-for-profit Hospitals" (The University of Wisconsin–Madison,1988), 215 pp. Supervisor: Werner G. Frank [Order No. DA8810487]

Tax-exempt revenue bonds are an important financial vehicle for not-for-profit hospitals. An important determinant for access to the capital markets is the bond rating assigned to these revenue bonds. The bond rating obtained by a hospital for its proposed debt issue leads to nontrivial economic consequences for the issuing entity. These health care entities are unique in that they are both business-type enterprises, as well as being not-for-profit charitable organizations.

This empirical study investigated the feasibility of developing a statistical model that would successfully classify hospital tax-exempt revenue bonds according to bond rating categories. The statistical analysis methodology chosen for this purpose was stepwise multiple discriminant analysis. This technique of data analysis is an appropriate vehicle for identifying the independent variables that cause the group to be maximally separated. The initial set of nine independent variables consisted of four income statement based measures, two balance sheet ratios, and three utilization statistics. These variables comprise both accounting and nonaccounting metrics as well as incorporating historical and forecasted measurements.

Discriminant analysis separated the hospitals according to a dependent variable consisting of four predetermined bond rating categories. Further analysis was performed by dichotomizing the dependent variable into two rating categories: (1) those bonds rated as A or above, and (2) those that were rated less than A. For both forms of the dependent variable, a holdout validation procedure was used to compute unbiased estimates of the misclassification rates.

It is concluded that the independent variables that were studied may capture much of what distinguishes one hospital from another, but only when the dependent variable possesses the much coarser two group classification scale. In this case the classification accuracy was quite high. Conversely, much lower accuracy rates were observed for the finer four-group classification model.

Copley, Paul Andrew, "An Empirical Investigation of the Determinants of Local Government Audit Fees" (The University of Alabama, 1987), 167 pp. Chair: Robert W. Ingram. [Order No. DA8810932]

For over a decade the financial reporting practices of local governments have received increased attention. Several studies suggest that there is an association between the quality of financial reporting and the level of audit fees. This study investigates this association by examining the determinants of audit fees for a national sample of city and county governments.

In particular this study draws from previous research in the area of audit pricing to develop a model to explain variation in local government audit fees. Further, the unique nature of the local government environment permitted the examination of several factors relevant to audit pricing that cannot effectively be investigated in the corporate setting. In particular, the effects on audit fees of increased levels of financial disclosure and of state regulation of local government accounting practices were examined.

The results of this study suggest that many of the determinants of corporate audit fees are applicable to the local government sector as well. The most significant of these determinants appear to be government size, factors affecting the auditor cost function, and factors associated with auditor loss exposure. Measures of local government inputs into the accounting system and measures of complexity in a government unit's operations were not found to have a significant association with audit fees.

A significant negative association between audit fees and a state requirement that local government financial statements comply with generally accepted accounting standards was found in some formulations of the model. Significant positive associations were detected between the presence of specific financial reporting practices and local government audit fees. The significant effects were not limited to reporting practices which may simply have been proxying for increased complexity in the local government's operations, but included several practices applicable to most local government entities.

Roberts, Robin Wendell, "Determinants of Auditor Change in the Public Sector" (University of Arkansas, 1987), 135 pp. [Order No. DA8818332]

Because of the role that the auditor plays in monitoring the activities of agents within an organizational environment where moral hazard problems exist, auditor changes should concern society. Specific reasons include (1) the possible economic costs associated with a change, (2) the possible effects of auditor change on auditor independence, and (3) the information the auditor change reveals about the auditing environment.

The purpose of the study was to extend prior auditor change research into the public sector by developing and testing empirically a model of public sector auditor change. Texas independent school districts were used to represent the public sector. Eleven characteristics or events, developed from previous theoretical and empirical research, were hypothesized to be related to public sector auditor change. The hypotheses were classified into three categories representing possible sets of influences on auditor change: (1) the client-auditor relations set of hypotheses, (2) the economic set of hypotheses, and (3) the political set of hypotheses.

Data for the fiscal years August 31, 1982–August 31, 1984, from 87 school districts that changed auditor and 271 school districts that did not change auditor were used to construct a logistic regression model to examine the relationships between auditor change and its hypothesized determinants. The logistic regression model was significant at less than the .0001 level. The model supported three research hypotheses. These hypotheses were that public sector auditor change is related to (1) an independent auditor's report of material internal accounting control weaknesses, (2) an independent auditor's report of school board violations of nepotism, pecuniary interest, or competitive bidding laws, and (3) a change in audit fees.

A conclusion of the study was that the possibility exists for school district officials to use their ability to institute changes in independent auditor to try to avoid the reporting of violations of Texas laws or regulations. Disclosure of the facts surrounding an auditor change by a Texas school district may decrease the possibility that school districts may exercise control over their independent auditor. An additional conclusion was that changes in audit fees are an important component of auditor change research. [Abstract shortened with permission of author.]

Cheng, Rita Hartung, "Toward a Positive Theory of State Government Accounting Disclosure" (Temple University, 1988), 267 pp. Major Adviser: Mary Anne Gaffney. [Order No. DA8902954]

The primary purpose of this dissertation was to develop and test a theory regarding policy choices of state government accounting disclosure. This study is the first to apply a comprehensive study of political markets to an accounting choice. Advances found in the political science and public choice literature were integrated with government accounting research findings in order to model the political environment. Ten theoretical constructs were posited as directly or indirectly affecting accounting disclosure choices: (1) socio-economic development and diversity, (2) interest group strength, (3) political competition, (4) strength of the governor, (5) power of the legislature, (6) debt market influences, (7) press strength, 8) external audit influence, (9) federal government influence, and (10) characteristics of the bureaucracy. The complex relationships among these latent constructs were used to develop a politico-economic causal model to explain accounting disclosure choices.

Several measures of quality of financial accounting disclosure were selected for the analysis. Current disclosure practices, past practices and change in practices from 1978 to 1986 were examined by univariate and multivariate statistical analyses.

Multiple observable indicators for each of the theoretical constructs were specified. LISREL was employed to estimate the parameters for the indicators and structural coefficients and to test the overall fit of the politico-economic model. Empirical support was found for the negative causal effect of socio-economic development on interest group strength, the positive causal relationship of interest group strength on political competition, the negative causal effect of interest group strength on legislative influence/bureaucratic accounting and auditing ability, and the negative causal effect of interest group strength on gubernatorial strength. Political competition was found to have a weak negative causal effect on gubernatorial strength. Several factors were found to positively affect the quality of financial reporting: the power of the governor, legislative influence/bureaucratic accounting and auditing ability, a strong press, and bureaucratic financial ability. Results confirm previous research findings and better explain the agency relationships that comprise the political market and the effect of these relationships on government accounting disclosure. Results are expected to contribute toward the development of a positive theory of state government accounting choices.

Irvine, Richard J., "An Examination of the Effect of the Single Audit Act on Small CPA Firms" (Louisiana Tech University, 1989), 317 pp. Supervisor: James G. Johnston. [Order No. DA89041939]

The problem was a study of how CPA firms were implementing auditing procedures for single audits that were in accordance with professional auditing standards as defined by the GAO and AICPA. Small CPA firms were selected as the research setting because the GAO reported that small CPA firms were more prone to audit quality problems.

A case study and interviews were selected as the methodology for the study. A qualitative study was used because the GAO acknowledged the absence of an absolute measure of audit quality. Ten small CPA firms were selected to participate in the study. Data were collected by questionnaires and by personal interviews. A demographics questionnaire was used to collect data to ascertain that each participating firm met the study's criterion of a small firm. Interview guides were used to collect data related to management practices and auditing procedures for the planning and supervision, internal control, and compliance components of a single audit. Questions used on these data collection instruments were developed from the audit quality control review guides that are used by the Regional Inspectors General in their quality control reviews of audit reports and audit work papers.

The study provided evidence that eight firms had reported audit management practices and audit procedures that appeared to be consistent with professional standards. One of the two remaining firms reported an audit management practice that was considered to be inconsistent with professional standards for the internal control component of a single audit. The tenth firm reported management practices and auditing procedures that were found to be inconsistent with professional standards for all three components of a single audit.

The conclusion of the study was that, given the management objective of maintaining the firms practice in accordance with professional standards, small CPA firms can utilize available sources of information and training to deliver an audit report and compile a set of audit work papers that can pass the audit quality control systems of the Regional Inspectors General.

Matika, Lawrence A., "The Contributions of Frederick Albert Cleveland to the Development of a System of Municipal Accounting in the Progressive Era" (Kent State University, 1988), 146 pp. Director: David F. Fetyko. [Order No. DA8907604]

After the Civil War, America began its first period of great technological advance. In a relatively short period of time, the country changed from a rural, agricultural nation to an urban, industrial one. The inability of nineteenth century society to cope with the problems caused by this transformation led to a protest and reform effort called the Progressive movement.

Political Progressives at the beginning of the twentieth century believed that one of the roots of the social ills in the United States was the corruption and inefficiency of government. Many organizations were formed to combat these problems, and many accountants were involved with these organizations. One of the accountants involved was Frederick Albert Cleveland.

This study examines the contributions of Cleveland to the development of a system of municipal accounting in the Progressive era. He developed the first comprehensive municipal accounting system.

The study concludes that Cleveland was a Progressive leader of the Progressive movement. He fit the accepted definitions of a Progressive and devoted most of his adult life to the advocacy of government reform, public service, and education.

The study also concludes that the accounting systems in use were inadequate, there was a large reform movement that advocated municipal reform, and accountants with adequate resources and expertise were involved in the movement. Given these factors, if Cleveland had not devised his system, some one else would have created an improved system.

The third conclusion of the study is that adoption of Cleveland's system would have helped the Progressives advance their goal of ending corruption, extending popular control, and increasing the influence of government.

The final conclusion of the study is that Cleveland's system constitutes the foundation for contemporary municipal accounting practices. There remains one material difference between Cleveland's system and contemporary practice: Cleveland advocated the use of the accrual basis of accounting, while the modified accrual basis is used today. However, the Governmental Accounting Standards Board is currently reviewing a proposal to require the accrual basis. If this proposal is adopted, there will be no substantive differences between Cleveland's system and contemporary practices.

Nikkhah-Azad, Ali, "Perceptions of College and University Auditors Concerning the Importance of Selected Factors Associated with Operational Auditing" (University of North Texas, 1988), 169 pp. Major Professor: B. Lumsden. [Order No. DA8908929]

The primary purpose of this study was to identify and analyze the perceptions of college and university auditors concerning the importance of selected factors associated with operational auditing. The secondary purpose was to determine whether the perceptions of certified auditors differ significantly from those of noncertified auditors.

Selected factors associated with operational auditing for colleges and universities were categorized in three attribute groups—organizational, personal, and environmental. The identification of organizational and personal attributes was based mainly on concepts set forth in the Standard for the Professional Practice of Internal Auditing published by the Institute of Internal Auditors (1978). Identification of environmental attributes was based on a review of the relevant literature, as well as on discussions with selected college and university auditors. Each attribute, whether categorized as organizational, personal, or environmental, was used as a basis for the identification of detailed factors associated with operational auditing. The findings of this study reveal that factors dealing with organizational attributes were perceived as considerably more favorable than were factors dealing with personal or environmental attributes.

With regard to the secondary purpose of this research, a total of 14 hypotheses were developed and subjected to *t*-tests to determine whether the perceptions of certified auditors differed significantly from those of noncertified auditors. Of the 14 hypotheses tested, there were no significant differences between perceptions of the two groups concerning the importance of independence, audit plan, audit program, audit supervision, continuing education, training, audit follow-up, objectivity, technical competence, experience, and interpersonal skills.

Certified auditors perceived attributes that deal with audit report and professional certification to be more important to operational auditing than did their noncertified counterparts. With regard to the importance of a knowledge and understanding of the higher education environment (i.e., knowledge of characteristics uniquely identifiable with institutions of higher education) to operational auditing, certified auditors perceived this attribute less favorably than did noncertified auditors.

Putman, Robert Lynn, "An Empirical Study of the Impact of Public Law 98-21 on the Financial Operating Environment of United States Hospitals" (Memphis State University, 1988), 176 pp. Major Professor: L. Gayle Rayburn. [Order No. DA8911449]

The purpose of this study was to assess the impact of Public Law 98-21 on hospital cost containment practices and efficiency of operations. Prior to the implementation of the law, hospitals were reimbursed by Medicare based upon a retrospective full-cost plan. This method of reimbursement provided no incentives for hospitals to contain costs or to operate efficiently.

Public Law 98-21, which was enacted in 1982 and implemented October 1, 1983, changed Medicare's reimbursement method to a prospective payment system (PPS). The PPS uses Yale University's case classification system, called Diagnosis-Related Group (DRGs), as a basis for its fixed-fee reimbursements. The plan includes 467 classifications of illnesses and diseases for reimbursement purposes.

The intent of P. L. 98-21 was to encourage hospitals to curb increasing health care costs by rewarding them for effective cost containment and efficiency practices. The two null hypotheses tested in the study were that the enactment and implementation of P. L. 98-21 had no significant impact on; (1) cost containment practices, and (2) efficiency of operations of United States hospitals. The hypotheses were tested for three size categories of hospitals; small (0-100 beds), medium (101-300 beds), and large (greater than 300 beds).

Four cost containment and three efficiency variables from 120 sample hospitals were subjected to a twenty-four year (1964-1987) time series analysis. The Box-Jenkins autoregressive integrated moving average (ARIMA) method was used to test for statistical significance of shifts in the time series in the intervention year, which was assumed to be 1984.

Findings of the study indicate that the law had no significant impact on hospital cost containment practices, but it did significantly affect their efficiency of operations. Results indicate that the implementation of P. L. 98-21 has caused hospitals to become more efficient, primarily through control of personnel costs. The law produced a more salient impact on the efficiency of operations of the smaller and medium-sired hospitals than the large hospitals.

Implications of the study are that P. L. 98-21 has been only partially effective, and that major revisions of the law should be considered.

Martin, Susan Work, "Modeling the Local Government General Fund Deficit" (Michigan State University, 1988), 132 pp. [Order No.DA8912611]

Multiple regression models were estimated to predict the 1981 general fund balances for a set of Michigan local units of government. Six alternative models are estimated from four years of data (1978, 1979, 1980, and 1981). Three single year models using 1978, 1979, or 1980 data are estimated. Three multiple year models using 1978 + 1979, 1979 + 1980, and 1978 + 1979 + 1980 are estimated. Thirty matched pairs of local government's (sixty units) audited financial statement data are used to estimate the model. One unit in each pair had a general fund deficit in 1981, the other had a surplus in that year.

Twenty independent variables were used from the following categories: assets, liabilities, budgetary control, tax base, taxing power, and borrowing.

The estimated single year models achieve a R^2 of 96.9%, 94.2%, and 93.2% for 1980, 1979, and 1978, respectively. When their prediction errors are scaled by local unit size, the single year models produce prediction errors of 94.5%, 84.6%, and 96.1% for 1980, 1979, and 1978, respectively. The multiple year models achieve a R^2 of 93.1%, 91.8% and 91.2% for 1979 + 1980, 1978 + 1979, and 1978 + 1979 + 1980, respectively and size scaled mean prediction errors of 85.3%, 64.2%, and 69.4%, respectively.

Among the independent variables used to estimate the models, the unfunded pension liability and expenditures variance emerge with consistently strong association with the future general fund balance across all six prediction models.

The model estimated with 1978 data (t-3) achieved a prediction error (96.1%) superior to the naive model (93.3%) when predicting the 1982 general fund balance in the hold-out sample with 1979 data. The t-3 model was also the most parsimonious of all six estimated models.

Deis, Donald Ray, Jr., "Toward a Theory of the Role of the Public Sector Audit as a Monitoring Device: A Test Using Texas Independent School Districts" (Texas A & M University, 1988), 98 pp. Chair: Gary A. Giroux. [Order No. DA8913347]

This dissertation investigated the role of the public sector audit as a monitoring device in the political environment in which bureaucratic agents and their sponsors interact. The primary objectives of the study were to determine (1) whether the audit provides evidence of control over information being exercised by bureaucrats, and (2) how the level of auditing demanded is affected by the presence of competing control mechanisms.

The research project used information pertaining to 202 independent school districts in Texas. These districts were split into two samples the largest 102 districts and a random sample of 100 districts. Ordinary least-square regression models were performed to statistically analyze the relationships between (1) the level of school district expenditures and factors modeled to represent a profile of the "median voter," (2) budget and staffing preferences and measures of fiscal, information, and audit complexity, (3) expenditures, the "median voter" profile and proxies for bureaucratic influence, and (4) 1986 audit fees and competing control mechanisms.

The major results of the study indicated that (1) bureaucratic influence is consistently exhibited in the sample of the large school districts, (2) for large school districts the level of audit demanded is affected by the presence of competing control mechanisms, and (3) the results, generally, do not hold for small school districts.

Smith, Carl Stuart, "An Analysis of the Application of Indirect Cost Allocation Methodologies in Higher Education" (The University of Connecticut, 1989), 147 pp. [Order No. DA8915617]

Over the past few years, American colleges and universities have been faced with declining enrollments due in great part to reduced numbers of high school graduates. With the reduced enrollments, financial managers of institutions of higher education have had to deal with determining what cost reduction and cost avoidance programs to adopt or identifying alternative revenue sources. While the evaluation of an academic program's contribution toward the curriculum offerings of a university had always been an inherent function of a university's faculty and administration, the monetary evaluation had not been a problem in the money abundant years of the sixties and early seventies. Thus, many schools were forced, reluctantly, to scrutinize costs and identify new revenue sources in a more comprehensive manner.

In order to evaluate cost-cutting and revenue producing alternatives properly, a financial analysis must be made in order to determine the amount of net cost saved or revenue produced associated with each alternative.

The purpose of this study was to answer the following question: to what extent does full-time equivalent enrollment relate to the utilization of indirect cost allocation methodologies in institutions of higher education?

In this study privately funded institutions listed in the directory of *American Colleges and Universities* with full-time equivalent enrollment of greater than 2,000 students were surveyed. Respondents were asked to indicate whether their institution utilized indirect cost allocation methodologies. The data received was statistically analyzed for significance.

The analysis of this data found that as full-time equivalent enrollment increases more institutions implement indirect cost allocation methodologies.

The study has implications for administrators of institutions of higher education who are contemplating a change in their indirect cost allocation system or implementing such systems.

Davis, Dorothy A., "An Empirical Investigation into Existing Budgeting Practices to Determine Diversity in Interpretations of the Law on Budgeting at the Municipal Level in Mississippi" (Mississippi State University, 1989), 231 pp. Director: Dora Rose Herring. [Order No. DA8917058]

Budgeting for municipalities is a legal part of the accounting process. Legislators in the state of Mississippi, through statutes, determine the process followed including budgeting style, taxing limitations, expenditure level, format, and timing. During the last several years, the specific interpretation of the law by the municipal officials has been a topic of growing interest. The decrease in the level of services while ad valorem taxes are increasing concerns citizens.

This research focuses of the general fund of cities over 7,000 in Mississippi. Comparison of existing budgeting with the law determines specific interpretations by the cities. Additional purposes are identifying potential methods used in collecting and maintaining a reserve along with trends over a period of time.

In Mississippi, the line-item budgeting process allows the taxpayer to see where all funds are spent and is the mechanism used to determine the ad valorem tax levy. Subtracting the estimated expenditures from the estimated beginning fund balance plus all estimated revenues except ad valorem taxes determines the tax levy. Use of this formula prevents cities from collecting any more than necessary for the services provided during the year. Adoption of the budget legally establishes the tax levy. If the elected officials adopt a budget with materially inaccurate forecasts or items omitted, the budget is not fulfilling the original objectives.

Both original budgets and financial statements for four years were gathered from 39 to 41 cities with a population over 7,000 in Mississippi to determine the budgeting practices followed. Analysis indicated that all cities carry a reserve or surplus in the general fund. This reserve appears to be maintained year to year through inaccurate forecasts on the budgets. Generally, revenues are underestimated within 5%, expenditures are overestimated between 5% and 10% and the beginning fund balance is underestimated by more than 100%. There was no evidence to support a relationship between the reserve and population, total revenue, or total expenditures.

Development of a prediction model for reserve was the final analysis phase. Analysis of this model provided further evidence to support the previous conclusions.

Bettner, Mark Steven, "The Effects of Perceived Accounting Competence, Machiavellianism, Past Budgeting Behaviors and Beliefs about the Effectiveness of Past Budgeting Behavior on Budgetary Attitude: An Empirical Analysis" (Texas Tech University, 1988), 138 pp. Chairperson: Donald K. Clancy. [Order No. DA8920935]

The purpose of this study was to examine variables hypothesized to influence budgetary attitude. The variables selected were perceived accounting competence, Machiavellianism, past budgeting behavior, and beliefs about the consequences of past budgeting behavior.

Studies of budgetary attitude have made significant contributions in the area of managerial accounting theory, and have focused on all aspects of the budgeting process. To avoid possible limitations of previous research, two focuses on budgetary attitude were selected for this study. The first focus was on attitudes toward the budget's value as a managerial tool. The second focus was on attitudes toward involvement in budgeting processes.

The subjects in this study were 282 budgeteers of a large state university. The subjects completed and returned a measurement instrument which provided input data pertaining to the study's variables of interest. Tests of the research hypotheses involving these variables were performed using structural equation modeling with LISREL.

Research findings indicate that budgetary attitude is strongly influenced by positive belief concerning the effectiveness of straightforward budgeting behavior. The data also indicate that positive belief concerning the effectiveness of straightforward behaviors are most frequently held by individuals high in perceived competence who have frequently engaged in straightforward budgeting behaviors in the past. Straightforward budgeting behaviors refer to the detailed compilation of accounting information and the formation of unbiased projections regarding resource generation and consumption.

The data do provide strong evidence that high Machiavellian individuals engage heavily in manipulative budgeting behavior, and regard such involvement as being highly effective. However, the data do not support the hypothesis that beliefs about the effectiveness of manipulative behaviors positively influence budgetary attitude. Manipulative behaviors pertain to the political and social aspects of budgetary involvement and do not necessarily require a minimum level of accounting competence.

The general implication of these findings is that increasing perceived accounting competence and directing manipulative behavior toward collaboration would make budgeting processes more effective.

Green, Sharon L., "A Behavioral Investigation of the Effects of Alternative Governmental Financial Reporting Formats on Analysts' Predictions of Bond Ratings" (University of Pittsburgh, 1989), 994 pp. [Order No. DA8921321]

In 1984, the Governmental Accounting Standards Board announced that a complete review of the financial reporting model for governmental entities was a "top priority" item in its initial project agenda. Debate over the appropriate format for governmental financial reports has led to a number of normative assertions that predict that a change in format would affect the usefulness of the reports.

The purpose of the research reported in this dissertation was two-fold: (1) to ascertain whether a change in the format (i.e., load) of current reports would produce the effects predicted by the normative assertions; and (2) if so, to ascertain which specific sources of load (i.e., load within the primary financial statements or load outside the financial statements) were responsible for observed effects.

Eighty-nine experienced municipal analysts participated in the study. Participants were mailed financial reports for two cities and asked to predict the outcome of a Moody's bond rating review for each city. In general, the results did not support the predictions of the normative assertions. However, analysis of significant interactions between the load factors revealed that, under a limited set of circumstances, a change in the format of current reports led to the predicted effects. Specifically, prediction accuracy was significantly increased when statistical, trend data were added to current GAAP-based reports. Prediction time was also significantly increased when the amount of data outside the financial statements was increased. In addition, the financial condition of the city was found to significantly interact with both prediction accuracy and prediction time. Prediction confidence, however, was not significantly affected.

Yuen, Alexander E. C., "The California Experience: An Empirical Study of the Usefulness of Municipal Financial Reports for Newspaper Reporters" (Golden Gate University, 1989), 246 pp. Advisor: Charles F. Vincent. [Order No. DA8923433]

A major strength of American society is a well-informed citizenry. Most citizens rely on the news media, especially newspapers, to keep informed about their city's fiscal condition. California's municipalities publish annual financial reports (AFRs) which average seventy pages and are based on fund accounting principles. These AFRs are not designed for the average citizen or for the newspaper reporter covering the "City Hall beat," who typically does not have a background in financial reporting or governmental accounting.

"Popular" reports are supplemental municipal reports prepared in an understandable format designed for the "man on the street." A questionnaire surveying California newspapers, mailed in the summer of 1987, was based on previous studies (Carlson 1982 and Crain 1978) and attempted to find out which specific disclosures reporters wanted if Californian cities were to publish "popular" reports.

The mail survey, with an overall response rate of 26 percent, indicated that current AFRs prepared by California municipalities are not a major source of information for newspaper reporters. Further, many California newspapers indicated that California municipalities should publish supplemental municipal "popular" reports.

Reporters would like cities to publish quarterly supplemental "popular" reports using charts, graphics, and narratives, and eliminating fund accounting principles. These "popular" reports would illustrate a cash flow statement, a balance sheet, and an operating statement that the average citizen and newspaper reporter could understand and use.

Alrawi, Hikmat Ahmad Abdulghafoor, "Accounting, Resource Allocation, Planning and Efficiency: Case Studies of the United Kingdom and Iraqi Universities" (University of Hull, United Kingdom, 1988), 702 pp. [Order No. DA8924054]

This study investigates the accounting, resource allocation, planning and efficiency of UK and Iraqi universities, concentrating on the efficiency with which universities manage their resource allocation in practice, which is seen in relation to university funding, goals and objectives, and governance. It evaluates financial planning and fund monitoring in UK and Iraqi universities in order to identify ways of improving their efficiency in these areas. In addition, a comparison is made between the two systems in terms of the efficiency or otherwise of their accounting and resource allocation. [Abstract shortened with permission of author.]

Lawrence, Carol Martin, "The Effect of Accounting System Type and Ownership Structure on Hospital Costs" (Indiana University, 1989),197 pp. Chair: Robert W. Parry, Jr. [Order No. DA8925155]

The purpose of this study is to investigate the impact of a hospital's for-profit/non-profit status and the nature of its accounting system on operating costs. A series of cross-sectional regression models is used in which the dependent variables are measures of hospital operating costs, including total cost per case, nursing cost per case, personnel cost per case, and capital cost per case. Independent variables represent the type of accounting system used by the hospital and its for-profit/non-profit status. Additional independent variables are included to control for other factors which are expected to affect hospital operating costs, including size, membership in a multi-hospital system, cost of living, case mix, competition, regulation, and teaching status.

The regression results indicate that for-profit status is associated with higher total cost per case, higher nursing cost per case, and higher capital cost per case. The use of an innovative accounting system is associated with higher capital costs but does not affect other cost measures. The research findings do not support the theoretical prediction that for-profit hospitals will be more efficient. The findings on the impact of innovative accounting systems suggest that the interaction of the characteristics of the host organization and the features of the system affects the effectiveness of the system.

Brannan, Rodger Lloyd, "The Single Audit Act of 1984: An Examination of the Audit Process in the Government Sector" (University of Nebraska at Lincoln, 1989), 222 pp. Advisor: James F. Brown, Jr. [Order No. DA8925229]

The Single Audit Act of 1984 (SAA) was designed to improve the quality of financial management in government entities which receive federal financial aid. Many members of Congress felt there was a real need to improve the systems of control in these affected units of government. However, the ultimate goal was to improve the incidence or quality of compliance. It is through compliance that legislators and administrators alike control the expenditure process. The audit is an integral part of the control process. Without the audit there can be no verification of compliance and the legislative and political process is undone. The Single Audit Act was implemented to bring a greater degree of control over the federal expenditure process.

This study examines if compliance has indeed improved under the SAA and what factors have caused this change in control. The audit is viewed as a vehicle to bring about behavioral changes in affected individuals. In this instance the question is whether or not the SAA has moved managers to improve control and consequently compliance.

The study consists of a survey which tapped the perceptions of highly qualified individuals who work with the SAA on a day to day basis. The results indicate that compliance has improved. Furthermore if one looks at the characteristics and qualifications of the individuals surveyed their perceptions seem highly credible. The analysis also revealed that the full model was a highly significant predictor of compliance. Unfortunately not all of the variables in the model were significant predictors. The study also revealed that the respondents had differing perceptions concerning the working of the SAA depending on their place or level of employment.

The study showed that the SAA has been successful in improving the incidence of compliance. However, individual factors may need to be emphasized by those who supervise the process to improve control even more. Although this research was not intended as a direct test of theory, the results provided empirical evidence as to the validity of the normative assertions. In addition, important information has been provided about the potential effects of a change in the format of current reports as an outcome of the GASB review.

Langsam, Sheldon Allen, "The Effect of Mandatory Inclusion of Component Units on the Reported Financial Condition of Selected Local Governmental Units" (University of Arkansas, 1989), 193 pp. Advisor: Leon E. Nay. [Order No. DA8925743]

The purpose of this study was to assess the impact of the inclusion of component units as required by GASB standards on financial ratios used to evaluate the reported financial condition of selected local governmental units. Thirteen ratios were calculated for each of the 66 governmental units included in this study, using financial information disclosed in each government's comprehensive annual financial report (CAFR). These same ratios were recalculated after excluding component unit financial information. After computing the two sets of ratios for each of the 66 governmental units, the Pearson product-moment correlation coefficient, the Spearman coefficient of rank correlation, the paired t-test and a comparison of computed ratios for individual governmental units with available credit industry benchmarks were performed.

Pearson product-moment correlation coefficients for the thirteen ratios employed in this study ranged from .879 to .979. The Spearman coefficients of rank correlation ranged from .889 to .968. These results imply that the inclusion of component unit financial data does not have a significant impact on financial ratios used to evaluate the reported financial condition of governmental units studied.

Results of the paired t-test indicated the mean difference between ratios were significant at the .05 level for eight ratios. Establishment of 96% confidence intervals around each mean difference suggested that the true mean difference for these eight ratios, although statistically significant, was probably not of practical significance to financial statement users.

Comparison of computed ratios with available credit industry benchmarks highlighted isolated instances in which the inclusion of component unit financial data had a noticeable effect on the *total revenues to total expenditures, direct long-term debt to net assessed valuation* and *debt service to total revenues ratios* for two reporting entities.

The findings of this study are important because it is the first time that a comprehensive set of financial ratios have been used with a large cross section of local governmental units to gather empirical evidence as to the actual impact of the inclusion of component unit financial information, in accordance with GASB reporting standards, on local governmental units.

Kilani, Kilani Abdulkerim, "The Evolution and Status of Accounting in Libya (Volume I and II)" (University of Hull, United Kingdom, 1988), 877 pp. [Order No. BRDX90144]

The main purposes of this study were to ascertain whether Libya's accounting Systems (enterprise, Government, social) provide the necessary information for its socio-economic development planning and to suggest means by which to improve accounting in the country.

Thus, this study is divided into three parts; namely, the evolution and state of accounting in Libya, the accounting information needs of Libya, and the potential improvement of accounting in Libya. In the first part, attempts were made to describe the Libyan environment and to determine the possible orientation of accounting in Libya. It is shown that Libya is a developing country, which in former years was subject to pressure from Foreign powers both politically and economically. This pressure has created a bias towards the UK/USA accounting systems. Laws and regulations, accounting education and the accounting profession, are all oriented towards the Accounting of these two countries.

In the second part, it is argued theoretically, that Libya needs accounting information which is related to economic decision making and to socio-economic development planning.

Based on the above findings and arguments of this study, it is reasonable to suggest that the current accounting systems in Libya do not provide information relevant to the Libyan environment, and improvement of these systems by introducing uniformity is urgently needed. A uniform accounting system along the lines of the Iraqi uniform accounting system is recommended, as well as other areas of improvement including PPBS, value for money audit, flow of funds statement, National Balance Sheet, and input-output tables.

The general characteristics of an appropriate new framework of accounting are discussed. All the above improvements should be based on societal accounting rather than on the Classical Accounting Theory. [Abstract shortened by UMI.]

McKenzie, Karen Sue, "Prospect Theory in Governmental Accounting: Implications for the Budgeting Process at the Local Level," (The Louisiana State University and Agricultural and Mechanical College, 1989), 182 pp. Director: Nicholas G. Apostolou. [Order No.DA9002160]

Small local governmental units are responsible for allocating resources on behalf of a substantial portion of all United States citizens. The research reported here investigates the effects of presentation format (or framing) on decision preference in a governmental resource allocation context. The subjects represent a population of governmental units which has not received prior research attention—small local governments. Budget preparers were asked to choose among objectively identical alternatives, which differed in presentation formats. The cases used to investigate the effects of presentation were modelled after Kahneman and Tversky's [1979] seminal work in prospect theory, which addressed violations of expected utility theory. The survey's approximately 50% response rate provided results indicating that the subjects of this study cannot be considered "rational decision makers" as defined by the well accepted expected utility theory. However, most of their decision behavior could be explained with the concepts of prospect theory. The implications of this research include the need for further investigation of the resource allocation process of small local governments. Future research should focus on development of a resource allocation system which is not prone to manipulation as a result of the mere presentation of the decision problem and its alternatives. The fact that approximately 25% of the United States population is served by these small governments suggests the need for continued research.

Dobitz, Carol S., "Fund Accounting Principles Advocated by Accounting Educators and Hospital/Municipal/College Chief Accountants" (The University of North Dakota, 1989), 299 pp. Adviser: Roger Bloomquist. [Order No. DA9003757]

The study was designed to determine appropriate content for the Fund Accounting topic offered in college accounting programs to aid in ensuring that accounting graduates have adequate preparation for accounting positions with nonprofit entities.

Two questionnaires, containing the same fifty-seven nonprofit accounting principles and different demographic variables, were developed with the input from a panel of experts. These were mailed nationally to Accounting Educators and Chief Accountants employed by nonprofit hospitals, nonprofit colleges, and municipalities. The respondents indicated: (1) the nonprofit accounting principles that are in current usage and (2) the principles respondents believed are appropriate.

The findings were based on the responses of 129 Accounting Educators and 153 Chief Accountants. The findings are as follows: (1) Accounting Educators and Chief Accountants of nonprofit entities sampled do not possess the same views regarding the nonprofit accounting principles that are being followed in actual practice and the principles that are being taught in college accounting programs. The three groups of Chief Accountants also possess different views as to which nonprofit accounting principles should be followed. (2) Accounting Educators and Chief Accountants of nonprofit entities sampled do not possess the same views regarding the nonprofit accounting principles which should be followed and should be taught in college accounting programs.

Based on the data obtained from Chief Accountants and Accounting Educators regarding their perceptions of the appropriate nonprofit accounting principles, a curriculum framework was developed. The framework was divided into three units, each covering one of the three types of nonprofit entities included in this study, namely, municipalities, nonprofit colleges, and nonprofit hospitals. The areas covered by the principles are: basis of accounting, fixed assets and depreciation, fund accounting techniques, financial statement reporting, and financial statement disclosures in notes and supporting schedules. Several of the principles that are recommended in the curriculum framework are: (1) accrual basis of accounting, (2) capitalize fixed assets at time of acquisition, (3) classify assets and liabilities into balanced fund groups using a fund system, (4) report each fund balance on the financial statement at the end of the period, and (5) disclose changes in accounting principles.

Soybel, Virginia Elizabeth Earll, "Municipal Financial Reporting and the New York City Fiscal Crisis" (Columbia University, 1989), 162 pp. [Order No. DA9005939]

This study examines empirically the municipal bond market's assessment of the relative risk of New York City general obligation bonds and the association between that assessment and the City's financial disclosures. This analysis is accomplished in three parts. First, the behavior of New York City bond yields relative to particular benchmarks from 1961 until the City's default in 1975 is examined. Secondly, a set of financial ratios are calculated using New York City's published financial statements and are analyzed over the same time period. The same ratios are then recalculated using financial statements that have been adjusted to conform with generally accepted accounting principles (GAAP), and the two sets of ratios are compared. Finally, the association between New York City bond yield premiums and both sets of financial ratios are tested to investigate the relationship between these ratios and the market's evaluation of the relative risk of New York City bonds.

The results of the study indicate that throughout the period from 1961 to 1975, the City's bonds were perceived as riskier than benchmarks of other municipal bonds, even those of the same ratings class. Tests of the association between New York City bond yield differentials and both sets of financial ratios show that, for those ratios that are significantly affected by the adjustments made to achieve conformance with GAAP, the yield differentials are significantly correlated in the expected directions with the adjusted ratios, but not with the unadjusted ratios. These results are consistent with the notion that while the City engaged in misleading accounting practices, the bond market was not completely misled.

Allen, Arthur Conrad, Jr. "Effects of Local Government Audit Quality on the Reliability of Accounting Numbers and Investor Decisions" (The University of Alabama, 1989), 117 pp. Chair: Robert W. Ingram. [Order No. DA9008137]

Prior research has indicated that users of accounting information believe that local government audits provide important information (e.g., Robbins and Austin [1986]). Despite the audit's perceived importance, other studies have found that some local government audits are deficient (e.g., Berry et al. [1987], U.S. GAO [1986]). This study investigated the effects of local government audit quality on the predictability of bond rating changes and the market reaction to bond rating changes.

Audit quality was linked to the reliability of accounting information. The reliability of accounting information was linked to (1) bond rating change predictability, and (2) the market reaction to bond rating changes. Audit quality was proxied by audit fees (controlled for nonquality elements) and auditor firm size (Big 8 firms vs.

Non-Big 8 firms).

To test the relationship between audit quality and bond rating change predictability, two logistic regression models were constructed. The difference between the two models was that the local governments in one model employed higher quality auditors (Big 8 firms) than the auditors (Non-Big 8 firms) employed by the local governments in the other logit model. The difference in the classificatory accuracy of the two models was in the expected direction, but not statistically significant.

To test the relationship between audit quality and the market reaction to bond rating changes, the two measures of audit quality were regressed on the measure of market reaction to bond rating changes. As expected, the Big 8 variable was significantly negatively associated with the market reaction to bond rating changes. However, the audit fees variable was not significant. Further analyses of the data showed that the results were sensitive to the time period in which the audit fees were gathered. In general, the audit fee variable became significant and the auditor firm size variable became insignificant as the precision of the audit fee data increased. This result provides some evidence that audit fees do proxy audit quality and audit quality does reduce the market reaction to bond rating changes. However, the magnitude of the reduction was small, as was the percent of variation explained.

MacQuarrie, Allan James, "Health Care Cost Containment in the New Environment of Prospective Pricing of Services: The Implications for the Accounting and Financial Function" (The Pennsylvania State University, 1989), 292 pp. Adviser: William L. Ferrara. [Order No. DA9018249]

In the new hospital reimbursement environment which recently moved to prospective payment for services, many accountants and health care industry experts have predicted that hospitals will begin to use cost accounting and budgeting techniques similar to those portrayed in cost accounting textbooks and utilized by many manufacturing concerns. Along these lines, the determination of job (DRG) costs, flexible budgets, and standard costs have been identified and were particular concerns of this exploratory study.

In this study, restricted to Pennsylvania hospitals, a questionnaire survey was used to determine the nature and scope of the cost accounting and budget systems that hospitals are currently using or planning to use. In order to more adequately explain the questionnaire survey findings and, in effect, to provide a richer description of the implementation and use of more sophisticated cost accounting and budgeting techniques in actual hospitals, ten case studies followed the questionnaire survey. Hospitals selected for case study were selected from those the questionnaire identified as being involved with more sophisticated techniques.

The major finding of this study is that most hospitals had not implemented sophisticated cost accounting and budget techniques and that even in those hospitals that had begun to use more sophisticated techniques such as standard costs and flexible budgets, simplistic methodologies were generally used in implementing these techniques. This study also suggests that (1) the use of unsophisticated DRG cost accumulation techniques was widespread, (2) very few hospitals had adopted any form of standard cost system, (3) the majority of hospitals had not implemented flexible budgeting systems, and (4) budget variance reports generally had limited utility to operating managers concerned with controlling costs and monitoring productivity, in part, because many budget variances commonly confirm information already received from more timely sources. The study also suggests that the hospital product costing systems observed in this study were influenced by the regulatory requirements of Blue Cross and Medicare and that Medicare cost reporting methodologies have been particularly influential.

Fettus, Sharon H., "Information and Congressional Decision-Making for Infrastructure Investments" (University of Maryland College Park,1989), 283 pp. Director: Lawrence A. Gordon. [Order No. DA9021498]

Need for economic restraint has put great pressure on the federal government's budgetary process. Concurrently, concern has arisen that the nation's infrastructure is rapidly deteriorating. Congress responded with P.L. 98-501, requiring "more specific information on the Nation's needs (that) would help determine the appropriate mechanism to address the problem."

The Larcker and Lessig multi-item instrument is used to determine whether information with augmented content and different format than that generated by P.L. 98-501 is perceived more useful for legislative decision making. The independent variables, substance and format, are manipulated at two levels. Data collection was based on a questionnaire mailed to staff for each member of Congress. Each questionnaire contained two sets of information rather than a complete replication of the treatments. Both main effects and interaction are, therefore, confounded in a BIB design.

ANOVA techniques were used to diagnose perceived usefulness. The gain in precision due to the use of smaller blocks is at the expense of loss of information on those treatment comparisons confounded with blocks. Interblock information was recovered by the calculation of weighted combinations of the inter and intrablock estimates of contrasts for each treatment.

The empirical results suggest that information, augmented with data more timely and relevant to current economic conditions, is perceived more useful than information mandated by P.L. 98-501. The second main effect, information format, was not significant. A significant interaction between the two factors is present. An ordinal ranking persists for the information substance factor, that augmented information is perceived more useful. A disordinal ranking, however, is present for the current format versus graphical reformatting, disallowing an independent interpretation.

This research hopes to further demonstrate the need for a national capital investment policy. P.L.98-501 recognized that the critical and necessary "first step" is better coordinated and more consistent information. This study suggests that the means of achieving that first step have not yet been realized.

Sanders, George D., "An Empirical Investigation of the Association of Municipal Tax Structure with Municipal Accounting Choice and Bias and Noise in Municipal Accounting Ratios" (The University of Alabama,1989), Chair: Robert W. Ingram. [Order No. DA9022272]

This study draws on theoretical work and empirical research in the public choice area to test the association of certain tax structure variables with accounting choices. The fiscal illusion hypothesis in the public choice literature suggests that governments use complex and invisible tax structures to increase demand for public services by inducing an illusion about the cost of such services. However, a more recent theory, sometimes called the fiscal stress hypothesis, holds that the increased consumption of public services observed in governments with more complex or less visible tax structures results from a lower tax price permitted by savings resulting from a more stable revenue stream.

This study posits that the differences in the motivations of government officials implied by the two hypotheses result in different predictions for certain accounting choices made by government officials. The accounting choices examined are the use of the cash basis of accounting, the use of the full GASB fund model, the number of disclosures in the annual financial report, and the bias and noise characteristics of accounting ratios. In general, it is predicted from the fiscal illusion hypothesis that cities with complex and less visible taxes will select accounting methods that reduce the quality of accounting information and, from the fiscal stress hypothesis, that cities with these tax structure characteristics will use accounting methods which improve the quality of accounting information.

With one exception, the empirical results are consistent with the predictions from the fiscal stress hypothesis. Cities with more complex or more invisible tax structures are found to be more likely to use accounting methods that have been shown to result in more useful (less noisy and/or less biased) accounting information. The sole exception to the results supporting the fiscal stress hypothesis is the association of noise and visibility. This result, while not as strong as the result for the complexity index, seems to indicate that noise may increase in accounting numbers as tax visibility decreases.

Gatian, Amy Elizabeth Williams, "User Information Satisfaction (UIS)and User Productivity: An Empirical Examination" (Virginia Polytechnic Institute and State University, 1989), 252 pp. Chairman: James O. Hicks, Jr. [Order No. DA9023155]

In this research the relationships between user information satisfaction (UIS) and user productivity were examined. Two users groups were used to test the following hypotheses: (1A) There is no relationship between UIS and perceptions of decision-making quality for academic department heads. (1B) There is no relationship between UIS and perceptions of decision-making quality for managers within the controller's office. (2) There is no relationship between UIS and objectively measured productivity for managers within the controller's office. (3) There is no relationship between UIS and a user's length of experience with a system. (4A) There is no relationship between UIS and a user's age. (4B) There is no relationship between UIS and a user's sex. (4C) There is no relationship between UIS and a user's level of education.

Data utilized in testing the hypotheses were collected with a packet of six questionnaires mailed to the controllers of 100 universities. Usable responses were obtained from 107 of 300 controller's office managers and 77 of 300 academic users. H_{1A}, H_{1B} and H_2 were tested with canonical correlation analysis. H_3, H_{4A}, H_{4B}, and H_{4C} were tested with multiple regression.

The findings can be summarized as follows: (1) Satisfaction with computer processing was correlated with making better operating budget decisions for both groups and helping academic users track activities in research, grant and designated gift accounts. (2) Satisfaction with system related problem finding was correlated with elimination of steps and making jobs easier for managers, and with helping academic users track activity in research accounts, and to feel they have benefitted overall from FRS. (3) Satisfaction with the linear combination of inputs and problem finding was correlated with financial transactions per full time employee equivalents (FTE), late internal reports per total internal reports and number of ledger accounts per FTE. (4) More frequent users of FRS were more satisfied. Additionally, UIS and mandatory system usage were positively correlated. (6) UIS and sex were moderately correlated. Specifically, males within the academic group were less satisfied with FRS than the females surveyed.

Mahoney, Daniel Paul, "Pennsylvania's Municipal Labor Market Before and After the Enactment of the Municipal Pension Plan Funding Standard and Recovery Act: An Empirical Study" (Syracuse University, 1990), 216 pp. Advisor: John C. Anderson. [Order No. DA9025474]

This study examines Pennsylvania's municipal labor market before and after the enactment of "The Municipal Pension Plan Funding Standard and Recovery Act" (Act 205) in 1984. This Act provided for mandatory pension plan funding (with amortization of existing deficiencies), more uniform pension plan disclosure, and a change in the allocation of state assistance to an "employee unit" basis (with police officers and fire fighters each counted as two "units" and non-uniformed employees as one "unit").

The study is concerned with the "supply" and "demand" effects of pension underfunding. A wage (supply) equation is used to model the wage at which municipal employees are willing to supply their services and an employment (demand) equation is used to model the number of public employees demanded by municipal officials and residents. This simultaneous supply and demand relationship is estimated for both 1982 and 1987.

In both analyses, pension underfunding is associated with an increased demand for the services of police and fire fighters as hypothesized. The results for the non-uniformed employee category supported the opposite contention. The results also suggest that the supply reaction to underfunding differs for alternative categories of municipal employees.

Pennsylvania's municipal police officers did not exhibit a wage response to underfunding. Rather, they appear to regard wages and pension funding as two distinct bargaining issues. Pennsylvania's municipal fire fighters exhibited a wage response to underfunding in the pre-Act 205 analysis (albeit based on a less informative measure of funding adequacy). Further, there was no indication that the municipal employee labor market discerned the difference in the alternative disclosure methods used in the pre-Act 205 era.

In the post-Act 205 era, fire fighters also appeared to bargain for wages and funding separately. The non-uniformed employees appeared to react to underfunding in the post-Act 205 era and seek compensating wages. This result is logical and expected. Due to ample state assistance, pensions become more of a "pass-through" benefit for police and firefighters. The state assistance is noticeably less generous to non-uniformed employee pension plans and, due to improved disclosure, they (or their representatives) should now be aware of the funding status of their plans.

Mattison, Dorothy McCall, "The Influence of Selected Variables on the Financial Performance of Not-for-Profit and for-Profit Hospitals: A Comparative Analysis" (The George Washington University, 1980), 188 pp. Director: Peter B. Vaill. [Order No. DA9027373]

During the past several decades, questions emerged concerning the relative financial performance of not-for-profit and for-profit hospitals. As the hospital industry underwent major economic changes, answering these questions became urgent. Some argued that the merit of profit-seeking hospitals is their greater incentive to control or lower costs, thereby enabling them to optimize profits. Previous studies relying on accounting and other operating data do not yield definitive answers about the relative performance (relative costliness and profitability) of not-for-profit versus for-profit hospitals.

This study investigated the influence of selected variables on the financial performance of not-for-profit and for-profit short-term, acute care, nongovernmental hospitals with an average stay of 21 days or less. In addition, this study attempted to determine whether financial performance of the two groups of hospitals is influenced differently by the selected variables.

The study applied multiple regression analysis to data obtained in 1985 and 1986 from the Health Care Financing Administration's Prospective Payment System Minimum Cost Data Set. The study analyzed 88 percent of the not-for-profit and 88 percent of the for-profit hospitals included in the above specified category. The two dependent variables examined in separate regression equations are return-on-investment (ROI) and cash to total assets (CASHASST). The independent variables include total equity to assets (EQUASST), depreciation expense to fixed assets (DEPFIXAS), allowances and discounts to gross patient revenue (DEDUCT2), fixed asset turnover (FIXASTU), net patient revenue to total discharges (CHARGES), and a number of other variables expected to impact significantly on ROI and CASHASST. The study subdivided the not-for-profit and for-profit hospitals into four subgroups based on profitability.

The analysis disclosed that both operating and financing variables exert a substantial impact on for-profit and not-for-profit hospital ROI and CASHASST. Among the most relatively important variables are EQUASST, DEPFIXAS, FIXASTU, and DEDUCT2. Differences in the influence of the independent variables on ROI and CASHASST were found not to be associated with whether the subgroups of hospitals were operated as for-profit or not-for-profit organizations.

Soderstrom, Naomi Siegel, "The Response of Hospitals to Incentives: The Case of the Medicare Prospective Payment System" (Northwestern University, 1990), 137 pp. Co-Chairmen: Bala Balachandran and Robert P. Magee. [Order No. DA9031992]

This dissertation examines the response of hospitals to the form of reimbursement and monitoring system under the Prospective Payment System for Medicare. In 1983, the Federal Government changed reimbursement for hospitals from a fee-for-service basis to reimbursement by admission. Under the reimbursement system, there are several strategies that hospitals can follow to increase profit. The strategies examined here are (1) providing inaccurate reports of diagnoses and (2) reducing the level of care given to each patient. Empirical evidence provides support for the contention that hospitals in good financial condition and/or with lower marginal costs have fewer errors in reporting and treatment of patients than hospitals in poor financial condition and/or with higher marginal costs. Error rates are also found to differ systematically across diagnoses, indicating that the form of monitoring currently in use should be reevaluated.

Montondon, Lucille Marie, "Study of Municipal Resource Allocation Decisions and Municipal Bond Ratings" (University of Houston, 1990), 150 pp. [Order No. DA9034555]

Factors related to municipal budgeting decisions were examined in this study. In addition, an investigation was conducted to determine if municipal budgeting decisions influence external risk assessment measured by municipal bond ratings.

The budget per capita was examined for three municipal departments. Independent variables were selected by applying the Supply and Demand theories of political science and economics to municipal governments. These theories suggest that resource allocation decisions are related to factors which are internal (Supply Theory) and external (Demand Theory) to the municipality.

Of the variables examined, only percent of local funding was found to be significant in all departmental budgets. Other variables showed varying explanatory power. Employees per capita were significant only in the police department budget, while choice of auditor was significant only in the fire department budget. No external political variables were significant for any department.

The entire General Fund was studied using the operating ratio as the dependent variable. This ratio is a measure of the proportion of the total general funds that are allocated to service-providing departments. Alternatively, this ratio indicates the proportion of funds allocated to administrative tasks, and provides a means of quantifying the administrative decisions of a municipality. Debt per capita and tenure of the mayor were significant and negatively related to the operating ratio.

The effect of budgetary allocation decisions on bond ratings was also examined. The operating ratio was used as a partitioning mechanism, aiding the municipalities into groups for further analyses. Grouping municipalities that allocate greater or lesser amounts to administrative tasks provided a means of detecting differing explanatory powers among the variables studied.

Accounting quality and debt per capita were significant in the subsample with higher operating ratios. On the other hand, assessed property value per capita was significant in the subsample with lower operating ratios. This finding suggests that differences in municipal resource allocation decisions are related to external assessments of credit worthiness.

Staples, Catherine Loving, "The Relation between the Media, Monitoring Devices, and the School District Budgetary Process" (University of North Carolina at Chapel Hill, 1990), 203 pp. Director: Marc A. Rubin. [Order No. DA9034761]

The information needs of government financial statement users have been the focus of several studies which suggest the existence of a government financial information cycle. Within the cycle, three potential user groups have been identified. The first group consists of government officials such as legislators, managers, and planners. This group may act as both a provider and a user of government financial information.

Citizens and corporations comprise the second user group. The media and analysts are identified as the third user group. Research suggests that information flows initially to the media group to be subsequently disseminated to the other users.

This study examines the media's role in the information cycle for the budgetary process for school districts. Better understanding the role of the media should improve the budgeting process.

Utilizing Virginia school districts, this study suggests that the media may affect the school district's budget process. However, school district size appears to be a relevant factor. For large school districts, the discretionary budget categories of summer school and adult education seem to be influenced by the media. Discretionary budgets can be cut more easily than nondiscretionary budgets. For small school districts, the nondiscretionary budget categories of fixed charges and administration appear to be explained in part by the media.

This research also examines the effect of the budget officials' time in office on the school budget. For large school districts, tenure affected only the operations and maintenance budget. The fixed charges budget was influenced by tenure for the small school districts.

The use of monitoring devices within a school district also is discussed. Studies suggest that financial monitoring devices will be utilized by politicians to monitor school districts with large student populations, debt balances, administrative salary expenses, and levels of political activity. The method of school funding allocation used by the board of supervisors is tested as a possible monitoring device since one method requires more supervision than does the other. This research appears to substantiate the earlier theories concerning debt levels, political competition, and monitoring devices.

Harris, Jeannie E., "Tax Expenditures: Report Utilization by State Policy Makers" (Virginia Polytechnic Institute and State University, 1990), 309 pp. Chairman: Sam A. Hicks. [Order No. DA9103526]

Tax expenditures are deviations from a normative tax structure which take the form of exemptions, deductions, credits, etc. Tax expenditure reports show estimates of revenues foregone from tax expenditures.

This study investigated report use in ten states by (1) examining tax expenditure reporting processes and report use and (2) applying three path models of technical information use to tax expenditure reports. Data were gathered from report preparers, legislative staff persons and legislators.

The adoption of recommended standard features was examined. Commonly adopted core features and innovative features were identified. Examination of tax expenditure reports and reporting processes supports the following findings: (1) The tax expenditure concept has broad acceptance. (2) Reporting achieves an educational objective by facilitating an understanding of tax structure. (3) Use of reports is consistent with the use of technical information in general. (4) Legislators and staff persons share similar perceptions on reporting. (5) The practice of formally comparing tax and direct expenditures has not been widely adopted. (6) Awareness of tax expenditure costs may protect revenues by fostering resistance to new tax expenditures.

In the three specified path models of information use, the dependent variable is level of report use. The independent variables in each model represent three theory [sic] of information use. The most paths were retained as significant in the information specific model, but the individual attribute model explained the highest percentage of variance in level of use (28.1%). The role constraint model was unsupported. A final combined model, explaining 94.9% of variance in level of use, shows that the information specific and personal attribute models are related. In the combined model: (1) report usefulness has the largest direct and total effect on level of use, (2) the exogenous variables, quality of report communication and fiscal analysis attitude affect report usefulness by affecting the intervening variables, relevance of report and technical quality of report. This suggests report preparers may influence marginally report use by improving report communication and technical quality of reports.

Shreim, Obeid Saad, "Value for Money Auditing: Its Development and Application with Special Reference to the U.K. Public Sector"(University College, Cardiff [Wales], United Kingdom, 1989), 967 pp. [Order No. BRDX91019]

Value for money auditing has been part of the National Audit Office and the District Audit Service audit work in the public sector in the U.K. for more than 50 years. A major part of this study was devoted to tracing the way in which value for money auditing was developed in the public sector in the U.K. and elsewhere. But since economy, efficiency and effectiveness were given statutory recognition in 1982 at the local government level and in 1983 at the central government level, widespread concern has been shown regarding the subject from a whole range of interested parties including politicians, pressure groups, the general public and, of course, the accounting profession. The focus of their attention was both on the auditor's appropriateness in delivering effectiveness and on bringing the feasibility of achieving effectiveness into question. Therefore, this study is aimed at investigating the appropriateness of the auditor in delivering effectiveness and looking into the viability of its achievement.

Evidence on these specific issues was obtained from a mail questionnaire survey of three groups closely involved with, or affected by, effectiveness auditing, (i.e., external auditors at the local and central government levels, financial officers at the local and central government levels, service department managers at the local level). The results established strong prima facie evidence that effectiveness audit in its full meaning is far from being achieved and that the auditor's role needs to be backed by the inclusion of people from disciplines other than auditing.

Hill, Nancy Thorley, "The Adoption of Costing Systems in the Hospital Industry" (The University of Wisconsin—Madison, 1990) 240 pp. Supervisor: Werner G. Frank [Order No. DA9106681]

This dissertation examines environmental, organizational and managerial factors that are significant in distinguishing hospitals which are more likely to adopt costing systems able to determine costs at the Diagnosis Related Group (DRG) level. A nationwide survey of hospital chief financial officers was conducted to gather data about the organization and its costing capabilities. Additional information was gathered from American Hospital Association publications. A series of cross-sectional binary and multinomial logit models is used in which the dependent variable is defined as the adoption or non-adoption of a costing system and notes the costing system type. Further dynamic analysis using an event history model includes data over a 10 year period. The dynamic analysis allows for inclusion of time-varying independent variables and also accounts for censored observations.

Environmental factors include measures of regulation and competition. Parameter estimates of four measures of hospital rate and revenue regulation indicate that as regulation increases, hospitals are more likely to adopt costing systems. Measures of competition, however, indicate that as competition increases, costing system adoption is less likely. For the included organizational factors, only bed size is consistently significant in the various models. Finally, parameter estimates for managerial involvement, as measured by administrative and accounting department involvement in costing system adoption decisions, indicate that as involvement increases, costing system adoption is less likely.

This research assesses one part of the management accounting system, the costing system, within the hospital industry. Empirical examination of 589 short-term medical hospitals indicates that the decision to adopt a costing system is contingent upon a hospital's specific environmental, organizational and managerial characteristics. The results suggest that hospital regulation (as measured by four regulatory variables) is the driving force in costing system adoption. This environmental factor plays an important role in costing system adoption. Competition and organizational structure also have significant impacts on costing system adoption, but they are smaller in magnitude.

Vijayakumar, Jayaraman, "An Empirical Analysis of the Factors Influencing Call Decisions Concerning Local Government Bonds" (University of Pittsburgh, 1990), 165 pp. Chairperson: James Patton. [Order No. DA9106765]

Given the rapidly increasing debt and interest burden of many cities, the subject of efficient debt management in local government has been growing in significance.

This study examines one important aspect of efficient debt management in the municipal sector, namely, the factors influencing the inclusion and exercise of call provisions in municipal debt.

The study first presents an overview of existing theoretical and empirical findings concerning call decisions in the corporate and public sectors. In addition, it provides an integrative conceptual framework and identifies the factors likely to influence the call decision. Based on this framework, the study develops and tests selected hypotheses examining the influence of these factors.

The empirical results indicate support for the theory and hypotheses developed. The results suggest that information asymmetry between borrowers and lenders in municipal bond markets is a possible reason for the inclusion of call provisions. In addition, the achievement of savings in interest is shown to be an important incentive for calls of bonds in the municipal sector. Limited support is also observed for the role of patronage in influencing the call decision.

The results show that factors such as the prevailing level of interest rates, the years to maturity outstanding for a bond, favorable changes in bond ratings, and political competition, all significantly influence the decision to call. The study does not however, find factors such as the size of the issue, changes in debt levels for the issuer, and the form of government of the city issuing the bond to be significant influences on the decision to call.

These results show that in addition to economic characteristics, political considerations also influence decision making in the municipal sector. The results of this study suggest that environmental factors such as political competition, unique to the public sector, need to be considered in examining managerial incentives in the public sector.

Samidi, Juhari Bin, "An Empirical Investigation of the Capital Budgeting Decision Process of Government-Controlled Enterprises as Compared to Investor-Owned Enterprises: The Case of Malaysia" (University of Arkansas, 1989), 264 pp. Advisor: Leon E. Hay. [Order No. DA9111161]

Commercial and industrial public enterprises in Malaysia have been established with the mission of supplementing the private sector in accelerating the nation's economic development process. Although many of these enterprises have been successful, a large number of them are having serious financial problems. The purpose of this study is to examine and evaluate the capital budgeting decision procedures which are workable among the successful public enterprises in Malaysia; so that over time their good practices can be disseminated more widely to other enterprises in the country.

The case study approach was used. Data collected through personal interviews with managers involved in the capital budgeting process of the selected firms were supplemented with data obtained from the firms' annual reports, financial statements and government documents. Matching private sector firms were selected for comparison of their capital budgeting practices.

Several of the major findings are: (1) the government-owned enterprises studied have well-defined capital budgeting policies and are better organized to perform capital budgeting activities than the matching investor-owned enterprises, (2) discounted cash flow (DCF) techniques, such as internal rate of return (IRR) and net present value methods, were used by the government firms; however, the accounting rate of return and the payback methods were still popular among the investor-owned firms, (3) the approval process for major capital projects is highly centralized, particularly for government firms, and (4) formal post-audit procedure is rare as such activity is considered culturally unethical.

Realizing the important role of capital investments in creating the desired economic growth and employment, the government agencies and officials responsible for public enterprises are recommended to pursue the following strategies: (1) An appropriate organization structure and system to plan and control capital investment activities should be established by all government enterprises which are actively involved in such activities. (2) Since capital investment is an important aspect of management accounting, the relevant government enterprises should increase their recruitment of adequately trained accountants into their organizations to perform such functions.

Johnson, Gary Gene, "Compliance Auditing in the Public Sector: An Empirical Investigation into the Extent of Noncompliance with State Laws by County Governments" (University of Arkansas, 1989), 171 pp. Advisor: Leon E. Hay. [Order No. DA9111217]

Local general governments are subject to audits. The scope of these audits extends beyond a determination of whether the financial reports are in conformity with GAAP to a determination of the entity's compliance with applicable laws and regulations. The focus of this study was on noncompliance with state laws.

Data for this project were obtained from the management letters accompanying the county audit reports in the State of Arkansas and from a survey of state auditors. A comprehensive list of instances of noncompliance was compiled from the management letters and integrated into a survey instrument in order to obtain a rating of the seriousness of each item. Data were also obtained from the survey concerning the effectiveness of audit procedures in detecting instances of noncompliance and causes of noncompliance.

Regression analysis was employed to evaluate the influence of three variables on the number of reported instances of noncompliance with state laws by functional area of county government and by the county as a unit. Results showed that four separate size variable measures had very little impact. In only one instance (county clerk) was a size measure significant in a final model. Variables associated with effectiveness of government officials to comply with legal requirements, and allocation of county resources exhibited the most explanatory power, but the highest r^2 was only .17.

ANOVA was used to test for differences in the number of reported instances of noncompliance between the functional areas of county government. Significant differences were found. Multiple comparisons based on the Tukey test identified the locations of the differences. Statutory responsibilities associated with each functional area were then related to the number of reported instances of noncompliance.

Correlational analysis applied to the data relating to audit procedures showed that the perceived effectiveness of a list of audit procedures in detecting instances of noncompliance generally correlate significantly with the effectiveness of the same audit procedures in detecting financial account errors.

Descriptive analyses were conducted on data relating to the causes and incidence of noncompliance, and on the means and standard deviations computed for the auditors' ratings of the instances of noncompliance.

ACKNOWLEDGMENT

CUMULATIVE INDEX
FOR VOLUMES 1–7

Research in Governmental and Nonprofit Accounting

Edited by **James L. Chan,** *The University of Illinois at Chicago* and **James M. Patton,** *University of Pittsburgh*

REVIEWS: "All individuals interested in governmental accounting standard setting process will find some food for thought in this volume."

—Public Budgeting & Finance

"... an important addition to any collection in the government and nonprofit area."

—Journal of Urban Affairs

Volume 1, 1985, 347 pp. $63.50
ISBN 0-89232-517-8

CONTENTS: Introduction, *James L. Chan.* **PART I. GOVERN-MENTAL ACCOUNTING POLICY RESEARCH. The Birth of the Governmental Accounting Standards Board: How? Why? What Next?,** *James L. Chan, University of Illinois at Chicago.* **Objectives for the Governmental Accounting Standards Board,** *Wanda A. Wallace, Southern Methodist University.* **A Digest of Authoritative Pronoucements on Governmental Accounting and Reporting,** *Robert W. Parry, Jr., Indiana University.* **The Governmental Financial Reporting Entity: A Review and Analysis,** *James M. Patton, University of Pittsburgh.* **Measuring and Reporting the Financial Condition of Public Organizations,** *Herman B. Leonard, Harvard University.* **Measuring the Periodic Performance of Govern-ment: Policy and Research Issues,** *Florence C. Sharp, University of Illinois and Robert W. Ingram, University of Iowa.* **Accounting Policies and the Measurement of Urban Fiscal Strain,** *Wanda A. Wallace, Southern Methodist University.* **Information for Municipal Bond Investment Decisions: Synthesis of Prior Research, An Extension and Policy Implications,** *Earl E. Wilson and Thomas P. Howard, University of Missouri at Columbia.* **Part II PROCEEDINGS. UNIVERSITY OF ILLINOIS AT CHICAGO SYMPOSIUM.** Governmental Accounting Standard Setting: Prospect in the 1980s. Introduction. Acknowledgements. Technical Program. List of Participants. Session I. Setting Governmental Accounting Standards: Strategies and Institutional Framework. Session II. Governmental Reporting Entity Issues. Session III. Long Term Assets and Liabilities with Emphasis on Infrastructure and Pensions. Session IV. Budgeting and Reporting Operations: Revenue Recognition, Expense/Expediture Measurement. Session V. Disclosure. Session VI. Recommendations for Considerations by the Standard-Setting Body.

J A I P R E S S

Volume 2, 1986, 273 pp. $63.50
ISBN 0-89232-628-X

CONTENTS: Introduction, *James L. Chan.* **PART I. GOVERN-
MENTAL AUDITING RESEARCH. The Timing of Initial
Independent Audits of Municipalities: An Empirical Analysis,**
Wanda W. Wallace, Texas A&M University. **The Information
Content of the Audit Report as Perceived by Municipal
Analysts,** *Susan Herhold Baskin, University of Illinois at Chicago.*
**Governmental Auditing Research: An Analytic Framework,
Assessment of Past Work, and Future Directions,** *Leonard
Eugene Berry, Georgia State University and Wanda W. Wallace,
Texas A&M University.* **PART II. HEALTH CARE RESEARCH.
Social Expectations and Accounting Practices in the Health
Sector,** *Mark A. Covaleski, University of Wisconsin at Madison
and Mark W. Dirsmith, Pennsylvania State University.*
**Measurement of Hospital Performance and Implications for
Accounting, H. David Sherman,** *Northeastern University.*
**Measuring the Economic Performance of For-Profit and
Nonprofit Organizations,** *Regina E. Herzlinger and William S.
Krasker, Harvard University.* **Future Directions of Health Care
Accounting Research,** *Bruce R. Neumann, University of
Colorado at Denver.* **PART III. RESEARCH ON HIGHER
EDUCATION INSTITUTIONS. Bureaucratic and Political
Models of the University Budgetary Process: Consensus on
Departmental Merit,** *Allen G. Schick, University of Maryland and
Peter Lorenzi, University of Kansas.* **Predicting Failure of
Private Colleges: Financial and Nonfinancial Determinants,**
*Victor W. Lomax, Jr., Savannah State College and Earl R. Wilson,
University of Missouri at Columbia.* **PART IV. MUNICIPAL
CREDIT ANALYSIS. Improving Models of Municipal Bond
Rating Changes: Surrogation of Subjective Bias,** *R. Penny
Marquette, University of Akron.* **Municipal Borrowing Costs and
the Differential Impact of Accounting Information Across
Rating Categories,** *Earl D. Benson, Western Washington
University, Barry R. Marks, University of Houston at Clear Lakes
and K.K. Raman, North Texas State University.*

Volume 3, 1987   2 Volume Set $127.00
Set ISBN 0-89232-699-9

PART A, 206 pp. $63.50
ISBN 0-089232-785-5

CONTENTS: Introduction, *James L. Chan.* **American
Accounting Association Government and Nonprofit Section
Outstanding Dissertation Award. A Theory of Demand for
Municipal Audits and Audit Contracts,** *Marc A. Rubin,
University of North Carolina at Chapel Hill.* **Governmental
Accounting Research: A Managerial Emphasis. An Informa-
tion System for Administering Welfare Programs,** *Thomas R.
Prince and Bala V. Balachandran, Northestern University.* **The**

J A I

P R E S S

Effects of Interest Group Competition on Funding Government Management Information System, *Vivian L. Carpenter, Wayne State University and the University of Chicago.* Contracting Strategies for Maximum Benefit in Sales Contracts with Government: The Installment Sale Alternative, *David A. Dittman, University of Minnesota, Raymond J. Krasniewski, Ohio State University and Margaret Smith, Duke University.* Information Systems for Road Maintenance Management: A Value for Money Approach, *Martin S. Putterill, University of Auckland.* Governmental Financial Reporting Issues. Disclosure Practices of Public Employee Retirement Systems: An Analysis of Incentives to Adopt Alternative Standards, *Mary S. Stone, Walter A. Robbins and David W. Phipps, University of Alabama.* Criteria for Identifying the Municipal Organizational Reporting Entity, *Craig D. Shoulders, Virginia Polytechnic Institute and State University.*

PART B, 1987, 280 pp. $63.50
ISBN 0-89232-786-3

CONTENTS: Governmental Accounting Research Methodology. The Role of Information in a Democracy and in Government Operations: Public Choice Methodology, *James L. Chan, University of Illinois at Chicago and Marc A. Rubin, University of North Carolina at Chapel Hill.* Analytical Agency Theory and Municipal Accounting: An Introduction and an Application, *Rajiv D. Banker, Carnegie-Mellon University and James M. Patton, University of Pittsburgh.* Agency Theory and Governmental Nonprofit Sector Research, *Wanda A. Wallace, Texas A&M University.* Behavioral Research in Municipal Accounting, *Susan H. Herhold, University of Illinois at Chicago, Robert W. Parry, Indiana University and James M. Patton, University of Pittsburgh.* Governmental Capital Markets Research in Accounting: A Review, *Robert W. Ingram, University of Alabama, Krishnamurthy K. Raman, North Texas State University and Earl R. Wilson, University of Missouri-Columbia.* Increasing the Use and Usefulness of Governmental Financial Reports: Papers and Proceedings of the 1985 Governmental Accounting Research Symposium of the University of Illinois at Chicago. Welcoming Remarks, *Marcus Alexis.* Setting Governmental Accounting Standards in a Multi-Constituency Environment, *James F. Antonio.* GASB Research on User Needs and Objectives of Government Financial Reporting, *Martin H. Ives.* Federal Government Reporting Study: Summary Report. The Office of the Auditor General of Canada and the United States General Accounting Office. Improving Governmental Accounting and Financial Management: The Illinois Experience and a Proposal for the U.S. Government, *The Honorable Roland W. Burris.* Improving New York City's Financial Reporting: A Ten Year Retrospective, *The Honorable Harrison J. Goldin.* The Use and Usefulness of Governmental Financial Reports: The

Perspective of Municipal Investors, *Leon J. Karvelis, Jr.* The Use and Usefulness of Governmental Financial Reports: The Perspective of Citizen-Taxpayer Organizations, *Cynthia B. Green.* The Use and Usefulness of Governmental Financial Reports: The Perspective of Public Sector Employee Unions, *James Gordon Ward.*

Volume 4, 1988, 260 pp. $63.50
ISBN 0-89232-787-1

Edited by **James L. Chan,** *University of Illinois at Chicago* and **Rowan H. Jones,** *University of Birmingham*

CONTENTS: Introduction, *James L. Chan and Rowan H. Jones.* **PART I. PAPERS BASED ON DOCTORAL DISSERTATIONS. Public Employee Retirement System Reports: A Study of Knowledgeable User Information Processing Ability,** *Stephen D. Willits, Bucknell University, Donald K. Clancy and Robert J. Freeman, Texas Tech University.* **The Impact of Financial Reporting Requirements of Municipal Officials' Fixed Asset Acquisitions Decisions,** *Frances H. Carpenter, Trinity University.* **An Assessment of the Ability of Accounting Numbers to Predict Municipal General Obligation Bond Ratings,** *Shari H. Wescott, University of Houston.* **The Importance of Selected Information Items to Municipal Bond Analysts and Their Disclosure in Municipal Annual Reports: An Empirical Assessment,** *Walter A. Robbins, University of Alabama.* **Revenue Recognition Criteria for State and Local Governments,** *L. Charles Bokemeier, University of Kentucky.* **PART II. ABSTRACTS OF DOCTORAL DISSERTATIONS IN GOVERNMENT AND NONPROFIT ACCOUNTING.**

Volume 5, 1989, 310 pp. $63.50
ISBN 0-89232-975-0

Edited by **James L. Chan,** *The University of Illinois at Chicago* and **James M. Patton,** *University of Pittsburgh*

CONTENTS: Introduction, *James L. Chan, The University of Illinois at Chicago and James M. Patton, University of Pittsburgh.* **Statement of Editorial Philosophy,** *James L. Chan, The University of Illinois at Chicago and James M. Patton, University of Pittsburgh.* **PART I. AMERICAN ACCOUNTING ASSOCIATION GOVERNMENTAL AND NONPROFIT SECTION OUTSTANDING DISSERTATION AWARD. The Determinates of Local Government Audit Fees: Additional Evidence,** *Paul A. Copley, The University of Georgia.* **PART II. GOVERNMENTAL AND NONPROFIT ACCOUNTING RESEARCH. Factors Influencing School District Financial Reporting Practices,** *Rajiv D. Banker, Carnegie-Mellon University, Beverly S. Bunch, Syracuse University and Robert P. Strauss, Carnegie-Mellon University.* **State Policy Regarding Local GovernmentAudi-**

tors, *Ramachandran Ramanan and Marc A. Rubin, University of North Carolina at Chapel Hill.* **Personel Reports and Users Information Needs,** *Penelope S. Wardlow and James T. Godfrey, George Mason University.* **Resource Allocation Decisions by Charitable Organizations: An Experience,** *Sarah A. Reed, Texas A&M University and Bruce S. Koch, North Texas State University.* **PART III. DATA DEVELOPMENT ANALYSIS. An Introduction to Data Envelopment Analysis with Some of its Models and Their Users,** *R. Banker, Carnegie-Mellon University, A. Charnes, W.W. Cooper, The University of Texas at Austin, John Swarts, USARC PAE-ARA, Ft. Sheridan, Illinois and Dave Thomas, The University of Texas at Austin.* **DEA and Ratio Efficiency Analysis for Public Institutions of Higher Learning in Texas,** *Taesik Ahn, Arizona State University, Victor Arnold, Abraham Charnes and William Cooper, The University of Texas at Austin.* **Comparisons of DEA and Existing Ratio and Regression Systems for Effective Efficiency Evaluations of Regulated Electric Cooperatives in Texas,** *A. Charnes, W.W. Cooper, The University of Texas at Austin, D. Divine, Price Waterhouse, T.W. Ruefi and D. Thomas, The University of Texas at Austin.* **An Approach to Testing for Organizational Slack Via Ankes's Game Theoretic DEA Formulations,** *A. Charnes, W.W. Cooper, The University of Texas at Austin and R.L. Clark, Clemson University.* **Econometric Estimation and Data Envelopment Analysis,** *Rajvi D. Banker, Carnegie-Mellon University.* **Incorporated Value Judgments in Efficiency Analysis,** *Rajiv D. Banker, Carnegie-Mellon University and Richard C. Morey, University of Cincinnati.* **Analysis of Cost Variances for Management Control in Hospitals,** *Rajiv D. Banker, Carnegie-Mellon University, Somnath Das, University of California, and Srikant M. Datar, Carnegie-Mellon University.* **NA International Assessment of the Efficiency of Air Force Accounting and Finance Officers,** *William F. Bowlin, SAF/ACCE, Washington, D.C.*

Volume 6, 1990, 262 pp. $63.50
ISBN 1-55938-119-1

JAI PRESS INC.
55 Old Post Road - No. 2
P.O. Box 1678
Greenwich, Connecticut 06836-1678
Tel: 203-661-7602

JAI PRESS

Advances in Accounting Information Systems

Edited by **Steven G. Sutton,** *Faculty of Management, The University of Calgary*

Volume 1, 1992, 213 pp. $63.50
ISBN 0-89232-575-1

JAI PRESS INC.
55 Old Post Road - No. 2
P.O. Box 1678
Greenwich, Connecticut 06836-1678
Tel: 203-661-7602